Discovering English with Sketch Engine

a corpus-based approach to language exploration

Second Edition

James Thomas

Second Edition

February 2016

VERSATILE

Copyright © James Thomas 2016

ISBN 978-80-260-8360-3

All rights reserved.
No part of this publication may be reproduced or transmitted
in any form or by any means, electronic or mechanical,
including photocopying, recording, or any information storage
or retrieval system, without prior permission from the author or publisher.

Cover design

Martin Hrdina

Typesetting

Peter Docherty

Contact

deske@versatile.pub

Discovering English with Sketch Engine

Second Edition

a corpus-based approach to language exploration

Using Corpora

to learn English

to learn about English

to learn about learning English

James Thomas

VERSATILE

http://versatile.pub

http://lulu.com/spotlight/versatilepub

This book is dedicated to the memory of Adam Kilgarriff.

Adam will be remembered, with gratitude and admiration. Without his restless spirit of inquiry, his intellectual vigour and his generosity, there would be no Sketch Engine and our understanding of language and linguistics would be the poorer. Adam's intellectual and practical work continue to empower and inspire a vast international community.

Table of Contents

	Preface	1
	Preface to the Second Edition	2
	Using this book and its accompanying resources	3
	DESKE Workbook and Glossary	4
	DESKE Online	4
	About the author	4
	Acknowledgements	5
	About Sketch Engine	6
	Introduction to Corpora and Language Study	6
	Word Sketch	14
	Not just words	14
	Selecting a corpus	16
Chapter 1	**Words and Phrases**	**23**
	Three levels of querying	23
	Asking questions simply	23
	Operators in Simple Query	36
	Learning language from language	39
Chapter 2	**Taking Ownership of your Concordance Page**	**41**
	View Options: Top	41
	View Options: Middle	44
	View Options: Bottom	45
Chapter 3	**What's on the menu?**	**47**
	Save	47
	Save as subcorpus	47
	KWIC/Sentence	47
	Sort	47
	Semantic Prosody	48
	Sample	51
	Filter	53
	Frequency	54
	Zipf's law	58
	Node Tags	60
	Serendipity	63
	Node forms	63
	Doc IDs	64
	Text Types	64
	Collocation	65
	Visualize	67
Chapter 4	**Thesaurus**	**69**
	Word Cloud	71

Chapter 5	Top Level Queries continued	73
	Morphology	73
	Inferring meaning	78
	Verbs of Motion	80
	Phrase	81
	Linear Unit Grammar	85
	Word Form	86
	Character	88
	Operators used in fields other than Simple Query	90
	Working with Affixes	91
	Corpus Query Language – a brief introduction	95
	Periphrasis	97
	Discovering English	98
Chapter 6	**It depends on the context**	**99**
	Lemma Filter	100
	Phrasal verbs	102
	Excluding items	104
	Reconstructing phrases	105
	POS Filter	106
	Fronting	107
	Bound and Free Morphemes	107
	Combining both filters	110
	Delexical verb structures	111
	Negative filter	113
	Hypernyms	114
	About lexical bundles	115
	About patterns	116
	About Word templates (1)	117
	Distinguishing bundles, patterns and word templates	120
Chapter 7	**Text Types**	**121**
	Filtering Text Types	123
	Mode: spoken and written	125
	Text types in web-crawled corpora	127
	Synchronic and Diachronic Corpora	128
	The Brown Family	129
	Subcorpora	132
	Text Types Frequency Distribution	133
Chapter 8	**Corpus Query Language – in detail**	**139**
	The Essentials of CQL	139
	Question Tags	140
	Word	141
	Part of speech	141
	CQL lemma queries	142
	Combining elements within brackets	142
	Strings of elements	144
	How to allow space between elements	146

How to exclude elements 147
How to make search items optional 148
How to search for punctuation 149
Escape 150
Within a sentence 150
Wildcards and/or operators 151
Syntagms 151
Searching for constructions 153

Chapter 9   Parallel Corpora **157**

Using parallel corpora 158
Conclusion 162

Chapter 10   Collocation **163**

Collocation Candidates 164
Functions 166
Hoey Procedure 169
Observing polysemy 170
Lexical Support 172

Chapter 11   Word Sketches **175**

False friends 177
and/or 179
Multi-word sketches 179
Size matters 180
Advanced Options 180
Prepositions in word sketches 181
Bilingual Word Sketches 181
Prepositions bound and free 182
Sorting Word Sketches 183
Clustering 184
Word Sketches and Lexicography 185
Word templates (2) 187
When is enough too much? 189

Chapter 12   Word Sketch Differences **191**

Chapter 13   Word List **195**

Filter Options 197
White list, black list 198
Output Options 199

Chapter 14   DIY corpora **203**

Creating a corpus from the web 204
Creating a corpus from selected documents 206

Chapter 15   Pride and Prejudice **209**

Afterword	213
References	214
Index of Names and Notions	219
Word Focus Index	224
Penn Treebank Tags as used in Sketch Engine	226
Abbreviations used in this book	228

Preface

Discovering English with Sketch Engine has been written for anyone who would like to extend their understanding of how English works through a guided discovery approach. This involves sending queries to carefully designed databases of texts and drawing conclusions from multiple examples sampled from many speakers and writers. This book is also for anyone who would like to know what questions can be asked about language and how to ask them.

These databases are referred to as **corpora** (singular *corpus*). One of the leading researchers in the field of corpus linguistics, John Sinclair (1933-2007), defined a corpus as "a collection of pieces of language text in electronic form, selected according to external criteria to represent, as far as possible, a language or language variety as a source of data for linguistic research[1]". Geoffrey Leech (1936-2014), one of England's leading 20th century grammarians, lovably defined a corpus as "a helluva lot of text, stored on a computer" (1992:106). Corpora allow users to ask questions of thousands of native speakers whose language has been sampled and stored.

To search a corpus, we use **concordancers.** These are programs which search corpora and return data which can be processed in many ways to reveal linguistic regularities or otherwise. This book uses Sketch Engine exclusively for these purposes. On every page, we see how **patterns of normal language** emerge as we convert data into information through a combination of analytical tools and intuition. This process often answers more than the original question. When information is integrated into one's thinking, knowledge is created as indicated in the diagram on the next page. In terms of pedagogy, this is referred to as Knowledge Creation, and derives from the work of Lev Vygotsky (1896–1934) and Jerome Bruner (born 1915 and still going). These ideas are pursued throughout this book.

Readers whose English is good enough to use this book do not need a language course that takes them on a graded, step-by-step march through the use of articles, conditionals, passive voice, discourse markers, question tags, modal verbs or any of the many etceteras that make up traditional grammar-oriented course book syllabuses. We do meet all of these along the way, somewhat kaleidoscopically, but at the same time, cyclically. A quick look at the **Index of Names and Notions** gives some idea of the coverage of such features of language.

In fact, this book focuses on **words in their patterns** as they appear in corpora across all levels of the Hierarchy of Language, as introduced on p.31. We explore words in constructions, from morphology to discourse. We investigate many of the aspects of words, phrases and clauses that are involved in forming sentences, paragraphs, texts and discourse. There is also a **Word Focus Index.**

---

[1] http://bit.ly/sinclair_corp_design

Sketch Engine and other corpus analysis tools have taken linguistics into hitherto unimagined realms which have in turn generated whole new sets of questions. Asking a corpus these questions generates a lot of data whose structuring reveals many hitherto unrecognised language patterns that contribute profitably to our understanding of language.

It is hoped that your experience with this book leads you to develop a sense for language patterns, that you acquire some of them, and that your hunger for understanding and acquiring them can be sated by the corpus skills you develop.

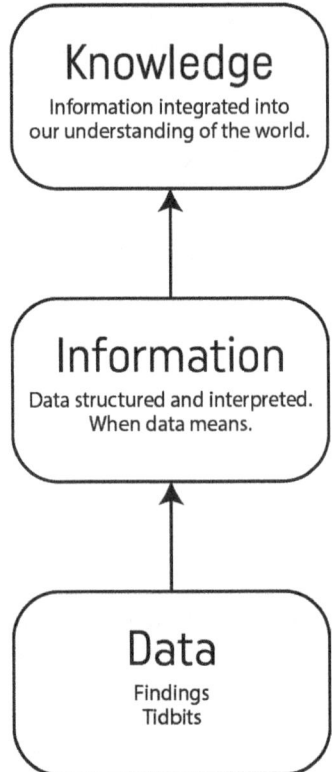

Preface to the Second Edition

The second edition keeps pace with developments in the Sketch Engine suite of tools and corpora. They have grown and matured in the short period since the first edition. The book also represents considerable development in its linguistic and pedagogical approaches. Many language questions have been refocussed, texts have been revised, graphics improved, the book re-indexed and the references expanded and repaired.

Using this book and its accompanying resources

Discovering English with Sketch Engine (DESKE) is above all an activity book. The reader is continuously tasked with investigating interesting and surprising instances of usage and more often, hunting for patterns of normal usage in a variety of corpora.

All of this work is done within Sketch Engine, for which the user needs to register. With a one month trial account, you have access to at least one corpus per language, and there are also some open corpora – this is enough for much of the work in the early part of this book. For teachers using Sketch Engine in a semester long course, there is the Teacher and Student Licenses, details of which can be found on their website under Prices.

The structure of the book is a step-by-step guide to using Sketch Engine, not the structured syllabus of a language course. There is a considerable amount of recycling as well, with some aspects of English being revisited in different parts of the book as a quick scan of the indexes will reveal. These recurring meetings with features of English is not unlike our everyday encounters with language.

There are hundreds of questions posed which need to be investigated online as your Sketch Engine skillset expands. It is therefore best worked through cover to cover with Sketch Engine open and a notebook or the Workbook at hand (see 3 below). Each new aspect of the software we meet allows us to ask new questions or interpret data beyond the scope of the given question. It is therefore expected that the reader will be constantly going from the known to the unknown at several levels while enjoying a rich learning experience.

DESKE rarely provides answers to the questions. The questions are triggers for thinking about language and for conducting searches. The reader is expected to look at the data and draw conclusions.

Some supplementary material for this book can be found at the Versatile website [2]: Bookmark it, as it links to pages containing:

1. all of the URLs that appear in the footnotes throughout this book.
2. a page of all the questions. You can download this and make notes in it as you work. You may benefit from a folder or file to organise the information you glean, and note your own questions that are triggered by your investigations.
3. a page with suggestions for using this book.
4. a feedback form to Versatile.

Teachers using this book with students in class or individually might find that sets of questions can be set for homework so that students have time to work things out, follow leads and prepare their own questions about the questions. Classroom time can then be devoted to presenting findings and discussing issues that have arisen, making the *teacher the guide on the side* rather than *the sage on the stage* (King 1993). This procedure has recently been branded, 'The Flipped Classroom', but was used by some of my secondary school teachers in the 1970s. And it wasn't new then!

Like many online resources that are used across diverse user communities, Sketch Engine is under constant development. This is partly in response to user requests, and partly driven by the vision of the Sketch Engine team. At the time of printing, the book reflects Sketch Engine as at March 2016.

This book is printed through the print-on-demand service, Lulu.com. One of the beauties of such a mode of publishing is the relative ease with which the book can be updated as the incremental changes in the software go online. This is in sharp contrast to the economies of scale that dictate large print runs to commercial publishers and the standard five-year interval between editions. For more on the decision to self-publish, see the Lulu page at Versatile.

---

[2] http://bit.ly/versatile_deske

Every care has been taken to ensure that this book is accurate and logically structured. But nothing is perfect, and as the saying goes, you can't please all of the people all of the time. Thus, feedback, comments and queries are welcome through the online form. Please note that this is *not* the contact address for Sketch Engine feedback – use the "Send Feedback" buttons on their webpages.

DESKE Workbook and Glossary

The second edition of DESKE has a workbook that provides readers with a structured space in which to make notes on the discovery questions, answer language and linguistic quizzes for which there is an answer key. Some tables and diagrams in the book have been reproduced as tasks, there are some discussion questions often oriented towards the application of corpora to language learning and teaching, and these questions have also been formatted as photocopiables for classroom slip-swapping discussions.

This book also contains a glossary of the book's terms related to grammar and syntax, vocabulary and semantics, discourse and pragmatics, corpus and general linguistics, language acquisition and education.

DESKE Online

At the time of writing, an e-learning course to support the book is under development. It is being created in Moodle and will contain such things as videos, language learning activities, linguistic terminology activities, discussion forums, a wiki and links to related readings.

Watch the Versatile website for news of its progress and launch.

About the author

James Thomas has been the head of teacher training in the Department of English and American Studies, Faculty of Arts, Masaryk University in Brno, Czech Republic since 2008. His first university appointment was in the Faculty of Education of the same university, where he mainly taught teacher training courses and some language courses. This was followed by a decisive period at the Faculty of Informatics when and where Sketch Engine was in its infancy.

Most of his courses involve working to some extent with language data, recognising the importance of leading language teachers and students to appreciate not only the relevance of data to everything from morphology through collocation, chunks, discourse and pragmatics, but also to the pedagogical value of guided discovery, for which the tools that allow direct contact with language data are invaluable.

In 2010 he was awarded the British Council ELTon for Innovation in ELT publishing for his co-authored book, *Global Issues in ELT*[3], and in the same year hosted the biennial Teaching and Language Corpora (TALC) conference. He is a committee member of that conference,[4] and chair of Eurocall's SIG, CorpusCALL[5]. For a list of activities and publications, see his Versatile page[6].

He is interested in seeing the widespread adoption of corpora in language teaching as a tool in deepening teachers' conceptualisation of language per se, so that they can ask better questions and search

---

[3] http://www.globalissues.eu
[4] http://ucrel.lancs.ac.uk/talc2014
[5] http://corpuscall.eu
[6] http://bit.ly/versatile_thomas

for answers in language data. He believes that rising to this challenge equips teachers with valuable professional skills, some of which they will choose to pass on to their students.

Acknowledgements

This book would hardly have seen the light of day without input, co-operation and feedback from a small band of supportive friends and colleagues around the world.

Alan Pulverness, a well-known ELT author and editor, teacher and presenter, has been both encouraging and supportive as a co-author in some projects and especially as the editor of the first edition of this book. He is based at Norwich Institute for Language Education [http://www.nile-elt.com]. Alan is the editor of the newsletter of the IATEFL Literature, Media and Cultural Studies Special Interest Group.

Martin Hrdina's work as the cover designer of this book and the others which are forming a series is greatly appreciated. He is also responsible for the overall look of Versatile.pub, for which I am extremely grateful, and proud.

Peter Docherty has recreated all the graphics from the first edition, positioned them as well as managing the references section. In the process, he has made numerous valuable suggestions.

The idea for this book arose out of a request to put together a set of worksheets to accompany a two-day seminar organised by Dr. Olga Dontcheva-Navrátilová at the Faculty of Education. Compiling a book from all the resources I had created over the years seemed like a relatively small challenge. It has been anything but.

Without the Sketch Engine team, there would be nothing. Under the stewardship of Miloš Jakubíček, they have tweaked a lot of the workings of this software according to my suggestions. They seem to be permanently online, responding to my requests for details as I have been writing. It is difficult to imagine creating this book without the support of Vít Baisa in particular.

Adam Kilgarriff was the owner of Sketch Engine. His intellectual vision guided its development, especially in lexicographic applications. His support for a book that exploits Sketch Engine for language education far exceeded my expectations.

There were two critical readers of the first edition who provided invaluable feedback:

Bernd Wick (MA), high school language teacher and lecturer (University of Tübingen), read the previous version and offered many valuable insights.

Alex Boulton, Professor of English and Applied Linguistics, Université de Lorraine made countless, invaluable comments. His thoroughness is admirable and his generosity boundless.

There are several authors whose work jolted me from where I was to where I am. Patrick Hanks has been inspirational not only through his writings but during a period when we both worked at the FI MU (above). Only a handful of the others have I known personally, despite having met them all at conferences and workshops: Tim Johns, John Sinclair, Michael Stubbs, Michael Hoey, Michael Rundell, Luke Prodromou, Mike McCarthy, Susan Hunston, Anne O'Keefe, Michael Halliday, Yukio Tono, Geoff Leech, Barbara Seidlhofer, Douglas Biber, Susan Conrad, Randi Reppen, Henry Widdowson, Anna Mauranen. And many more.

Among the many more must be counted the Teaching and Language Corpora committee (TALC), whose commitment to our biennial conference creates the premier platform for lively debate, cross-fertilization of ideas generated by the ever-growing international community, and for the publication of articles, books and journals. The committee that was active during the last decade consists of the following: Guy Aston, Alex Boulton, Lynne Flowerdew, Ana Frankenberg-Garcia, Agnieszka Leńko, Bernhard Kettemann, Natalie Kübler, Ute Römer, Chris Tribble. And me. New committee members include Yukio Tono and Maggie Charles.

About Sketch Engine

Sketch Engine is a corpus query tool. It lets you explore many corpora in many ways. Having started life as downloadable software, it is nowadays a website with a multi-functional concordancer and many corpora for many languages, which are ready to be explored through its many tools. At the time of writing, there are corpora for sixty languages. The c. 25 corpora in English range in size from very small, such as the early, ground-breaking Brown Corpus with little over one million words to the approximately 20 billion word enTenTen Corpus [2013]. There are also tools for creating corpora from your own data and for quickly generating corpora from the web.

It is the brainchild of Pavel Rychlý and Adam Kilgarriff. They met in 2001 when Rychlý had already developed tools for fast corpus access as part of his PhD and Kilgarriff had already created the first version of 'Word Sketches', corpus-based summaries of a word's grammatical and collocational behaviour. They started working together at that time and were co-developing Sketch Engine until late 2014 when Adam was diagnosed with cancer. He died on May 16th, 2015, leaving family, friends and colleagues in awe at his stoicism and greatly saddened by his death at the age of 55. He leaves an extraordinary legacy, spanning the fields of computational linguistics, lexicography, and language teaching.

> Language is never, ever, ever, random.
> Adam Kilgarriff (2005).

The current generation of monolingual learner dictionaries from Cambridge University Press, Oxford University Press, Macmillan and Collins not only derive their data for describing the meanings and uses of words from corpora, but use Sketch Engine to do so. Being used extensively in lexicography, Sketch Engine is entirely compatible with the increasing focus on vocabulary in contemporary language teaching.

The Chinese character in the logo means *culture* and *language,* among other things.

In addition to Sketch Engine as we know it, there is a new learner-oriented version called SKELL – Sketch Engine for Language Learning, with a simple, user-friendly interface. It is currently available with English and Russian corpora. For more on SKELL, see its homepage: http://skell.sketchengine.co.uk.

The Sketch Engine tools, corpora and other resources are developed in Brno, Czech Republic.

Introduction to Corpora and Language Study

Corpus studies empirically confirm the patterned nature of language at every level of the Hierarchy of Language from morphology, through words, phrases and sentences to text, as well as on the stylistic, contextual and pragmatic stages where they perform. Using corpora helps learners make consciously the decisions that native speakers make subconsciously: they can observe, choose and use native speaker patterns of normal usage.

A pattern-oriented, user-friendly and widely applicable conception of language has emerged, requiring new approaches to data and interpretation. This is no less true for pure linguistics than it is for applied linguistics fields such as translation, lexicography, cognition, forensic linguistics, text mining, interlanguage studies and language teaching. Most branches of language study now use concordances in the hunt for all sorts of patterns, reports of which ripple through the global conversation via conferences, articles, books, and online discussion groups, all the while strengthening and updating our understanding of language.

> Wilhelm von Humboldt (1767–1835) is credited with being the first European linguist to identify human language as a rule-governed system, rather than just a collection of words and phrases paired with meanings. (Wikipedia)

A concordancer is to linguists what microscopes, telescopes, time-lapse photography and data-mining are to their respective fields. They all reveal patterns of behaviour that are unrecognisable through human perception alone. Once invented, such instruments provide new data which lead to scientific breakthroughs. As the tools constantly develop, new avenues of research open up. It is no exaggeration to say that they influence our understanding of the world, especially when they end up in the hands of every interested man, woman and child. There are floods of amateur weather watchers collecting data for meteorologists, swarms of birdwatchers providing ornithologists with migration data, and now torrents of 'word botchers'[7] hunting for the patterns we choose in specific contexts and the linguistic exploitations we more consciously choose in even more specific contexts.

> As I write this (5.2.15), the BBC reports: Scientists working on Europe's Planck satellite say the first stars in the Universe lit up later than was previously thought - it's actually a very big change in our understanding of how certain key events progressed at the earliest epochs.

Underpinning this patterned view of language is Neo-Firthian linguistics. In a paper on Firth, Widdowson (2007:410) writes:

> Analyses of corpora by computer have now revealed detailed and hitherto unsuspected patterns of idiomaticity, of collocation and colligation in texts, and in so doing have provided descriptive substantiation of the insights that Firth expressed over fifty years earlier.

J.R. Firth (1890-1960) was a British linguist who most famously said: *You shall know a word by the company it keeps.* Thus patterns of lexical words in each other's company (collocation and patterns of words in their grammatical company (colligation) are cornerstones of his work and of this book. He also attached great significance to context in its widest sense following the work of the anthropologist Malinowski (1884-1942). Malinowski (1923) found that providing English translations of the Kiriwinan language could not convey the meaning adequately. Even when accompanied by a description of the 'Context of Situation', a fuller description of the 'Context of Culture' was still needed. However, being men of their time, when electronic corpora were not even a distant dream, Firth's language data tended to derive from intuition, while Malinowski's data derived from interview and observation, as is the anthropologists' wont.

Firth's most influential followers were Michael Halliday (1925) and John Sinclair (1933-2007). Halliday, the father of Systemic Functional Grammar (SFG), introduced the term *lexicogrammar* which refers to the unity of lexis and grammar, as the two poles of a single cline, or continuum. Because the two ends are organized differently, different techniques for describing them evolved: the dictionary and thesaurus for lexis, and the 'grammar book' for grammar. Both techniques may be used at various points along the cline, but with diminishing returns. For example, we can describe lexical items in terms of systems of features but the level of generality is quite low (Halliday and Matthiessen 2004:44). And we can describe grammar in terms of the lexis that instantiates it. It is for this reason that grammarians and lexicographers are referred to as lumpers and splitters respectively: grammarians group their observations into holistic groupings, whereas lexicographers divide them into discrete units. The number of separate meanings for a word in a dictionary evidences how general or specific lexicographers choose to make their entries.

In reference to 'lexicogrammar', McEnery and Hardie[8] point out that Halliday "introduced this somewhat cumbersome term simply to make explicit the point that vocabulary cannot be discounted. Some version of this position is accepted by a very wide range of schools of linguistics, the main exception being Chomskyan linguistics." Halliday describes language not in terms of rules, but as sets of systems that involve choices made according to describable criteria: Language is "a network of systems, or interrelated sets of options for making meaning". (1985:15). Both of these aspects of Halliday's work recur throughout this book.

---

[7] spoonerize *birdwatcher* and you get *word botcher*, a kindly reference to people with a linguistic bent.
[8] M.A.K. Halliday, "Systemic Background," 1985. *On Language and Linguistics*. Continuum, 2003.

John Sinclair defined his influential *Idiom Principle* (1991) thus:

> The principle of idiom is that the language user has available to him or her a large number of semi-preconstructed phrases that constitute single choices, even though they might appear to be analysable into segments.

So, while Halliday views language as meanings generated by the interplay of vocabulary and grammar, constrained by context, Sinclair sees speakers and writers expressing their ideas by assembling chunks of language whenever possible, otherwise it becomes necessary to utilise the patterns in which words typically function (see Word templates p.117 and p.187). Some of Sinclair's colleagues, in particular Hanks and Hunston, have separately developed their own *word grammars* that account for patterns within and between the collocation and colligation of individual words and sets of words.

Native speakers acquire a vast repertoire of chunks and patterns because they meet them often enough in their contexts of situation for them to become the optimal way to express a given notion. This is evident even among very young children. Native speakers hear and read them every day: exposure. We say and write them every day: reinforcement. These receptive and productive processes *prime* us for them, and account for why our language is "FASI": fluent and accurate and sophisticated and idiomatic.

In one sense, the most basic pattern is *collocation*, when defined broadly, and it is the construct on which Michael Hoey's influential theory of Lexical Priming (2005) is built. This draws on evidence from psycholinguistics and cognitive science, and has its empirical foundation in corpora. It has quickly become a cornerstone of contemporary linguistics.

There is more than an overlap between grammar and vocabulary – there is an interdependence. As Michael Stubbs wrote: "It is not the words which tell you the meaning of the phrase, but the phrase which tells you the meaning of the individual words in it" (2001:18). He admits that this may be an exaggeration, but as we will see throughout this book, it is not a wild claim at all. After all, it is not far from Firth's widely quoted statement about words and the company they keep. Nor Kilgarriff's. Nor Hanks'. Nor Sinclair's. Nor Hopper's. Nor Hunston's. Nor Biber's.

The interdependence of grammar and vocabulary can be seen in both corpus-informed dictionaries which also contain grammatical information, and corpus-informed grammars which also contain lexical information. Two recent grammars of English are corpus-based descriptions, namely, the *Longman Grammar of Spoken and Written English*[9] (Biber, et al. 1999) and the *Cambridge Grammar of English* (Carter, McCarthy 2006). Halliday's *An Introduction to Functional Grammar*, first published in 1985, received a corpus makeover in its third edition (2004) co-authored with Christian Matthiessen.

Contemporary dictionaries and grammars describe language through the analysis of specific features that occur in large samples. This corpus analysis has had a great impact on these 'mediated' language teaching resources, as Bernardini (2000) refers to them (see p.14). The impact can be seen in the large amount of information about word grammar, frequency and pragmatics in contemporary dictionaries. And as grammars divide their attention between grammar patterns and words, they realise a lexicogrammatical view of language, compatible with Halliday's view that grammar and vocabulary are two ends of a single continuum. LGSWE's lexical index is 25 pages long, each divided into three columns. These descriptive dictionaries and grammars illustrate each feature with one or two authentic sentences.

A group of Neo-Firthian linguists, including Hanks, Hoey, Hunston, Rundell, were among the many involved, under Sinclair's stewardship, in the COBUILD project, which produced the first corpus-based English language learning resources, the most enduring of which is the COBUILD English Dictionary (Sinclair 1987). The title is an acronym: Collins Birmingham University International Language Database.

---

[9] frequently referred to as LGSWE in this book

This is a monolingual learner dictionary (MLD) and every MLD since has been developed through corpus-based descriptions. As McEnery and Hardie (2012:142) of Lancaster University say,

> It is perhaps unsurprising that a school of thought with roots in lexicography should emphasise the absolute centrality of the word – as opposed to some other unit of linguistic description, such as the phoneme, morpheme, phrase or clause – to the understanding of language.

It is equally unsurprising that Sketch Engine, which has been developed for lexicographical purposes, should be compatible with a broad lexical focus in contemporary language education. This is why this book, DESKE, is able to assume a lexical focus: the majority of patterns that we explore revolve around specific words and phrases. And like many of these contemporary resources, the current book has a conceptual and a lexical index.

The many types of patterns and structures we explore include word grammar, idioms, fixed phrases, semi-fixed phrases, collocation, colligation, word templates, sentence stems, compound nouns, phrasal verbs, syntagms, collostructions and lexical bundles. There is considerable overlap in what these terms refer to. Their value to translation and language learning cannot be overestimated.

Nor can the role of context be overestimated, as some lexicogrammatical patterns are likely to differ in different modes or mediums. some patterns in spoken language differ from those in academic prose, which differ from those in journalism, which differ from those in fiction, etc. See, for example, the explorations of syntagms (p.151). In addition to patterns of normal usage, there are patterns of abnormal usage, which are by definition less frequent in the language, and often express metaphorical, figurative ideas. Hanks (2013) refers to this creative, playful use of language as *exploitations*. Being patterns, they can also be discovered and explored. As Yogi Berra is said to have said,

As we often find, using corpora answers questions we had not even thought to ask. Long live serendipity! It is worth bearing in mind the words of Louis Pasteur (pictured above):

> *Dans les champs de l'observation le hasard ne favorise que les esprits préparés.*
>
> [In the fields of observation, chance favours only the prepared mind.] (1854)

Corpus consultations answer language questions and reveal patterns of normal usage that even linguists *don't know that they know*. This is a reference to the one level that Donald Rumsfeld did not get

to when he made his famous 'known knowns' statement in 2002 [10]. (Forgive me for not including a photo of the architect of the Iraq War.) Rumsfeld said that there are known knowns … there are known unknowns … but there are also unknown unknowns. His philosophy did not venture as far as the unknown knowns, i.e. the things we don't know that we know. Robert Frost (pictured left) hinted at an analogous notion when he said: I write to find out what I didn't know I knew. There are many aspects of language that we do not know we know, especially those which have been acquired subconsciously, and for native speakers this is almost the entire language.

Texts in corpora

Corpora are compiled for specific purposes which determine the selection criteria for the texts. For example, corpora may be created from emails, 18th century British poetry, sitcom scripts, research papers from a particular field, power drill manuals, the work of particular authors, a single novel, a

---

[10] See Wikipedia: There are known knowns. And now a film, *The Unknown Known* (Morris 2013).

decade of a newspaper, transcripts of radio phone-in programmes, transcripts of doctors interacting with patients, transcripts from law courts or parliament. Note that when studying spoken language, we are dealing with transcriptions – only a small proportion of publicly available corpora include multimedia files[11]. There are also corpora which contain the extant texts of dead and endangered languages [12]. Thus it can be seen that 'text' refers to both transcripts of what was spoken and documents that were written. They are inherently and inevitably historical.

Specific corpora are particularly useful for extracting terminology and observing how it works, and for exploring their fields, tenors and modes (see table on p.123), to use Halliday's three labels for his Context of Situation. The possibilities are limited only by the range of human communication itself.

However, to represent a whole living, vibrant, evolving language, samples of a cross-section of many varieties are compiled into a so-called reference corpus[13]. The British National Corpus (BNC), released in 1994, is the most frequently consulted reference corpus, and not only in this book. In the 21st century, there are much larger corpora, such as the enTenTen [2013], which contains 200 times as many words in it than the BNC. It is worth bearing in mind, that the biggest corpus in the world is tiny: three occurrences in a corpus may mean thousands of times a day in the real world. Fillmore expressed his view on the value of corpora, regardless of their sizes, thus:

> I don't think there can be any corpora, however large, that contain information about all of the areas of English lexicon and grammar that I want to explore; all that I have seen are inadequate. The second observation is that every corpus that I've had a chance to examine, however small, has taught me facts that I couldn't imagine finding out about in any other way. (1992)

This brings us to the important issue of *attested language*. Science does not invent data based on intuition or assumptions and then study it. Similarly, corpora do not contain language that has been created for the purpose of exemplifying language, which is what 'unattested' language is. This is found in language coursebooks, older dictionaries, style manuals and in grammars. For example, the Wikipedia article on Anaphora is rich in colourless illustrative sentences that would put a student to sleep and make a corpus linguist sleep furiously.

While the linguist's intuition was the primary 'data' in some 20th century linguistics, sophisticated access to vast quantities of authentic, attested language has consigned the 'armchair linguist' to history. The COBUILD Dictionary (2nd ed.) (Sinclair 1995) provides the following pragmatic meaning of *armchair*:

> An armchair critic, fan or traveller knows about a particular subject from what he or she has read or heard about rather than from practical experience.

modifies		
	13,400	-0.00
quarterback	609	5.70
traveler	443	4.40
critic	400	3.95
general	258	2.96
expert	231	0.77
table	197	0.37
travel	192	1.29
fan	186	0.16
warrior	180	3.53
traveller	169	4.09
psychologist	143	3.49
detective	122	3.77
philosopher	118	3.71

The next screenshot shows nouns that form compounds with *armchair*. It does not include *armchair linguist*, as this compound occurs only five times in this mega-corpus, but it nicely shows how COBUILD's lexicographers used such data in constructing their definition. It also suggests that sitting in your comfortable armchair, instead of venturing into the 'real world' and getting your hands dirty has never stopped some people from pontificating. The most instructive of the five 'armchair linguists' examples in enTenTen comes from the UCLA.EDU domain:

---

[11] See for example, SACODEYL.
[12] See, for example, *Comparing corpora from endangered language projects* (Haig, Schnell and Wegener 2011)
[13] See bit.ly/ref_corp_leech for a transcript of a talk Leech gave, *The Importance of Reference Corpora*.

Corp ex.1 *For example, in linguistics there is (or used to be) a rift between so-called "armchair linguists" who use their own knowledge of language to provide data and linguists who use corpus-based techniques to collect data (basically like what Google n-grams does).*

In this context, *provide data,* is a euphemism for *invent data,* which is a collocation that does not appear in the BNC but does occur 40 times in enTenTen[14], as we explore later in this book.

Attested language basks in its richness. It is rich in references to real people, places, events and many aspects of culture in its widest sense. Native speakers spend pretty much all of their lives exposed to attested language. When we are speaking our mother tongue, we are constantly making subconscious language choices which are based on the experiences of a lifetime of exposure to attested language. These are our primings and they come from multiple environments, the country, region, neighbourhood and family where we acquire language, as well as from our education, the literature we read, the media, and the language of the people we mix with socially and professionally. These influences shape our language and our world view. Roland Barthes', as noted in the Encyclopedia of Contemporary Literary Theory, view is that:

> Fillmore's caricature of the armchair linguist (1992): He sits in a deep soft comfortable armchair, with his eyes closed and his hands clasped behind his head. Once in a while he opens his eyes, sits up abruptly shouting, "Wow, what a neat fact!", grabs his pencil, and writes something down. Then he paces around for a few hours in the excitement of having come still closer to knowing what language is really like.

> Language is never transparent; it partly creates and gives a structure to the world which the individual encounters. So French-speakers and English-speakers live in different worlds, as do people such as Christians and Freudians who use different vocabularies. Barthes considered part of the thinker's moral responsibility to be aware that language is never innocent or free of ideology. (Makaryk 1993: 245)

Most people who study foreign languages experience a new awareness of their mother tongue, which in turn influences how they use it. With everyone's exposure to language being different, we are all primed differently, and this is why everyone has an idiolect. Hoey concludes that,

> if each person constructs their language out of the primings acquired from a unique set of data, there can be no right or wrong in language (and no absolute distinction between native and non-native speaker, though the latter will have acquired their primings by strikingly different routes (2005:181).

A corpus contains texts expressed in the primed idiolects of each of its authors. Thus, when we search a whole corpus, we identify patterns that are common to all its varieties. This 'floral' Venn diagram indicates that every circle contains elements that are unique to it, that some elements are shared with

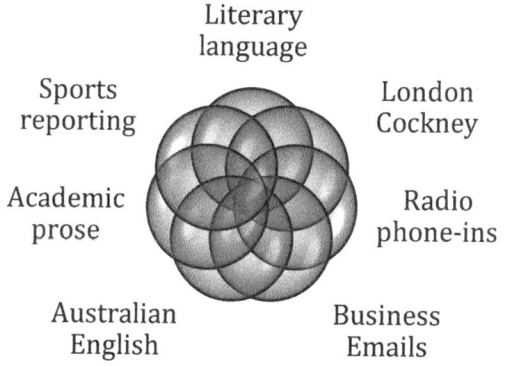

[14] ske.li/ett_invent_data

some of the others, and in the centre or core, that there are elements common to all of them, i.e. core English.

Written texts are lightly spiced with deviant uses of language such as spelling mistakes, incorrect verb forms, wrong prepositions, bad punctuation, poorly structured sentences and dubious relationships between their elements. Remember that many people are not taught to write, and yet we do. In spoken language we find utterances that are incomplete, that start and finish in 'ungrammatical' ways, there is overlapping, non-sequiturs, slips of the tongue as well as mistakes that result from real-time processing. Mistakes are not corrected before texts are included in a corpus, as this would chip away at their authenticity. To invoke a cliché, this is all part of the rich tapestry of language.

In both written and spoken language, corpora also abound in what is sometimes referred to as *taboo language* and we encounter texts whose subject matter some may find irksome. Correcting and cleansing texts according to some social mores is, by definition, the very antithesis of studying authentic language. No-one in their right mind, with the exception of language teaching publishers, would think that language can be faithfully represented through anodyne, innocuous texts. Michelangelo chipped away long and hard to find a naked man with disproportionately large hands imprisoned in a chunk of Carrara marble. See what we lose when this masterpiece is 'figleafed'!

One type of corpus that does contain a great deal of non-standard language is the so-called learner corpus. These corpora of student writing are tagged manually according to taxonomies of errors. Analysis of this data demonstrates that foreign language learners at different stages of development make predictable mistakes – these are classified as patterns in *interlanguage*, a now ubiquitous term coined by Selinker in 1972. The corpus analysis of non-native speakers' systematic deviations from normal usage is nowadays a major sub-field within Second Language Acquisition and is facilitated by corpora.

> The birds, wheatears, have nothing to do with wheat or ears. Their original name was 'white arse'. Victorians and vicars birdwatching in mixed company blushed when they spotted one. So their name was subtly figleafed.
>
> Website source: http://bit.ly/white_arse

Corpora are thus goldmines of language created for genuine, communicative purposes. The gold we mine is presented to us firstly in sentences containing the search item, while post-processing typically results in lists of words and numbers, as we saw in the above 'armchair' screenshot. No human could assemble unaided all their experiences of a word or phrase and draw empirical conclusions about them. Thus part of the joy of corpus work is coming across aspects of the language we were simply unaware of; another joy is finding things we didn't know that we knew.

Of the thousands of English corpora that have been created in the last 25 years, one in particular deserves comment. The British National Corpus has a special place in the development of corpus use, especially in many branches of English linguistics at the end of the 20th Century.

British National Corpus

The British National Corpus has long been the gold standard for British English, providing representative data about grammar (in its widest sense) and vocabulary (in its widest sense) in a representative cross-section of many fields (domains) and modes (mediums). Work on building the corpus began in 1991, and was completed in 1994. It is a snapshot of British English in the late 1980s and early 1990s and is therefore a *synchronic* corpus.

No new texts have been added to the BNC since then, which on one hand means that its data is stable and the same search will always yield the same data. On the other hand, it contains no new coinages since that time. Recent linguistic accretions such as *friend* as a verb, as in 'a social networker *friends* another social networker' are not represented. And *email* gets a mere 34 hits, the same as *Luddite*, coincidentally. Even the word *website* is not in the BNC, although *web site* is – once – in its c.100 million words.

Sketch Engine has three versions of the BNC, as can be seen in the screenshot on p.16. The first one is a sampled, smaller version containing approximately the first 10 million words of the original. The

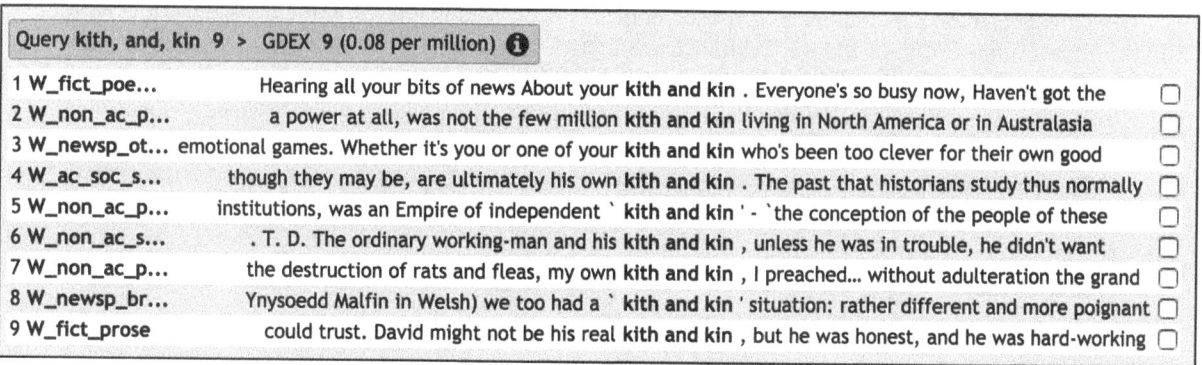

second is the second edition of the BNC, known as BNC 2, and uses the original part of speech (POS) tagging system, CLAWS. The third is the version that has been retagged using another tagging system called the Tree Tagger and is the only one used in this book. Aspects of tagging are introduced in *Not just words* on p.14.

As we progress through this book, we will learn a lot more about the BNC. For more information straight from the horse's mouth, see the BNC's own website [15].

Concordancers

Concordancers are a specific type of search engine that searches corpora to provide data about words, phrases, grammatical constructions and text types. Some do more and some do less. The work a concordancer can do depends not only on how it is designed and programmed, but on the data the corpora contain. As recently as 2012, McEnery and Hardie write: "The computer's role ends with supplying the analyst with a set of (probably sorted) concordance lines" (p.126). Not so with Sketch Engine: concordance lines are not only sortable, but can be delivered according to a variety of algorithms. Requests for collocates are rewarded with a list of single words and frequency information using a variety of statistics. Each collocate can be clicked on to see the concordance of the collocation. Tables of collocates of a single word can be generated in columns based on the grammatical relationship between the node (a.k.a. the search term) and its collocates. Lists of strings of words (bundles) and parts of speech (syntagms) can be generated and their significance can be compared with other corpora.

---

[15] http://www.natcorp.ox.ac.uk/corpus/creating.xml

The structuring of data into information is the most important thing that Sketch Engine software does. Concordancers assist in the analysis of large quantities of language data and often reveal otherwise imperceptible patterns. Some users may be searching for quick answers, while others may be studying language from multiple examples in an inductive way. As in much research, findings rarely lead to black and white conclusions: one of the characteristics of a good language learner is their tolerance of ambiguity, or *fuzziness* as computer scientists are wont to say.

We find, for example, that the word *kith* occurs in the phrase *kith and kin* 9 out of the 14 times that this word appears in the British National Corpus. We can conclude that this must be its canonical form. The other examples show that *kin* is never far away, as seen in this complete screenshot. There are no examples of *kith* without *kin* but *kin* without *kith* is plentiful. Such observations from data require some interpreting that can lead to a statement of linguistic tendencies, not absolutes.

Concordance

A concordance is a page or screen of lines of text that contain the search word. This screenshot of *kith and kin* shows an extract from the British National Corpus as it appears in Sketch Engine.

The most common presentation of language data in concordancers has the node, highlighted and centred: this is referred to as the Key Word in Context (KWIC) format. The set of lines is known as a **concordance**. A concordance shows both the context and co-text. Context refers to the text to the left and right of the node when we read the extracts horizontally. Studying language in linear sequences is referred to as syntagmatic analysis. Co-text refers to the words and structures that accompany the node, which can be observed by studying concordances vertically. This is useful data in paradigmatic analyses, as it reveals collocation and colligation patterns.

Word Sketch

Sketch Engine is so named because of its powerful feature, the word sketch. This is a one-page profile of a word's collocational behaviour. It is presented as a table of a word's collocates grouped in grammatical relations – it is a stunning overview of a word's paradigmatic and syntagmatic relations. While concordances are standard presentations of corpus data in virtually all corpus tools, word sketches are rare. *Just the Word*[16] (Whitelock) presents data in its own word sketch format but uses BNC data only. Word sketches are available in almost every corpus in Sketch Engine, including those that users make themselves. is devoted to word sketches.

Not just words

In addition to words, corpora typically have several layers of metadata – some associated with individual word forms, others with the texts that constitute the corpus.

Those associated with word forms are (a) lemmas, (b) part of speech tags and (c) semantic tags.

Lemmas

A lemma is a set of conjugating verb forms, e.g. *fly, flies, flew, flown, flying* or a set of declining noun or adjective forms, e.g. *brick, bricks; axis, axes; sheep, sheep; good, better, best*. A lemma does not include possessive forms of nouns, at least not according to Penn Treebank lemmatizing, the tagging system used in almost all of the corpora available through Sketch Engine. For example, *father's* does not appear on the list of word forms of *father*. The issue of lemmatizing is discussed in detail from p.75 where we start to distinguish various word forms.

---

[16] http://www.just-the-word.com

Part of speech tags

A part of speech (POS) tag is a code that indicates a word's part of speech in the context in which it appears. *Mushroom* appears in the following sentences as singular, plural and proper nouns as well as a past participle and an –ing verb.

Corp ex.2   *Life, for me, is certainly not too short to stuff a **mushroom**.*

Corp ex.3   *John Smith's bright idea has literally **mushroomed** beyond all expectations.*

Corp ex.4   *Actually they're quite clean these **mushrooms**.*

Corp ex.5   ***MUSHROOM** MEMORIES.*

Corp ex.6   *Toy towns: fantasy villages are **mushrooming** in Europe's hot spots.*

You might like to hazard a guess as to which of these five tags belong with *mushroom* in these five sentences. The first letter of a tag indicates its general POS and the following letters indicate the sub-categories.

NN   NNS   NP   VVG   VVN

POS tagging permits specifying the POS of a particular word when searching e.g. *mushroom (vb)*, of a word in the context of parts of speech e.g. *mushroom + preposition*, of sequences of POS e.g. *Noun + and other* Noun(s), and of the constituents of grammar structures such as the second conditional or past perfect. Open this link [17] to see the mushroom sentences with their tags.

Semantic Tags

Semantic tags are attached to lexical words. They are the headings of semantic types that can be found in ontologies, one of which can be seen on the website of Hanks' *Pattern Dictionary of English Verbs* (PDEV) [18]. In Corp ex.7, we see the lexical words in this sentence identified with semantic types. These are followed by a single-letter POS label. This example comes from a corpus currently in beta mode:

Who /0 should /0 **select** /cognition.v and /0 define /stative.v the /0 **criteria** /communication.n ? /0

Corp ex.7   Who /0 should /0 **select** /cognition.v and /0 define /stative.v the /0 **criteria** / communication.**n** ? /0

Text Types

In general corpora it is often important to know if search results represent spoken language, legal texts, personal mail, etc. Burnard states, "without metadata the investigator has nothing but disconnected words of unknowable provenance or authenticity" (2005 : 31). Sketch Engine provides the option to search for a language feature within specific text types, and to show the text types in which the search results were found. Summaries of the text types can also be generated. These features are discussed at many points in this book. A fuller exploration starts on p.64.

---

[17] http://ske.li/bnc_mushroom_pos
[18] http://www.pdev.org.uk/#onto

Types and Tokens

This sentence from the BNC has 22 tokens. But some of them occur more than once, e.g. cut/ting. The number of different words is the number of types.

Corp ex.8   *It's a funny thing - I cut my fingernails all the time, and every time I think to cut them, they need cutting.*

When a word list of a corpus or text is generated, the program reduces all repeated tokens to types, that is, every instance (token) of every word is counted but the list displays each word only once as a type, usually with the number of occurrences (Scott and Tribble 2006:12-13).

The type/token ratio is the ratio of the total number of different words (types) to the total number of words (tokens) in a sample of text. It is an important indicator of vocabulary density and diversity.

Selecting a corpus

The idiom, *horses for courses* expresses the need to match a task with people who have the appropriate skills. In our data-driven study of English, it is similarly important to use corpora that are relevant to our needs. In this book, we are primarily interested in the patterns of core British English, which makes the BNC the workhorse for our study. In addition, we work with the London English Corpus (LEC), CHILDES, and LEXMCI which represents British, American and Irish English, as well as the corpora created by crawling the internet, namely ukWaC, enTenTen and the New Model Corpus (NMC).

Language	Name	Words
English	TED_en	2,882,085
English	Brown Family (CLAWS + TreeTagger)	6,975,474
English	CHILDES English Corpus	22,693,506
English	British National Corpus	96,052,598
English	British National Corpus (TreeTagger)	96,267,546
English	OPUS2 English	1,139,515,048
English	ukWaC	1,316,556,457
English	enTenTen [2013]	19,717,205,676

When you sign in to Sketch Engine, the corpora which appear in the top box your Home page are those you have used most recently. This screenshot shows my most recently used eight. Being a dynamic list, it will change as you use different corpora.

There are two icons in the right column: clicking the left one leads to a page in a Sketch Engine wiki with information about the corpus. Clicking the right icon opens the corpus, as does clicking on the name of the corpus itself.

Click on **All corpora** to choose from about 90 corpora in 66 languages, at the time of writing.

Click on **Parallel Corpora** to work with corpora in two languages at once. The sources of the translations include the United Nations, the European Parliament and film subtitles.

Another set of corpora called **My corpora**, appears once you have created one with other Sketch Engine tools. See p.203 to learn how to make your own – it is surprisingly easy and fast. As you work through this book, you might be interested in comparing your findings in standard corpora with findings in corpora related to your fields of interest.

When other registered users create their own corpora and share them with you, they will be listed in another box at the bottom of the browser called **Other users' corpora.**

Permalinks

A valuable feature of Sketch Engine is the very, very long URL generated for each search. As the user performs various operations such as taking a sample, sorting and making a list of collocates, the URL changes. For example, here is the URL for the page that appears after searching for *trailblazer*. It shows the lemma of *trailblazer* in the BNC TT, in sentence view (as opposed to KWIC view) and sorted according to David Lee's Classification whose references will appear on the concordance page.

https://the.sketchengine.co.uk/bonito/run.cgi/view?q=alc%2C%5Blc%3D%22trailblazer%22%7Clemma_lc%3D%22trailblazer%22%5D;corpname=preloaded%2Fbnc2_tt_1;viewmode=sen;attrs=word&ctxat_rs=word&structs=g&refs=%3Dbncdoc.genre&pagesize=1000&gdexconf=&iquery=trailblazer&attr_tooltip=nott;fromp=1

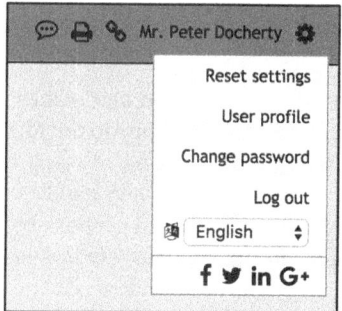

This *trailblazer* URL has 287 characters. In order to cite it in a paper, presentation or in this book, to tweet or dictate it, send it as a text message or via Facebook, it needs to be considerably shorter. Sketch Engine's URL shortening tool reduces it to a few characters only. To create permalinks, click on the link icon beside your name as in this screenshot.

For the above URL it produced this: http://ske.li/cf, which can be copied and pasted anywhere. Clicking on it redirects to the full URL in a browser.

Alternatively, you can customise it by typing something informative into the yellow field before clicking *Get Permalink*. For example, typing bnc_trailblazer_sent into the yellow field generates http://ske.li/bnc_trailblazer_sent.

It is a good idea to start customized permalinks with a consistent corpus identifier, and then something indicative. For example:

1. ett_friend_affixes_freqlist: *frequency list of the affixes with 'friend' in the enTenTen corpus*
2. bnc_arresting_wlt: *word form, lemma and tag listing of 'arresting' in the BNC*
3. cztt_zkouzka_colls: *collocates of 'zkouska' in the CzTenTen corpus.*

Furthermore, since registered users can retrieve a list of their permalinks by clicking *Show your stored links*, it is more helpful if they are meaningful. Once you click *Show your stored links*, you can bookmark it in your browser.

Note that permalinks to searches, sorts, etc, on your subcorpora will not work for other people, because your subcorpora are a part of your personal account (see p.132).

The unmediated use of corpora in language pedagogy

Corpus use has not made major inroads into language classrooms. Many of the 15 million English teachers in the world today, according to the British Council Annual Report (2010), have never heard of corpora, while many who are familiar with their use by lexicographers and grammarians are not aware that they can use them themselves, as could their students. There are also many who are aware but have dismissed them for reasons pertaining to teachers' views of language, of language acquisition and of teaching, as discussed in the following paragraphs.

We live in an era of guided discovery, task-based learning, learner autonomy, social constructivism and constructionism, peer correction, experiential learning, etc. We live in an era of blogs, wikis, shared documents, and TGIF (Twitter, Google, Instagram, Facebook) and many other types of online tools and devices, etc. Classrooms have data projectors and interactive whiteboards connected to the internet. Students have their own devices. So do teachers. We live in an era of collocation, multi-word units, word templates, pragmatic competence, functional grammar, cognitive grammar, etc. We live in an era where fuzziness is tolerated, and which prefers language systems and patterns to rules. We live in an era where tasks and texts have multiple affordances, i.e. opportunities to learn many things at the same time working with a single resource. We live in an era of Bloom's Taxonomy, which places remembering discrete pieces of information as the lowest order thinking skill and creativity as the highest. And in an era that acknowledges that groups can do things that individuals can't.

The use of corpora in language teaching is perfectly compatible with the era just described. In fact it sounds like an ideal environment in which learners could study, learn and acquire language through direct interactions with language data, referred to as an *unmediated* use of corpora (Bernardini 2000:225). There is no shortage of corpora and concordances, online and off. Even without such devices, learners can do tasks from corpus printouts (see Johns 1994 and Boulton 2010). Most course books, grammar books, journals, teacher resource books, teacher training courses, conferences and workshops perpetuate the approaches of a bygone era. But to challenge teachers' views of language, of language acquisition and of teaching is impractical, disrespectful and even subversive.

Given that the ground is fertile yet unploughed, let us now consider what can be sowed and reaped. Firstly, it is fair to say that students put themselves in the hands of their teachers, as patients do doctors and passengers do drivers. It might be precarious, but this is what we do. In the name of many a language teaching methodology, students have willingly participated in activities involving mindless drilling, learning long lists of irrelevant words, running around the classroom, interviewing passers-by, miming an egg, acting out poems, and entering trance-like alpha-states. Tasking students with looking at 40 examples of the phrase, *the umpteenth time,* to learn something about its behaviour should not be a big ask. It is not the students' view of language and learning that is being challenged.

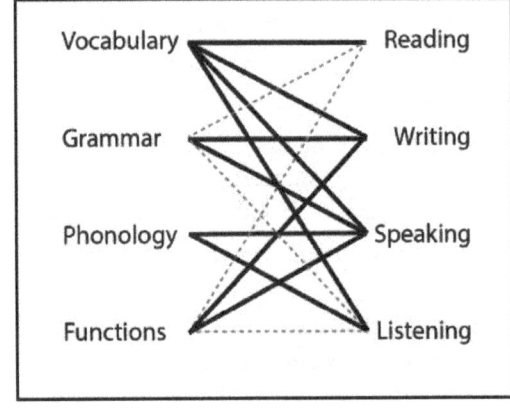

Teaching foreign languages involves teaching students the fours systems, namely vocabulary, grammar, functional language and phonology, so that they can develop the four skills of reading, writing, speaking and listening. As this diagram indicates, the four skills are dependent on the four systems. Getting better at the skills requires developing the four systems. Corpora are such rich sources of information about vocabulary, grammar and functional language that lexicographers, grammarians and discourse analysts respectively count them among their primary data sources. Teachers would gain much from joining the party.

Teachers and students can also use them to find out if *the high street* is used in American English, if *to lecture someone* means the same as *to give a lecture*, if *furthermore* is used in spoken English, if the past tense of *speed up* is *speeded* or *sped up*, if *data* has singular or plural agreement, which sports use *pitch, court, field*, if there are any adverbs typically used with past progressive or future perfect, what the differences are between *swear at, swear to, swear that, swear by*, what other adjectives accompany *clueless*, if and when first person pronouns are used in academic prose, if *the future holds* and *the problem lies* are patterns of normal usage, what things we *grit, clench, grind,* if *shoulder, elbow, wrist* are used as verbs. Given that the data comes from a large, sampled set of native speakers, if the answer to any of these questions is yes, it is important that the learner find out more about them, so that they interpret what they read and hear in the way that it was intended – and so that they write and speak fluently and accurately and sophisticatedly and idiomatically (FASI). After all, native speakers acquire their own language through exposure to large quantities of "used language" (Brazil 1995; O'Grady 2010), an expression that Sinclair and Mauranen describe as language that had been authenticated by its participation in communication, in the incrementation of shared experience (2006:144).

Corpora typically contain a large amount of authentic language data, and such a quantity of such a quality is often considered a drawback – *the curse of quality*. This need not be the case. The entirely understandable criticism of using authentic language with learners is based on the fact that such language contains rare words, unfamiliar phrases and constructions, recent coinages, cultural references and irony, all of which can be expected in language that has not been doctored, compromised or figleafed for learners – *the curse of quality*.

The entirely credible retort to this is the simple fact that it is rarely necessary to read whole concordance lines, let alone concordance pages. When tasked with answering any of the above questions, for example, it is often enough to scan the immediate context of the search word, as we did with *kith and kin*. In the case of Sketch Engine, concordance pages can be generated using the Good Examples (GDEX) algorithm (p.44), which presents the top concordance lines in 'learner-friendly' language. Corpus tools also summarise the data in word sketches, collocation lists, phrase, bundles, etc. And as far as *the curse of quantity*" is concerned, corpus tools provide random samples, make subcorpora, and generate lists and tables that summarise the results of a search.

It Is also objected that using corpora in class is time-consuming. Leaving aside the documented findings that teachers squander valuable class time in non-productive, 'busy' work (see Thornbury's *T is for Time*[19]), teachers need to be aware of how much studying, learning and acquiring are taking place simultaneously when learners are engaged in corpus-based guided discovery tasks. Such are its affordances. The following claim by Jean Piaget (1896-1980) adds another dimension to this. (Warning: sexist language ahead).

> Each time one prematurely teaches a child something he could have discovered for himself, the child is kept from inventing it and consequently from understanding it completely (1972).

In the name of metacognitive strategies, teachers can also raise students' awareness of what they have learnt and how. In addition to the language learnt through corpus tasks, this discussion is a practical speaking activity as well as preparation for learner autonomy.

It is also objected that learning to use corpus software is a steep learning curve. And so it is. As is learning to use an iPad, a word processor, a fancy washing machine, the wireless 2TB storage device I recently acquired along with its 73 page manual. Even dictionaries:

> Dictionaries are easy to use in a rudimentary fashion even on first encounter, though only training will help learners to make the most of them (Boulton 2015:277).

The basic features of these things can be used just as soon as they are out of the box, but it takes considerable familiarity with them before even half of their features are being properly used. Becoming and remaining a professional in any field requires study and diligence. We all hope that doctors and mechanics and engineers and fire/road/food safety inspectors have the most up-to-date equipment and know how to use it.

---

[19] See the blog, An A-Z of ELT blog (Thornbury): T is for Time.

Sketch Engine is the most complex, multi-faceted publicly available corpus resource. Not only can It do more than many of the others put together, it does things that none of the others do. This book starts with explorations of a lot of language through using the basic features of Sketch Engine, and introduces its features step by step to demonstrate how more and more language can be studied.

Data-driven learning

Sinclair's above-mentioned COBUILD project was undertaken at Birmingham University. In another corner of the university, Tim Johns (1936-2009) was doing his pioneering work in what he termed data-driven learning. He described it as ...

> an approach to foreign language learning that takes seriously the notion that the task of the learner is to 'discover' the foreign language, and that the task of the language teacher is to provide a context in which the learner can develop strategies for discovery – strategies through which he or she can 'learn how to learn' (1991).

Two lexically-oriented approaches to language teaching, Data-Driven Learning (Johns) and the Lexical Approach (Lewis), would have fared far better today than they did in the 1980s and 1990s when computers, corpus data and corpus tools still had much development ahead of them. This book hopes to contribute to their rehabilitation.

Both assume inductive learning procedures:

> Data-Driven Learning: identify ➔ classify ➔ generalise
>
> The Lexical Approach: observe ➔ hypothesize ➔ experiment

More recently, Carter and McCarthy (1995) proposed their three "I"s:

> Interlanguage Approach ➔ Illustration ➔ Interaction ➔ Induction

Flowerdew advocates adding a fourth 'I', namely teacher *Intervention*, as an optional stage between interaction and induction (2009:407). This puts teachers in the role of Vygotsky's more knowledgeable other (1978). Chujo et al. (2012) have piloted a four-stage DDL approach with elementary students: (1) hypothesis formation through inductive corpus-based exercises; (2) explicit explanations from the teacher to confirm or correct these hypotheses; (3) hypothesis testing through follow-up exercises; and (4) learner production.

Johns, on the other hand, claimed:

> What distinguishes the DDL approach is the attempt to cut out the middleman as much as possible and give direct access to the data so that the learner can take part in building his or her own profiles of meanings and uses (Johns 1991:30).

This refers to learning language directly from language rather than from mediated resources such as textbooks, grammars, dictionaries and teachers. This unmediated approach sees new roles for teachers when students are working with corpora: for one thing, it bestows a new significance on metacognitive strategies training. Metacognitive strategies involve planning for learning, thinking about learning and how to make it effective, self-monitoring during learning, and self-evaluation of learning after the language activity is completed (O'Malley and Chamot, 1990).

Johns' work has had an enduring impact on the application of corpus data to language learning, but mainly for the converted.

In pedagogical terms, metacognitive strategies require higher order thinking skills (HOTS), which are said to promote learning. HOTS require the learner to ask the right questions, create queries, use the tools available and finally arrive at an answer. These processes represent deep learning experiences.

This diagram represents the six levels of cognitive activity as formulated in the Revised Bloom's Taxonomy (Anderson et al. 2001).

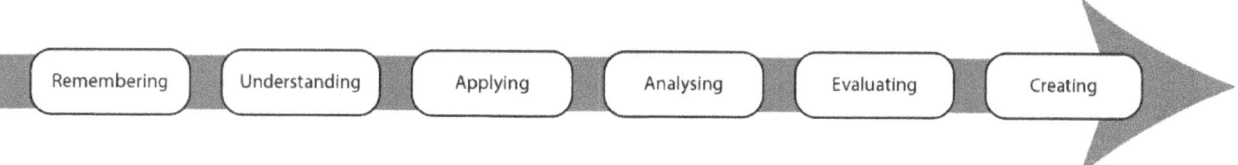

Without further ado, let us begin. Follow the registration instructions for Sketch Engine at bit.ly/versatile_ske_reg. Then return here, and go to the next page.

Your Notes

Chapter 1   Words and Phrases

Three levels of querying

Most of the language questions in this book can be addressed in most of the corpora available in Sketch Engine. But as we are focussing on the core features of British English, DESKE mainly uses the British National Corpus (Tree Tagger) for its discovery tasks.

Open it by clicking on its name in the table on the Home Page[20]. It may be necessary to click the **All Corpora** button to see it the first time you visit the page. Once a corpus has been used, it is promoted to the Recent list. Clicking on the name of a corpus takes you to a Query form with three levels:

1. The top level is **Query types** where we search for words and phrases, which in some ways resembles an internet search. The top of the top is Simple Query, and we will explore this first.
2. The second level lets us filter a top level query within a **Context**. This means that we can search for something in the context of other words and/or parts of speech, e.g. searching for *dictionary* in the context of *look* and a preposition, as we do in Question 151. We have already seen *kith* in the context of *kin*.
3. The third type allows us to specify the **Text Types** in which the word and/or context items occur, e.g. in spoken language, in academic texts, in legal texts, or spoken by women.

Asking questions simply

A good research question is one that you can envisage finding an answer to – never just ask the question. Always imagine the possible answers and how you would find them out (Wray and Bloomer 2012:1).

Simple Query field

We click on the **Query types** button to toggle between the Simple Query only and the full 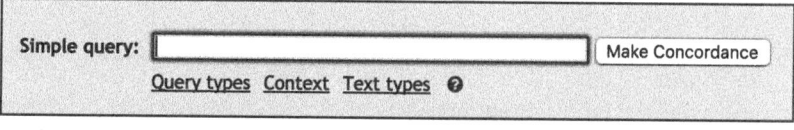 form. When you type a word or phrase into the Simple Query field and click Make Concordance, it searches the corpus and returns page(s) of the search results. Let's ask our first question.

Question 1   Does *whose* only refer to people or does it also refer to non-living things?

   Before answering any of these questions, make a note of what your intuition tells you.

[20] https://the.sketchengine.co.uk/auth/corpora

Type *whose* into Simple Query, click **Make Concordance** and look at the nouns and pronouns on the left of the node to see what it refers to.

Anyone who is under the impression that *whose* is limited to people only, as *who* is, tends to use *which* or *that* instead of *whose*. English does not do this.

> g about. A man **whose** actions and mot
> body of the boy **whose** motorbike had
> pelargoniums, **whose** leaves can deve
> ng laboratories **whose** market is Ameri
> ineyard owners **whose** irrigation suppli
> to an alleyway **whose** walls were form

Question 2   Do we say *people who* or *people that*?

Simply type one into Simple Query and the other into another Simple Query in another browser tab. Click between them to compare your findings.

Given that one of them is about ten times more frequent than the other, we'll take that as the pattern of normal usage. For further information, look down the concordance page at what follows *people that* – this is revealing.

Question 3   How is the idiom *kick the bucket* used?

Type the idiom into Simple Query and see if its context (read across) and co-text (read down) provide any clues as to its meaning. This is worth considering whether you know its meaning or not.

It is also important to observe how it is typically used. It is worth observing its position in sentences, its lexical company, i.e. frequently co-occurring words, and its grammatical company such as verb tenses, modality, prepositions, etc. It is also worth observing in what types of texts it is used, as we will study later in this book.

As the table below shows, *kick the bucket* yields very different quantities of data in three corpora, yet similar quantities in the spoken and written parts of the BNC.

Why might there be such a range of results?

The last column in the table shows the **Hits Per million** (HPM). This is a number that appears beside the raw frequency of hits at the top of the concordance page. It tells us that for every million words in the corpus, the item occurs this often. It is most useful when comparing searches in different corpora and subcorpora.

Can we conclude that this idiom is equally common in spoken and written English? No, we cannot. Six hits in 10 million is very different from seven hits in 90 million.

This is referred to as *normalization*.

kick the bucket	Corpus size in words	Hits	HPM
BNC (whole)	96,267,546	13	0.12
BNC Spoken	c. 10,000,000	6	0.51
BNC Written	c. 90,000,000	7	0.07
LEXMCI	1,448,180,339	95	0.06
enTenTen	11,191,860,036	2,769	0.20

One observation we can make here is that it is relatively least frequent in LEXMCI than the others.

There are many words and phrases that express dying in English. Recreate this table for *pass away*, *bite the dust*, and/or others that you know. And make similar observations about its context and co-text.

Give some thought now to what you have learnt in the process of answering this question.

Question 4   **Do problems *lie*? If so, what is meant by this?**

It often happens that we meet items of language that surprise us, and asking the thousands of native speakers whose language has been sampled in a corpus might not only answer the question, but provide other quite useful usage information, serendipitously.

In the Simple Query field type the two base forms (lemmas): *problem lie*. And click Make Concordance. What data is returned? What sorts of things precede and follow this pair of words? What information do you now have?

Here are several other quirky collocations that may be equally revealing:

shed light, burning issue, fall pregnant, lend support, loss interest, shed tear, ignite passion, strange bedfellow, smoking gun, exercise caution.

Compare their HPMs in different corpora as in the previous question.

Question 5   **Do people respond to something with the phrase *that's a moot point* to mean that they don't believe what was just said?**

Before doing anything, including consulting a dictionary, what does your intuition tell you?

Type *moot point* into Simple Query and be prepared for some very clear patterns.

Is it ever used in the plural?

What does its position relative to the full stops and commas tell us?

Is there a salient verb?

Is it in the past often enough to be called a pattern?

Moot Hall, Keswick UK

Is it used with modal verbs?

Is there any reported speech?

Does the language appear to be mostly spoken or written?

In the process of making these observations, have you answered the original question?

Question 6   **Can you say *handsome woman* in English?**

You can say anything. Try the question, *Do you say handsome woman* in English?

Students are routinely taught that *handsome woman* is not 'good English', but when you type this collocation into the Simple Query field, be prepared to find that it does indeed occur. At issue is not the collocation, but the semantics of *handsome*. An internet image search of various adjectives that describe men as physically attractive yield quite different pages of thumbnails, e.g. *handsome man, sexy man, gorgeous man*. Try the same adjectives with *woman*.

To find more such adjectives, click on Thesaurus in the left panel of Sketch Engine and enter *handsome*.

The features of *handsome*, although most common in men, also appear in a certain type of woman, namely a handsome one. We revisit this question several times (see Word Focus Index).

As we can already see, data has to be interpreted before it becomes information. We are now going to work through one example. In the process, we observe some features of Sketch Engine, start to see how language is the data from which we draw conclusions about patterns of normal usage and how these are sometimes exploited by language users. We also consider the relevance of these things to language learning.

Question 7 **Does anyone really say *while holidaying*?**

Perhaps a language teacher made it up to demonstrate something, or perhaps it appeared in translation software. If you are ever suspicious of a construction, even in your own writing, don't hesitate to check it in a corpus.

```
Simple query: while holidaying          Make Concordance
               Query types  Context  Text types  ⓘ
```

Remember that the BNC is more than 25 years old – it is sometimes fairer to ask, *Did people say ...?* rather than *Do people say ...?* Enter the phrase into imple Query and click the Make Concordance button.

The data is quite revealing. The screenshot below shows all five concordances of *while holidaying*. Don't worry if yours looks different – in the section below, View Options (p.41), we learn how to customise the appearance of concordance pages.

How many times does *while holidaying* occur in the BNC? In what sorts of texts? Is it ever at the beginning of a sentence? What precedes it? What immediately follows it?

Query while, holidaying 5 > GDEX 5 (0.04 per million) ⓘ	
1 W_newsp_ta...	feared they would die after being snatched **while holidaying** in France. The prisoners - who killed a ☐
2 W_news_scr...	Gloucestershire Royal Hospital, died 10 days ago **while holidaying** in Egypt. The tourist bus in which she ☐
3 W_newsp_ot...	married and guide dog Peter was best `man'. **While holidaying** in Scotland the couple became committed ☐
4 W_newsp_ta...	fend off the local romeos from his daughter **while holidaying** on the enchanted island. It's heavy breathing ☐
5 W_newsp_br...	was playing whist, and two years later, **while holidaying** with an uncle in the Netherlands, she picked ☐

Our search item occurs five times in the whole BNC of 100 million words. Five of anything is not significant as the 0.04 per million tells us. The word *while* occurs 54,791 times in the BNC, which is 484.9 times per million words. Open this permalink [21] to see verbs that frequently occur after while. These data shed some more light on the significance of *while holidaying*.

Would you expect the alternative construction, *while on holiday(s)* to occur more frequently? Try it. Bear in mind that the first recorded use of *holiday* as a verb is as recent as 1869 [22], which makes it less entrenched in the language than most common vocabulary.

---

[21] http://ske.li/bnc_while_vb
[22] See *holiday* in Merriam Webster online

It would be fair to conclude that *while holidaying* is possible, it is not probable.

Given that there are millions if not billions of words written and spoken in English every day, the paltry 100 million words of the BNC really is a tiny sample. Chances are that if it occurs five times in the BNC, it occurs thousands of times in authentic usage every day.

The probability that *while* and *holidaying* would occur together (contiguously) would be the same as the probability that any two words would co-occur:

- if all words were equally frequent in the language or in the corpus
- and if their parts of speech did not influence their likelihood of co-occurrence, e.g. adjective + noun is probable in English whereas adjective + adverb is not.

Returning to our concordance page, the text to the left of the **node** (the search item), usually indicates that something happened while holidaying; the text on the right usually says where, as can be expected in unmarked word order (see below). In one case only, does it start a sentence.

When you click on the node, a wider context box pops up as in this screenshot. Click on the arrow head at the top to close it.

≫

< previous many mourners turned up to say a final goodbye to nurse, Sharon Hill, that some had to stand outside Gloucester crematorium for the service. Sharon, who worked at Gloucestershire Royal Hospital, died 10 days ago *while holidaying* in Egypt. The tourist bus in which she was travelling was fired on by terrorists. The mourners were led by Sharon's parents, John and Sheila Hill. After the service, the rector gave his reaction next >

Across the top of any corpus search, a **breadcrumb trail** appears. As various operations are performed on search results, e.g. sorting, sampling, filtering, the breadcrumb trail expands. You can click on any breadcrumb in the trail to return the data to previous states.

Unmarked and marked features of language

Deviations from the normal, standard, typical way of doing something are said to be *marked*. Markedness can only appear when there is a situation which permits choice. For example, to avoid sexist language, authors will use he or she. This occurs 1,721 time in the BNC, whereas she or he occurs 54 times making it a marked choice. The choice may be made consciously or subconsciously. Wearing red shoes with your suit instead of the black ones you usually wear is a marked choice, and is likely to have an effect especially on those familiar with your typical attire.

In English, unmarked word order revolves around S V O M P T, the acronym for Subject, Verb, Object, Manner, Place, Time. The verb and the object and any of the adverbial elements (M P T) form the predicate, which provides new information about the subject. The bold element of Corp ex.9 shows the S V O and the following example shows S V O O, the second O being the indirect object.

Corp ex.9   Thus **he met Catharine Hanson**, *a handsome woman of 29 and immediately led her to his bedchamber.*

Corp ex.10   **Canano introduced me to two handsome women**, *one of whom was his mistress.*

Subject – Verb – Complement is also standard, since the verbs in this structure are copular verbs, which are among the most frequently used verbs, e.g. *be, become, appear, seem, look like*.

Corp ex.11   *Nona Thorp was a handsome woman but she had withdrawn into herself, ...*

Marked word order involves restructuring and it indicates the speaker's attitude to the information and its place in the discourse. For example,

Corp ex.12   One of the most **handsome women** I ever saw was in the Rhondda valley.

Corp ex.13   I thought what a very **handsome woman** she was.

Vocabulary choices often display degrees of markedness: the connotations of a word or phrase often motivate choosing *bright* over *clever*, when describing a student, for example. Troponyms also express degrees of markedness, for example, in the series,

go → walk → stroll → amble

each one being more marked than the one before. Each one contains an additional element of meaning: if someone is *walking*, it does not mean that they are *ambling*, but if they are *ambling*, they are surely *walking*. Analogous issues arise when we explore hypernyms on p.114.

If *troponym* is a new term, have you inferred its meaning from this exercise?

Question 8   **Would you expect each of the troponyms to be less frequent than the one to the left of it?**

In other words, the more marked, the less frequent.

Use Simple Query to observation serve the occurrences of these words. As they all appear in various parts of speech, the results will be mixed.

	go	**walk**	**stroll**	**amble**
Frequencies				
Hits per million				

What are some reasons for this wide range?

Question 9   **Would you expect that these frequencies impact on the order in which native speaker children *acquire* them, or learners *learn* them?**

First Language Acquisition (FLA) questions can be investigated using the CHILDES corpus, which is available through Sketch Engine. Corpus study of Second Language Acquisition (SLA) is mostly conducted via learner corpora.

The normal, standard, typical way of doing or saying something is more frequent than any of the marked variations on the linguistic menu. This means that language learners have more exposure to them and are primed for unmarked forms first.

These verbs of motion are followed up later when we have more corpus skills under our belts.

Question 10   **One swallow does not a summer make. What is this curious word order?**

Why is the verb at the end?
Is this marked word order a pattern of normal usage?
Is it a fossil from English's Germanic past?
Which meaning of *make* does this structure realise?
Is this a proverb or an idiom?

The BNC does not have enough data for this archaism. Make a Simple Query search in LEXMCI for *does not a*, where it yields 123 hits, 79 of which have the structure with noun phrases: NP does not a NP make[23]. Use your browser's Find (CTRL F) and search for *make* to see the prevalence and position of *make* on the concordance page. The pattern is clear. For example,

Corp ex.14   *However, chutzpah alone does not a good film make.*

Corp ex.15   *Of course, one battle **does not a war make**, ...*

The contracted form also occurs, although less frequently than the full form:

Corp ex.16   *One election loss **doesn't a failure make.***

Corp ex.17   *Having a girlfriend **doesn't a straight man make**!*

Do these examples[24] with the contraction appear to be spoken language?

Using Sort Right in the left panel, you see the lexical patterns as well.

See p.35 for forming queries with apostrophes.

But why don't we say, *One swallow makes not a summer?* What is the function of *does* in this proverb: negation or emphasis? See the paradigm under Periphrasis (p.97) for more on the roles of *do*.

In Shakespeare's day, the periphrastic *do* had not yet settled into its modern-day usage. *Romeo and Juliet* was written around 1595. See what they were saying then:

JULIET   *O think'st thou we shall ever meet again?*   (Do you think ...)

ROMEO   *I doubt it not; and all these woes shall serve*   (I don't doubt it)
For sweet discourses in our time to come.

He also instructed Mercutio, *Nay, good goose, bite not.* (Don't bite me)

Many fixed expressions in English also come from the King James Bible (1611) and retain their echoes of times past.

Man doth not live by bread alone. Deuteronomy 8:2-3, Matthew 4.4, Luke 4.4.

But does our idiom date from this period?

Let us consider this earlier form: Search LEXMCI for *doth not a*.

The seven examples contain contemporary references, e.g. *girlband, scouts*. What does this suggest? There is only one example of *doth not a* in the BNC, also with contemporary references.

Corp ex.18   A: *A little smoke and a couple of pills doth not a junkie make.*
B: *Yeth Shakeshpeare, you're right. It dothn't. Oth courth noth -*

Speaker B is clearly amused by what he or she takes as Shakespearean English. But why all the '*th*'s?

---

[23] http://ske.li/lexmci_not_make
[24] http://ske.li/ett_does_nt_a_make

For comparison, search for the unmarked form, *does not make a,* in LEXMCI. It seems that many instances of the structure, NP make + a + NP, are delexical verbs, e.g. *make a profit, make a contribution*. Delexical verbs are described on p.111.

Does our target structure, **NP does not a NP make**, have its own underlying meaning? Could it mean, *indicate, constitute, justify the label of...*, or something else?

You could similarly investigate *thought not,* the standard expression of which is *didn't think so.*

In searching for answers, we have found many questions. This idiom is not only interesting structurally and historically, its meaning is relevant to our guided discovery activities: *one swallow does not a summer make* is an underlying principle in pattern hunting: an insignificant number of occurrences does not permit us to declare something a pattern of normal usage.

One last word from the author, Michael Frayn quoting from the Kings James Bible, found in the BNC:

Corp ex.19   *If after the manner of men I have fought with beasts at Ephesus, what advantageth it me, if the dead rise not?*

Constrained options

The corollary of Kilgarriff's statement quoted above, *Language is never, ever, ever random*, is that every choice we make is constrained by a continuum of factors that range from purely grammatical conventions to the pragmatic considerations that are embedded in the context of the culture.

The sentence you have just read took much longer to write than to read. It is a long sentence containing a number of infrequent words sometimes in standard constructions, sometimes not. For a native speaker of English, such elements as *make a choice, factors range from A to B, context of culture,* placed no demands on the writing process. Structuring the sentence with three clauses, however, certainly took some juggling and a string of choices were made to achieve this result.

Halliday's view is that users select from options that arise in the environment of other options, and the power of language resides in its organization as a huge network of interrelated choices.

Michael Lewis' *The Lexical Approach* (1993) divides grammar for pedagogical purposes into Patterns, Facts and Choices. **Patterns** are the regularities within a language such as morphological forms (plural s, past –ed), unmarked word order (S V O M P T) and the gerund following prepositions. **Facts** on the other hand, relate to individual items. For example,

- the use of the subjunctive after certain words (mandative subjunctive)
- irregular forms of about 200 mostly high frequency verbs
- the comparative and superlative forms of some high frequency adjectives
- the irregular plurals of some mostly low frequency nouns, *man, woman* and *child* being notable exceptions.
- some verbs are most frequently used in the passive
- words have different meanings which are mostly realised by their patterns. This is convincingly demonstrated in the Pattern Dictionary of English Verbs, (Hanks)[25] which makes many appearances in this book
- cognates might have quite a different meaning or use in other languages

The specific exemplars of these have to be learned as language facts.

---

[25] http://www.pdev.org.uk

Choice presents the greatest challenge for non-native speakers because selecting the most probable form from possible forms involves weighing up the *constraints* on each one. As we move up the Hierarchy of Language, as represented in this diagram, there is a greater freedom of choice. As Roman Jakboson (1896-1982) put it:

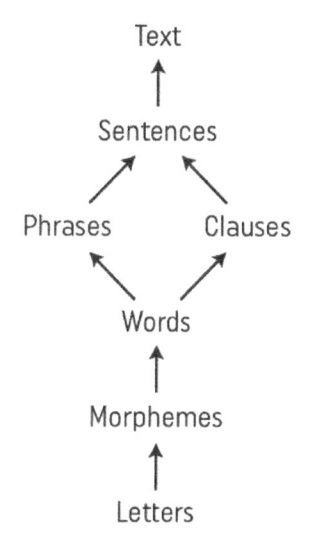

```
        Text
          ↑
      Sentences
        ↗   ↖
  Phrases   Clauses
        ↖   ↗
        Words
          ↑
      Morphemes
          ↑
        Letters
```

In the combination of linguistic units there is an ascending scale of freedom. In the combination of distinctive features into phonemes, the freedom of the individual is zero: the code has already established all the possibilities which may be utilized in a given language. Freedom to combine phonemes into words is circumscribed; it is limited to the marginal situation of word coinage. In forming sentences with words the speaker is less constrained. And finally, in the combination of sentences into utterances, the action of compulsory syntactic rules ceases, and the freedom of any individual speaker to create novel contexts increases substantially, although again the numerous stereotyped utterances are not to be overlooked (Jakobson 1971:53).

Choice may well be considered a fuzzy thing in language, but in fact, as the options are whittled away through a process of elimination, few if any remain. After all, every communicative act has a perlocutionary force, such as persuading, convincing, enlightening or getting someone to do something, and each of these has its own lexicogrammatical realisations (locutionary acts): never ever random. Perlocutionary force is an aspect of Austin's (1911-1960) influential theory of speech acts (Austin 1962), a cornerstone of the field of pragmatics. Choice not only entails things selected, but things rejected.

Another choice we make is how we refer to people, e.g. *Shakespeare, Will, the Bard, a man, he, the playwright*. Which one does a language user choose at any given moment, and what motivates the choice? In Pragmatics, this is called Reference. It is problematic in collocation study, as we will see.

> Found in the BNC: An example of a chain of co-referential items is Mrs Thatcher → The Prime Minister → The Iron Lady → Maggie. Halliday and Hasan do not discuss this type of referential linkage and Hoey (1988: 162) points out that co-reference 'is not strictly a linguistic feature at all but a matter of real-world knowledge'.

Corpus data inevitably show patterns in the choices that have already been made.

Other Simple Query searches

word	Frequency	
P | N is welcome	118	████████████████
P | N is welcomed	40	█████
P | N is welcoming	6	▌
P | N is Welcome	1	▏
P | N IS WELCOME	1	▏

We can now work through some more questions that can be asked and answered using Simple Query only. Note that **lemmas** entered into the Simple Query field search for all inflected forms (see Morphology p.75), whereas **word forms** you enter return that word form only. For example, searching for *be welcome* returns the combinations of all eight conjugated forms of *be* as well as its contractions, plus all three forms of *welcome*, whereas *is welcome*, searches for all forms of *is*, of which there is only one, and all forms of *welcome,* as can be seen in this screenshot. To see this frequency list for *be welcome*, open this permalink [26].

---

[26] ske.li/bnc_be_welcome

Words and Phrases

Question 11   **Is *open door* an adjective + noun or a verb + noun? Or something else?**

The minimal use of inflection in contemporary English leads to many word forms being used in different parts of speech. This is referred to as conversion and is discussed on p.74. *Open door* is a pair of words that looks like a typical verb + noun combination, but which turns out to be used in a variety of POS combinations.

There are 412 hits of *open door* (3.6 per million) in the BNC. It is mainly an adjective + noun as in Corp ex.20. The following example shows a compound adjective describing *policy*. We then see it is a verb and its object, conjugated and declined respectively. This literal use of *to open a door* contrasts with its figurative use in the last example. Interesting, isn't it? When inanimate subjects open doors, marked meanings can be expected.

Corp ex.20   *To the right, a partially **opened door** led to a connecting office.*

Corp ex.21   *Harding, the man who implemented BNFL's **open door** policy has said goodbye.*

Corp ex.22   *… he would prowl the ward, **opening doors**, locking me in a bathroom.*

Corp ex.23   *Our album **opened doors** for us all over the world.*

These variations are problematic for error tagging software: be prepared for unexpected, unreliable results.

Question 12   **I've come across *boldly go* a few times and wondered if it is more than a collocation.**

Type the phrase into Simple Query. There are not very many hits in the BNC, which tells us something. There are a few words in the contexts which give a good clue as to the source of this phrase.

Does *go* conjugate or is the word form part of the fixed phrase?

It is interesting to find that *go* is very rarely preceded by an adverb that describes how something or someone went. Open this permalink [27] and look at the list; it was generated using the Frequency tool, which we study on p.54. For more information about *boldly go,* see its very own entry in Wikipedia [28].

Question 13   **In the Introduction, someone was said to *sleep furiously.* Where did this counter-intuitive description of sleeping come from?**

People do like to play with language. This is extracted from a very short and highly improbable sentence created by the American linguist, Noam Chomsky, to demonstrate that syntactic correctness of a sentence, even if the content is semantic nonsense, meets the *grammaticality* requirements of a language (1957).

While *sleep furiously* does not occur in the BNC, a search for it in enTenTen yields enough data to reveal how it was originally used, how people commented on it, and how people have exploited it. Its Wikipedia page reveals even more [29].

---

[27] ske.li/bnc_ly_go
[28] See Wikipedia: Where no man has gone before.
[29] See Wikipedia: Colorless green ideas sleep furiously.

Question 14   **I've heard the phrase, *Just when you thought it was safe to ...* and I wonder how it might be used. Is it ironic?**

Let's search for *just when you* and see where it leads. In fact, the raw unsorted data doesn't easily lead us anywhere. Click on Sort Right in the left panel and click through the five pages. Who said language wasn't patterned?

Question 15   **I've also heard *in my point of view*. I thought it was *from*...**

In the BNC there is one example with *in* and 69 with *from*. Let that be a lesson to you! A single instance does not a pattern make.

Now search the internet for *in my point of view*. What do you learn?

Forming Simple Query searches is similar to querying Google and Yahoo, etc, but the results are very different because the internet is a vast, random and unregulated collection of documents of many types, changing moment by moment. This is in stark contrast to a corpus designed for language study and analysis. Thus the internet is able to say what is possible in English while a corpus search tells us what is probable. This contrast appears in classroom language: note the difference between *Can you say this in English?* and *Do you say this in English?* as we saw in Question 6.

Question 16   **How is the word *germane* used?**

Resist the temptation to look this word up in a dictionary, at least until we have worked through the steps below. In any case, we ask questions that dictionaries do not answer.

Search for *germane* in the BNC using Simple Query. It is indeed a rare word.

It is mostly followed by *to*. Search now for *germane to* in Simple Query[30]. Is *to* a preposition or an infinitive marker when used with *germane*? Or both?

Which verb precedes *germane*? Always, often, sometimes?

What sorts of things are the subjects?

By this stage, you have probably inferred the meaning and worked out the pattern that *germane* is used in.

How would you express this notion in other words?

People's needs for precision and concision vary. These needs certainly influence the choices we make when writing and speaking. It can take a long time to weigh up the pros and cons of a particular expression. The French author, Gustave Flaubert, placed such high demands on himself, or went to such great pains to find *le mot juste*, that his overall output was much smaller than that of his contemporaries.

Le mot juste refers to the most precise and appropriate wording for a specific concept in a particular context. Interestingly, this is a lexical gap in English, i.e. when there is no expression for a concept, which makes it impossible to search in a corpus. We borrowed this one from French. As the old joke goes: you can always rely on English for the *mot juste.*

Question 17   **What other words and phrases has English borrowed?**

English vocabulary owes a great deal to both French and German. The estimated

---

[30] ske.li/bnc_germane_to

percentages of English words that derive from these two languages ranges from c. 25% to 30% each.

The pronunciation of 'ch' exemplifies these sources. When 'ch' is pronounced č, the word typically has a Germanic origin, e.g. *church*. When pronounced š, the word is most likely to be of French original, e.g. *nonchalant*. The third pronunciation of 'ch' is **k**, which signals its Greek origin, e.g. *stomach*.

Some well-known French borrowings include: .

coup d'état, denoument, faux amis, faux pas, laissez-faire, nouveau riche, sangfroid.

Some well-known German borrowings include:

angst, doppelgänger, ersatz, gemütlichkeit, schadenfreude, wunderkind, zeitgeist.

> **Loan word.** Both form and meaning are borrowed, or assimilated, with some adaptation to the phonological system of the new language. (Crystal 2006:286)

Make a list of at least five categories of 'word knowledge' that would enable someone to use these words appropriately when speaking and writing. As we work through this book, keep an eye on your categories and the French and German lists and build up a dossier for each word.

Question 18 — When might one use *curiouser* instead of *more curious*?

Search for both forms of the comparative of *curious* in two separate browser tabs. The formal aspect of language we observe in c*uriouser* relates to what we know about the formation of the comparative in English as we explore on p.107.

To what extent do the frequencies of occurrences of these two forms determine which form to use and in what contexts? Despite there being 20 hits of *curiouser*, they are in fact duplicates of ten occurrences. Click on Left under Sort in the left panel to see how they duplicate. Click on Doc IDs under Frequency to see the ten documents duplicated.

While frequency is a decisive factor in determining what is normal (as anyone in a minority will attest), there are other factors at work ensuring that language is not bland, mechanical and colourless.

In the concordance page, the sentence which continues, *Cried Alice ...* is the original. Even its author admits that his character was not speaking good English:

> "Curiouser and curiouser!" Cried Alice (she was so much surprised, that for the moment she quite forgot how to speak good English)." From *Alice in Wonderland* (Ch. 2), Lewis Carroll, 1865.

As with *boldly go, does not a ... make, sleep furiously* and many such exploitations of the language, scanning the contexts and co-texts often provides a good hint as to how *curiouser* slipped into the language and how it is used.

When might you use *curiouser* instead of *more curious*?

Question 19 — Is *Pacific Ocean* written with this capitalisation?

And what about *Czech Republic*, *East Timor*, and other such compound country names. Enter them in lower case. From the concordance page, click Node forms under Frequency.

From the concordance page, observe their relationship with the definite article. Can you determine a pattern here?

Question 20 **Is *Internet* written with this capitalisation?**

Search for this in the BNC, Simple Query field, and see how it is capitalised. Search in more recent corpora to find out if this practice persists.

As we saw on p.**Error! Bookmark not defined.**, *web site* occurs once only in the BNC. However, the word *web* occurs hundreds of times, but is it in the internet sense? And is capitalisation an issue? Search and explore.

The word *Internet* is not infrequent in the BNC. In the first edition of this book, both *internet* and *web* were used 13 times without any conscious choice on the part of the author. Boulton (2015:267) points out:

> Though there is a technical difference between the *Internet* and the *world wide web*, the two are commonly used interchangeably, as here.

And as here. Sometimes the preference for *web* is dictated by the compound *web crawling*, which is rare with *internet*.

Punctuation in English and in Sketch Engine

Welcome to punctuation, a right royal pain in corpus work, and none more so than the apostrophe. It is used for contractions e.g. *they're, who'd, can't* and possessives *Megan's, sufferer's*. Search for these five words.

Behind the scenes, corpora store words with apostrophes as two separate tokens.

To search for words with apostrophes, it is therefore necessary to separate the two parts, e.g. *pianist 's, they 'd, hangover 's*. To complicate matters even further, the full negative contraction is separated from the base word, e.g. *do n't, could n't, wo n't*.

Question 21 **Does the phrase *who'd have thought* stand alone? Or is it a part of a sentence? If so, how is it followed up?**

Enter the search into Simple Query. Try it in various corpora.

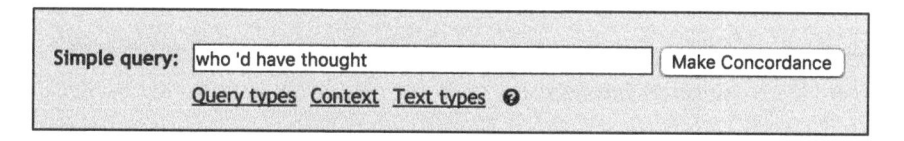

Simple query: who 'd have thought   Make Concordance
Query types Context Text types ?

Question 22 **Is it the norm to use apostrophes with decades?**

Search for both *1970s* and *1970's* in the BNC using the Simple Query field.

It is necessary to include the space when searching: 1970 s, 1970 's. As with wrong spelling, other instances of incorrect usage appear in corpora because they occur in the data that was included. But as we are primarily interested in identifying patterns of normal usage, 1970's occurring 98 times vs. the 3,046 occurrences of 1970s unequivocally answers the question. When something occurs 98 times in the BNC, it shows that many native speakers think that this is the correct written form. This little example further exemplifies the danger of searching the web to check for the existence of a construction: it is virtually impossible to search for something that gives no results. Everything is possible.

> in the 1950s, 1960s, 1970s and 1980s. These firm
> ate 1960's and early 1970's increased the UK den

Question 23   **Is it true that English never uses a preposition to end a sentence with?**

Search for *of* followed by a full stop. Leave a space in between. Sort the concordance page using Left under Sort in the left panel. This reveals some quite salient patterns.

In terms of pronunciation, there is a systematic difference between *of* at the end of a sentence or information unit, and *of* in *the NP of NP* structure. In terms of teaching pronunciation, anything 'systematic' makes it teachable as a pattern, rather than being an isolated fact. The same pronunciation pattern applies to *can* when it is part of a verb phrase (VP) and when it is at the end of an information unit.

Repeating this searching and sorting procedure using other prepositions reveals valuable lexical patterns for learners of English.

To follow up *never use a preposition to end a sentence with,* see this link[31].

Question 24   **Is *why* followed by both *can't* and *cannot*?**

For example, do we say *Why can't I come, too?* and *Why cannot I come, too?*

Once again, before answering, what does your intuition tell you?

Operators in Simple Query

Operators such as **question marks** and **asterisks** are used in searches for various substitutions. Note that these work differently in other search fields, as we shall see.

Question mark: d?g finds lemmas that begin with d, followed by one letter followed by g. Since Simple Query is a lemma search, the results will include inflected forms, for example, *dog, dogged, dogs*. Click on Node Forms in the left panel to summarise the findings. z??k allows two letters between them, while m???y three, ???n?tion, etcetera.

Question 25   **Are *wh-* words followed by both *can't* and *cannot***

To follow on from the previous question, enter into Simple Query, wh? cannot, and in a separate search, wh? ca n't. Do any patterns emerge from these observations?

Question 26   **Is the spelling of words with either *–ise* or *-ize* a difference between UK and US English?**

As the LEXMCI corpus has 100 million words of US English in addition to much British and Irish English, the question mark can be put to good use in this corpus.

Select verbs that might have this spelling variation and search for them with the question mark in place of the alternating letter, for example,

compromi?e, organi?e, televi?e, bowdleri?e, epitomi?e, ostraci?e, summari?e.

Corpora provide data that can indicate such tendencies, but it is necessary to read further afield. Interestingly, this spelling difference is not related to a US-UK divide,

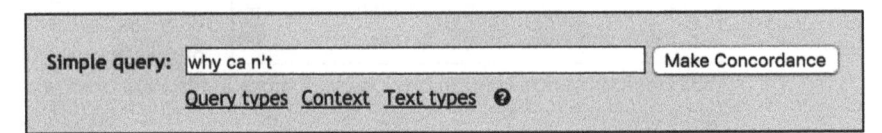

[31] http://public.wsu.edu/~brians/errors/churchill.html

rather Cambridge prefers *ise* while Oxford prefers *ize*, making both acceptable in British English. You can read more about this at these links[32]. There are some words which only have one correct spelling. For example, *summarise, prize*.

Do these spelling tendencies extend to other parts of speech?

For example, search for *televi?ion, reali?ation*.

Question 27 **Do you love me**

Who wants to know? How do people respond? How do people handle the response?

We cannot use a question mark in a question as it functions as an 'operator'. To find out how people follow up a question, enter it without the punctuation. We learn how to include punctuation in queries in and around Question 236.

Question 28 **'What's the difference between ...?'**

If this is a chunk, we should be able to observe plenty of examples in corpora. It may exist in both the contracted and full forms. The first example here is a request for information, whereas in the second it is a formula used in English jokes. Search for this chunk without the question mark and identify its uses.

Corp ex.24 *What is the difference between information and data?*

Corp ex.25 **What's the difference between** *a prostitute and a cockerel?*

Asterisk: d*g finds lemmas that begin with d and end with g. Any number of letters may appear in between. For example, *during, drug, deteriorating*. Try also combinations such as *t*n*tion* and list the node forms.

Question 29 **What is your favo*rite ...**

This search returns quite different results in 20th and 21st century corpora. Try the BNC and LEXMCI or enTenTen. Note also the use of *ou* in the target word when searching in these corpora.

Question 30 **What do we do with words like *thingamabob*?**

In the BNC, type *thinga** into Simple Query field to get the concordances. Click on Sort Node in the left panel to group them. Click on the line which has *thingamabob* preceded by *a thing group*. Clicking on the red node opens the wider context box. This particular example is of interest because it is someone talking about this linguistic phenomenon. Click on the blue metadata code and see that this is not just any old[33] *someone*.

Can you tell if these words are most typically used in speech or in writing?

What parts of speech are they? Do they refer to people as well as things?

Is the speaker in the following corpus example old, tired, drunk, deaf, lazy, uninterested? Clicking on the metadata code provides a clue.

Corp ex.26 *I went to that little shop on the corner, you know the one, bought by Miss **Thingambob** when poor old Mr **Whatshisname** went to Australia or somewhere with his asthma.*

---

[32] Further reading: http://www.metadyne.co.uk/ize.html and http://www.oxforddictionaries.com/words/ize-ise-or-yse
[33] see the phrase *just any old* in the enTenTen corpus: http://ske.li/lexmci_any_old

Asterisks can also be used between words. For example, type *have a * day* in Simple Query, then click Node forms in the left panel. Do all the expressions wish someone well?

The asterisk permits one item only which can be useful for finding missing words in phrases and exploring possibilities. It is useful for observing pronouns that occur in phrases, e.g. *take * breath away*, and finding out if phrasal verbs are separable, e.g. *let * down*. But we find that using the the Context Filter far more useful. See Chapter 6 *It depends on the context*.

Moving on from operators, let us now see what the BNC tells us about some more rare words.

Question 31 **What is the pattern that *cahoots* operates in?**

Type it into Simple Query. With so few lines to look at, the company left and right is clear. Looking at the concordance of *cahoots* may also tell you something about its meaning and usage – it is a type of *co-operating*, but does it have positive or negative connotations?

While intuition plays a part in answering our questions, quantitative data turns our impressions into qualitative information. Open this permalink[34] for a Frequency listing: a summary of data, no matter how large or small, is a step in converting data into information.

The quantity of data returned for any query obviously varies greatly not only because of the size of the corpus, but also on other factors: *cahoots* is unlikely to appear in a corpus of academic prose.

The almost 2.4 million words in the LEC corpus (2011), a sample of the English spoken in London, will provide far more focussed data for its tenor, field and mode (see p.123) than its near contemporary NMC (2008), a general English corpus many thousands of times larger, captured from the internet – horses for courses.

Question 32 **How ecstatic is life in London?**

Another question you'd never thought to ask! The word *ecstasy* occurs in the LEC 15 times and 438 times in NMC. Which of the word's meanings appear in the two corpora? How can you tell which meaning is meant?

The answers depend on the patterns in the context and co-text, and on the extent to which the data corresponds to the choices under consideration. The raw frequency of patterns with rare words differs significantly from those of common words and obviously, the bigger the corpus, the greater the chance they will appear. The mere existence of an item does not make it significant, as we saw on p.33 when discussing the internet as a source of language information.

Question 33 **What wayward items might appear in the BNC?**

Search the corpus for the following items. To learn more about their source, click on Text Types under Frequency in the left panel. This is putting metadata to good use and indicates the degrees to which some things are possible and probable in language.

accomodation, seperate, asshole, old fart, cotton candy, spag bol, would of done,

Speaking of these oddballs which do appear in the BNC, let us now consider some that do not.

---

[34] ske.li/bnc_cahoots_freq. We start making such lists on p.52.

zine, blog, road rage, regift, emoticon, sexaholism, snail mail, vertically challenged, metrosexual, merkin, sunshower, website, fess up, shirkaholic, bling

Are there any items here that you cannot live without?

The basic reason why words do not appear in the BNC is that they are not used in the texts included in the corpus. As obvious as that sounds, it is important to bear in mind. Some words are technical words and have limited use, others are rarely used, others are very slangy, new to the language or outside core English. But the simple reason is that they were not in the right place at the right time. Remember, there are no texts in the BNC after 1994 [35].

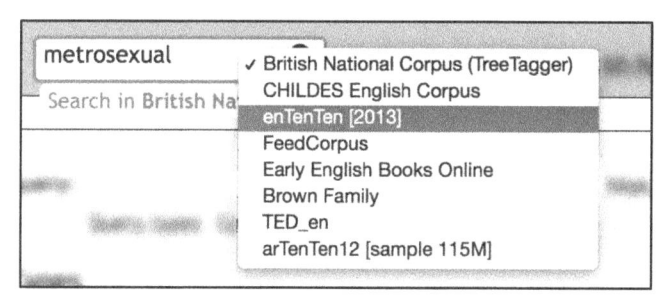

Search for some of the words above. To study items that are not in the BNC, try the much larger and more recent corpora such as enTenTen, FeedCorpus and LEXMCl which also have a wider geographical spread. To perform a Simple Query in another corpus, you can use the search field in the top right of the Sketch Engine interface as in this screenshot.

The dropdown list of corpora contains the most recent eight that you have accessed.

For other recently coined expressions that could be explored using corpora, see **New words in English** at the BBC/British Council site [36].

Question 34   **Did *tweet* mean something before the social medium, Twitter?**

Compare the use of *tweet* in the BNC and the NMC, two corpora of British English of approximately the same size. Does the meaning from the BNC still appear in the more recent NMC? Is Twitter's logo related to either meaning of *tweet*?

Question 35   **How do company names compare in the BNC and the NMC?**

e.g. Google, Amazon, General Motors, McDonalds, Kodak, Apple, Shell.

Learning language from language

This brings to an end our introduction to the Simple Query field, which we will be using throughout this book. By this stage, we have used the Simple Query field to obtain language data that can answer questions about many aspects of language.

We have looked at the meanings and uses of specific words and phrases, the grammatical and lexical company they keep, compared the frequencies of near synonyms, inferred the meaning of phrases from multiple contexts, explored the cultural relevance of some phrases, compared the significance of patterns of normal usage and the use of rare words. We have distinguished possible and probable language. We have investigated some interesting linguistic minutiae such as articles, apostrophes and the morphology of adjectives.

In the process, we met a number of general linguistic concepts that are important to language users generally, and are valuable foundation constructs in data-driven learning. To quote Boulton, "DDL can sensitise learners to issues of frequency and typicality, register and text type, discourse and style, as

---
[35] http://ske.li/bnc_pubdate
[36] http://www.teachingenglish.org.uk/articles/new-words-english

well as the fuzzy nature of language itself" (2009). The over-riding concept here is frequency, from which flow patterns of normal usage, marked and unmarked use of language, norms and exploitations, collocation and anything else that derives from Firth's notion of *knowing a word by the company it keeps* (1951).

Not unrelated to frequency is the issue of corpus size. We have found so far that corpora contain a wealth of linguistic elements that constitute the data from which we construct information. The language is as alive as the real world in which it was created, and therefore requires us to use critical thinking when drawing conclusions.

In the process, we learnt some of the basics of using Sketch Engine and familiarised ourselves with the main parts of the interface. And in accordance with the title of this book, we are finding the answers to language questions through guided discovery tasks.

Most of this has been gleaned from the BNC. Remember that most of the questions can be asked of any corpora, including those you make yourself. Sketch Engine has tools for building your own corpora, so if you would like to make a corpus now, turn to p.203 and make one. This will enable you to ask the questions in the rest of the book of your own data and compare them with corpora provided by Sketch Engine.

Before continuing with our explorations of the top level queries, we need to learn how to customise the interface. This is the stuff of the much shorter Chapter 2.

Chapter 2   Taking Ownership of your Concordance Page

In this section, we learn how to customise the concordance pages and discover what language information can be derived from different presentations of the data.

Regarding the phrase, *take ownership of something*, it used to be mostly used to refer to something tangible: after a transaction, something becomes yours. However, it occurs only four times in the BNC compared with 167 hits of *take possession*, 14 of which are *take possession of goods*, 13 of which belong in legal contexts: they are tagged with W_ac_polit_law_edu[37]. In the more current and much larger LEXMCI corpus, *take ownership* yields 1,083 hits from British English and 14 from American English.

Question 36   **What do we *take ownership of* nowadays?**

We ask this question because its answer tells us how its usage has changed since the BNC was compiled. Open this link[38] showing the right collocates of *ownership* in LEXMCI. They form lexical sets of intangible items which far outnumber tangible items.

It becomes clear that taking ownership of intangible abstractions such as *responsibility, issue, development* and *learning* involves a sense of being in control through mental/cognitive processes. Would you consider this a metaphorical extension of obtaining tangible things?

It is now time we took ownership of our concordance pages and customised them to suit our needs. To do so we click on View Options in the left panel.

View Options: Top

Click on the View Options button. It takes you to a new screen in the main panel that allows you to change the concordance view. In the Top Section of View Options, the features are determined by the metadata in the corpus – Sketch Engine is programmed to

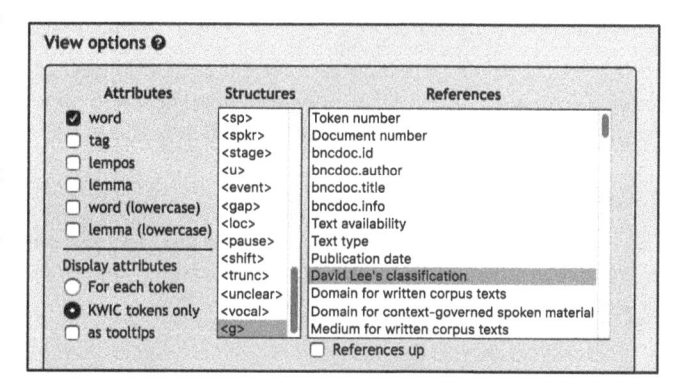

---

[37] ske.li/bnc_take_possession_goods
[38] ske.li/lexmci_take_possession_coll_r4

represent this dynamically. These screenshots are from the BNC – other corpora have different attributes and this Top Section varies accordingly.

Attributes

The Attributes column allows you to change the default display.

Selecting the other attributes shows, for example, the nodes' POS-tags and lemmas.

Lempos is a portmanteau word: lemma + POS (part of speech). Click on **Corpus Info** in the top part of the left panel to see a list of lempos suffixes.

Under Display Attributes, choose between displaying them for the node only, "KWIC tokens only", or for every token in the concordance line, "For each token".

KWIC stands for Key Word in Context. This is an unfortunate term, since the search item is elsewhere referred to as the *node*, a perfectly reasonable term. Furthermore, key words in a text are those that carry the bulk of its meaning they are useful for determining the topic of a text (Geeraerts 2010: 174).

Showing tags can be used to find out why a corpus line has unexpectedly matched a query: a common culprit is an incorrect POS-tag. In this 'broken' screenshot, the node is marked as a past participle in all cases (VVN), despite some being adjectives (AJ0).

```
Query broken 6,894 > GDEX 6,894 > Positive filter 6 (0.05 per million)
1 W_fict_prose      at Peter. She had missed; the bowl had broken /VVN . It was a blue-and-white pottery bowl
2 W_newsp_ta...     eat again. It was a long, noisy night of broken /VVN sleep. Mortars and grenades pounded the
3 W_fict_prose      ears. He grinned, showing a row of black broken /VVN teeth. `Here's to thee, gal. I likes spirit
4 W_fict_prose      can tell. From the feel I'd say both are broken /VVN . Ambulance coming?' `On its way. We'd
5 W_fict_prose      know. I don't know. A car crash? No bones broken /VVN , old boy. Lucky to be alive, you might
6 W_non_ac_s...     be honest, though, this separation has broken /VVN my heart. I don't think it's something
```

Structures

The Structures column allows you to change from the default display to show the beginning and end tags for structures such as sentences <s> and paragraphs <p>. They are used when searching for patterns that might occur at the beginnings of sentences and paragraphs, for example.

One of the most useful is <g> which stands for *glue*. With this selected, punctuation will not be separated from letters and numbers by a space on concordance pages. However, it is still necessary to separate punctuation when forming queries with punctuation, as we have already seen.

To see lists of all the structures and attributes in a corpus, click on Corpus info near the top of the left panel. Clicking on some of them reveals hyperlinks, and clicking on these shows the relevant list in the Word list tool. This is how http://ske.li/bnc_pubdate was generated.

References

The References column allows you to select the text type metadata about the source texts which appears in blue to the left of each concordance line, as in the screenshot above.

The items in the View Options list are those included in the metadata when the corpus was created. It

```
bncdoc.id              CMJ
bncdoc.author          Trollope, Joanna
bncdoc.year            1992
bncdoc.title           The rector's wife.
bncdoc.info            The rector's wife. Sample containing about 30175 words from a book (domain: imaginative)
Text availability      Worldwide rights cleared
Publication date       1985-1993
Text type              Written books and periodicals
David Lee's classification  W_fict_prose
```

is usual to select one, but more are possible, in which case you use CTRL click. It is also possible to select none of them, also using CTRL click.

Click on the blue letter(s) and number(s) to the left of a concordance line to have this metadata pop up. If there is a lot of metadata, the pop up window will scroll vertically.

David Lee's Classification

This is only available for the BNC but is generally found to be more useful than the original system: see the Index of Names and Notions for other references in this book.

Question 37 **Which of the following structures of *give* are most frequent in which register?**

Give it me, give me it, give it to me.

Enter these in the Simple Query field one at a time or in separate tabs. Make sure David Lee's Classification has been selected in View Options – References.

```
10 S_intervie...   Monday, she used to borrow it, forget to  give it me   back and . I could always ask me mother
11 W_ac_soc_s...   and me book from the social and said he'd  give it me   back once he'd cashed enough to pay the
12 S_conv          extra as well whenever I ask for it she just gives it me  I just say I've spent it all. But I never
13 W_fict_prose    just parted from her lover? `Why not? He   gave it me   to spend, presumably so he could spend
14 S_speech_u...   with me, then you can send in this, you can give it me   back at lunchtime, and I can send it into
15 W_non_ac_h...   besought the Lord our God that he would    give it me   . See now what his power is, for the day
```

Does the order of objects influence the meaning in any way? Is this a marked, conscious choice or is it constrained by text type, the speaker's attitude, etc?

Is there any other interesting company, such as punctuation or modal verbs?

Ditransitive verbs have two objects: e.g. give sth to sb. What other ditransitive verbs might be candidates for this variation in order?

Question 38 **Is *moot point* genre-specific?**

We studied some aspects of this phrase in Question 5. Now with David Lee's Classification, the metadata adds another piece to the puzzle. See this link [39].

Much of the language already explored in this book could be researched again with the added layer of text classification.

[39] ske.li/bnc_moot_point

View Options: Middle

Page Size

The Page Size box allows you to specify the page width and length for the display. KWIC Context size allows you to specify the width of the concordance window in number of characters.

Although dramatically increasing the Page Size may slow down the initial retrieval of the concordance, having many lines on one page reveals patterns as soon as it is sorted. 1,000 is good, if you have nothing against scrolling!

Jump to ...

If the number of hits exceeds the page size you set, a **Jump to** droplist appears at the top of the page after it has been sorted. This is very handy for getting past punctuation quickly, as well as going to a specific letter, or where you have sorted by References, to a particular reference.

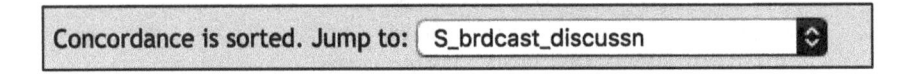

Sort Good Dictionary Examples

A set of criteria for selecting illustrative sentences is available here: *Choosing Illustrative Sentences*[40]. These criteria served as a basis for an algorithm that automatically selects *good dictionary examples*, a.k.a. GDEX. Selecting this in View Options and specifying the number of lines tells the program how many 'good examples' to present first. If you make the number of GDEX lines the same as Page size, your first page of concordances will contain all the 'good examples'. This is also shown in the breadcrumb trail.

GDEX is of great value to language teachers and learners, as well as for the lexicographers for whom it was originally programmed.

It is not used extensively in this book because so many of the tasks rely on Sketch Engine's post processing tools such as collocations, word sketches and frequency listing in particular.

---

[40] http://bit.ly/maelt_ill_sents

View Options: Bottom

Sentence copying

Selecting the checkbox for **one-click sentence copying** adds icons to the right of each line. Clicking on that icon copies the whole sentence to the computer's clipboard. You can then paste it into a word processor document, database, web page, etc.

Checkbox for selecting lines Selecting this in View Options places a column of checkboxes down the right side of the concordance page, as can be seen in the screenshot below. Once you select individual lines of interest, a new button appears in the left panel under Filter: **Selected lines.** Click on this to shorten your page to the selected lines only. This is very useful if you want to make a screenshot, or a print out, or **Save** a manually selected set of lines, e.g. the *broken* screenshot on p.42. Permalinks can be put to good use in this situation.

This works with the concordance lines on the current page only. If you need to select more lines, increase the Page length.

Allow multiple lines selection: this adds icons for copying more than one line at a time to the clipboard. The icon can be seen in the next screenshot beside the Checkboxes for selecting lines.

Show line numbers Select this to see each line numbered, as in the left column of this screenshot. This is very helpful when you need to refer to a specific line, as often happens in lectures and classrooms. It is also useful when mentioning a line in an article that contains a screenshot.

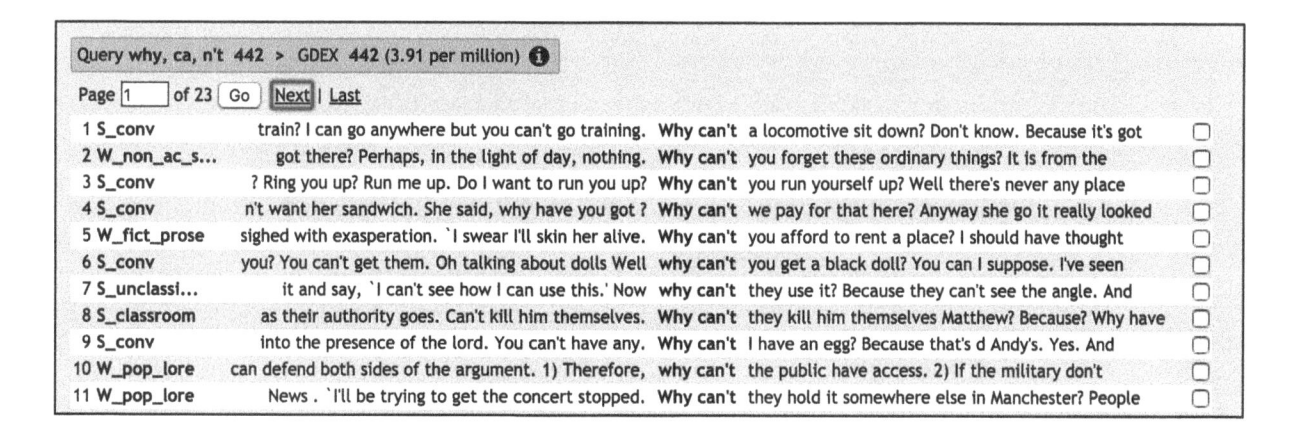

Shorten long references Select this to show only the beginning of long references, as is the case in this screenshot. This is especially useful with web-crawled corpora, whose references are often URLs. The full reference appears when the mouse hovers over it.

XML template for one-click copying is a feature used for specific projects only.

Save and Change Options

This button takes you back to your concordance page with your changes implemented. These changes made do not affect only the current corpus, but all.

Special note about copying sentences

When you copy sentences, it is often best to paste them into a simple text editor such as Notepad first. This strips away formatting such as background colour, red node word(s), thereby cleaning it for use in other programs. It may also be necessary to remove spaces between the node and the words either side of it, and before punctuation. In some word processors, Paste Special pastes text without any formatting, which makes the text editor step unnecessary.

We interrupted the Query types to bring you some important information about customising the interface. We will return to the rest of the top level queries after we do one more thing, Menu Items.

Chapter 3 What's on the menu?

The following menu items are used extensively to manipulate the results of a search. They appear in the left panel once you do a search. You can place the menu at the top instead: click Menu Position at the bottom of the panel. This may be preferred when working on a narrow monitor.

```
Save
Make subcorpus
View options
    KWIC
    Sentence
Sort
    Left
    Right
    Node
    Shuffle
Sample
    Last (20)
Filter
    Overlaps
    1st hit in doc
Frequency
    Node tags
    Node forms
    Doc IDs
Collocations
Visualize
❓
Menu position
```

Save

Click on **Save** to save the current data as a file on your computer. This can then be opened in spreadsheets, databases, word processors, etc. You can specify whether the output is text or xml, how many pages, whether a heading is included, whether the lines are numbered, whether the KWICs are aligned in the output as well as the maximum number of lines. Where it saves depends on your browser settings.

Save as subcorpus

After you have performed a search, and perhaps processed the concordances, you can save the result as a subcorpus. This can be selected for a wide range of further processing.

KWIC/Sentence

This lets you choose between the standard KWIC concordance view (which appears by default) and full sentence view.

If you selected **Icon for one-click sentence copying** in View Options, the full sentence will be copied whether in KWIC or in Sentence view.

Sort

As we have already seen, sorting is an important step in converting data into information. The examples we have looked at so far have mostly returned relatively small concordances. More frequent words and phrases yield a great deal of data and it may be necessary to use the Sample button (p.51), make searches more specific using the Filters (p.99), or use other tools such as Collocation (p.65) and Word Sketches (p.175).

The five buttons under Sort in the left panel perform the following automated sorts.

Left and right

The default order of lines on a concordance page after a search is Document IDs – this cannot be expected to reveal any patterns in the language. As we saw above, the right sorting of *just when you* (Question 14) was very revealing. Right Sorting sorts the words on the right of the node alphabetically, which reveals patterns in what follows the node, e.g. punctuation, bound prepositions, wh- words, to-infinitive, words that form compounds with the node. Left Sorting reveals patterns before the node, e.g. words forming compounds, prepositions, punctuation. These sorts exemplify the company words keep very nicely.

Question 39 — **What things are said to be *unthinkable*?**

Sometimes we come across a word in the course of our normal reading and we would like to be sure that we understand it in the way that it is meant. Unless it is a key word in the text, it is not likely to appear more than once. To get a feel for how it works generally or variously in the language, we need some more examples.

"You are not allowed to think this," sounds rather Orwellian, doesn't it? How intrusive must a ruling class be if they can tell us what we can and cannot think! But does *unthinkable* mean 'cannot to be thought about'? Would *can* refer to permission or ability? Let's investigate.

Do a Simple Query search for *unthinkable*. Right sort the page and look down the list. What typically follows it? Since there are not many nouns, it is not typically an attributive adjective. Rather, we see punctuation, conjunctions and relative pronouns, all of which indicate that it typically occurs at the end of information units. It also occurs in a fixed chunk, and is followed by several prepositions only.

There are also quite a few time references: *decade, month, year, time, until, now, previously,* which begs another question.

Left sorting the concordance page reveals quite different patterns. The high frequency of the verb *be* preceding *unthinkable* marks its predicative use. This term relates to the above-mentioned role of the predicate. Several other copular verbs play a role in this, too e.g. note the use of *seem*. You might like to consider the difference between *seeming unthinkable* and *being unthinkable*?

What verbs and verb phrases are most prominent?

Are there any salient adverbs describing *unthinkable* ?

Another significant colligation is *the*. How often does this occur directly before *unthinkable*? This is easy to calculate if line numbering is turned on. Is *the unthinkable* followed by nouns?

Open this permalink[41] to see the concordance lines with *unthinkable + noun*. The last breadcrumb indicates that they have been right sorted. There is a general air of doom and gloom in these 25 lines. This is referred to as negative semantic prosody.

Semantic Prosody

Firth noted in his 1948 work on phonology that there are many ways in which a sound can be influenced by its environment – he referred to this as prosody. By analogy, some of his followers applied his term

---

[41] ske.li/bnc_unthinkable_noun

to meaning (semantics) – semantic prosody. For example, the objects of the verb *to harbour*, include *grudge, resentment, bacteria, terrorist, hatred, prejudice*. Adjectives in the vicinity include *ineffective, deep-seated, irrational, hostile, illegal*. This negativity around the verb is its semantic prosody: *harbour* itself is not negative, unlike *resentment, hatred, hostile, illegal*. Thus, a list of collocates[42] of *harbour* is quite revealing, as we will explore later. See McEnery & Hardie (2012:136).

Question 40   **Is *whatsoever* typically used in negative contexts?**

Make a Simple Query search. Click the button to right sort the words alphabetically.

If you have your page length set at 1,000, the patterns that emerge from sorting are easy to recognise. If you have line numbering turned on, counting numbers of each phenomenon is easy.

What chunks emerge from a Left Sort[43] of *whatsoever*?

We also observe that more than half of the occurrences of *whatsoever* are followed by punctuation? This is not the first time we have made this observation – Hoey regards this as a pattern of normal usage: see this textbox. His list of ten priming hypotheses is immediately followed up with:

> The tenth of Hoey's priming hypotheses (2005:13) reads:
>
> Every word is primed to occur in, or avoid, certain positions within the discourse; these are its **textual colligations**.

> Very importantly, all these claims are in the first place constrained by domain and/or genre (2005:13).

In the following chapters, we will verify this claim by constraining many searches by such features.

Question 41   **In the name of language observation, what can we discover about the word *hamper* from a left sort?**

What part of speech is it usually?

Does the verb form prefer passive or active? If *hamper* is typically used in passive voice, a Right Sort should confirm this. Does it? By what means?

What things are *hampered* and by who(m) or what?

What adverbs typically boost it? Are they adverbs that typically associate with positive or negative things?

Does *hamper* appear to have positive or negative prosody?

Question 42   **What words in the context of *hamper* as a noun indicate a different meaning from the verb form of the word?**

In View options, show tags. When *hamper* is a noun, it has a totally different meaning and prosody. What words realise this?

Question 43   **Do marriages *break up* or *down*?**

Search for *marriage break* in Simple Query to see a concordance page with both words inflected. Sort Right the concordances and observe the patterns that emerge.

---

[42] ske.li/bnc_harbour_v_colls
[43] ske.li/bnc_whatsoever_left_colls

Do related nouns such as *relationship, friendship, union, affair* also break up and/or down? Does any pattern emerge?

Another approach is to make separate Simple Query searches for the two phrasal verbs, *break up* and *break down*. Left sorting will help identify the subjects.

Question 44 **Where do English people *go out to*?**

Does American English use *go out to* in the same way?

Using LEXMCI corpus which distinguishes US and UK English, search for *go out to* and note any destinations. Does the *to* appear to be part of a three word phrasal verb, or does it start the prepositional phrase indicating destination, or something else? Using text types, observe its use in UK and US English.

Question 45 **Why does *wont* return so many concordance lines?**

There are two basic reasons for this. Perform a search for this word without an apostrophe. Sort to the left and observe some patterns of normal usage, sort to the right and observe some more. The patterns are mostly colligations [44].

In some cases *wont* is a typo, but in most cases it is a word in its own right. Can you infer its meaning? And can you describe the relationship between the grammar patterns and its meanings and uses?

Sorting Node, References and Shuffle

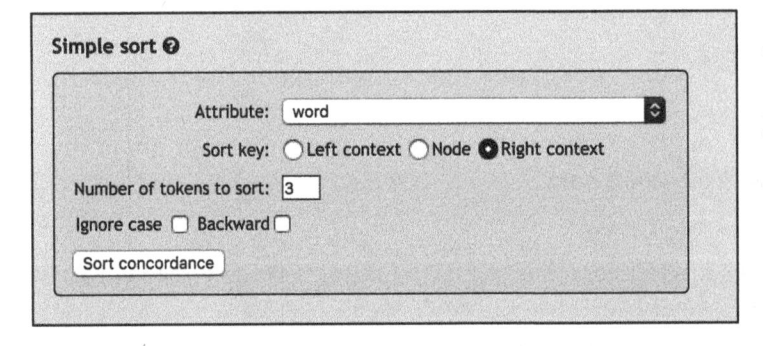

Earlier, we investigated *open door*. As we know, Simple Query items that are lemmas are conjugated and declined. To group all the possible forms of a search such as *open door*, sort by **Node**. We immediately see that of the 412 hits in the BNC, the first 314 are in their base forms. Is this just the case with *open door*? If we investigated other collocations, such as *shed light, fall pregnant* and others mentioned at the end of Question 4, and found that they most frequently occurred in their base forms, what will we have learnt?

Sort References rearranges the lines according to the metadata selected in View Options. David Lee's Classification shows that 13 hits of *open door* are spoken and over half are from fiction. Bear in mind the table in Question 3, when comparing such findings.

We use **Shuffle** to arbitrarily order the lines so as to avoid the bias which may result from only looking at the first portion or after sorting.

Simple and Complex Sorting

The automated sorts discussed so far are single level only: alphabetical. If we wanted to sort, for example, by David Lee's Classification and then alphabetically to the left, we need to use the Multi-level sort. In fact, this was used for the *moot point* example mentioned above. See the result of that sorting here [45].

---

[44] ske.li/bnc_wont
[45] ske.li/bnc_moot_point

When you click the Sort button itself in the left panel, you are presented with both a Simple Sort form as pictured on the previous page, and a Multilevel Sort form as pictured here.

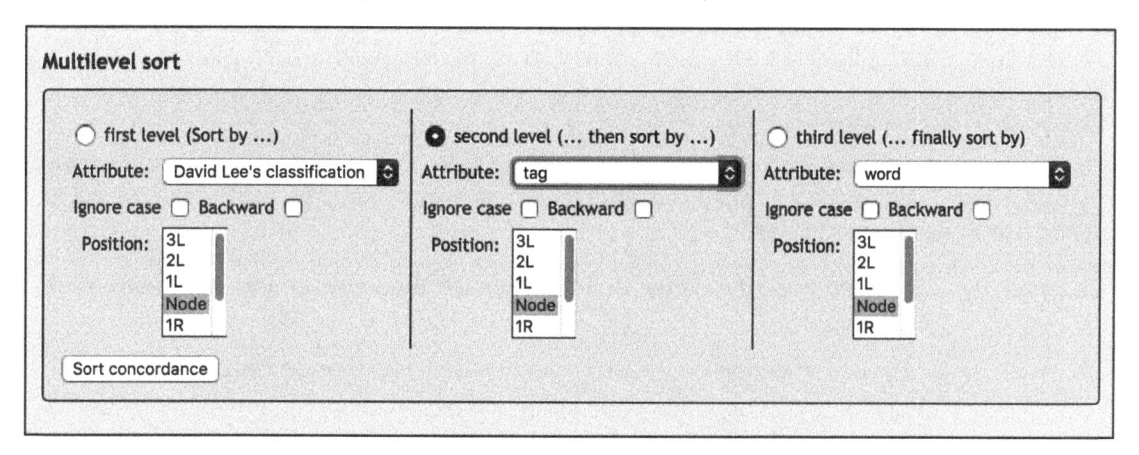

The Simple Sort has a dropdown list of Attributes derived from the metadata in the corpus.

Question 46 **Are the BNC's references to the Irish political situation spelled with a capital T or two?**

Simple Query: *the troubles*. Click Sort. Simple sort attribute: Word.

Sort key: node. And leave **Ignore case** unchecked.

As you scroll down the concordance page, it is clear where capitalisation begins. With line numbering turned on, it is clear how many are capitalised and not.

Question 47 **In which text types are *The Troubles* discussed?**

Using the Multi-level Sort, make the first level word – node.

Second level: 'Domain for written corpus texts' – node.

In the resulting concordance, the capitalised node starts halfway down the page, which can be marked using the Select Lines checkbox.

Question 48 **Is *open* typically a verb or adjective with *door* in fiction?**

To answer this question, our first level Attribute must be the domain. Use David Lee's Classification. Position: Node. The second level Attribute will be tag, also Node. Make the third level Attribute *word*, 1R. Making it 1L will show patterns in the determiners, which was not the question, but is not uninteresting.

The page will thus be sorted. W_fict_prose starts at about Line 50. To see the tags, it is necessary to go to View Options.

Selecting *backward* shows the element in reverse alphabetical order, e.g. David Lee's Classification listing starts with W_items (written) instead of S_ items (spoken).

Sample

Most corpora are only samples of the language they were designed to represent, as it is not usually possible to gather all the examples of a text type. An exception to this is a corpus of a specific text type, e.g. all Shakespeare's plays in a corpus designed to study the language of Shakespeare's plays.

But we are usually satisfied with observations made from a sample, which is a premise of much research.

It is not unusual for thousands of corpus lines to be returned for a search. Analysing the first lines whether the first 100 or the first 1,000, is not advised, since the default order is the document ID numbers in the corpus. To get a random sample, use the Sample button. It makes sense to make the sample size the same as your page length.

You can specify the size of the sample (i.e. the number of lines). For example, if you search for *play* (verb) in the BNC and decide that you do not want to analyse over 35,000 lines, use the sample tool to reduce it to a manageable number.

Question 49 **Does *be bound to* refer to anything else than something like 'being tied with rope'?**

Let's look at *be bound to*. Take a sample of 250. Right sort and patterns appear.

Do you see any instances of something being literally *bound*, e.g. with a rope? Is there any sense of being emotionally bound to someone? Chemicals also bind to each other. Open this concordance page[46] to see *bound to* followed by a determiner and then some.

However, more striking in a concordance of *bound to* is bound to + verb, as this frequency list reveals[47]. What can you observe about its subjects[48]?

Corp ex.27 *Breakfast **was bound to** arrive early enough for them to have time to talk afterwards.*

Corp ex.28 *well sooner or later er this mixture of languages is gonna spoil the English language isn't it? **Bound to**. Yes it**'s bound to**. No what the they'll do, they'll put all the words that are used into a computer er from all these things won't they?*

Thus two different meanings and functions are realised when the object of *to* is a noun phrase and when *to* itself is the infinitive marker. In the latter case, it is functions as a modal verb expressing the speaker's view of the likelihood that something will happen or would have happened. In linguistics, this is referred to as epistemic modality.

This relationship between meaning and structure is of great interest to contemporary linguistics but has made little headway in contemporary language teaching. My fledgling work on word templates that appears later this book is one attempt to find a pedagogically palatable path to this grammatical study of vocabulary. See especially p.117ff.

Question 50 **I've heard people say that they are *open to* various things. Any things at all?**

When you search for *be open to* in Simple Query, you potentially get all eight forms of BE and all four forms of OPEN. Let's try it. There are too many hits for a human to process. First, make a Sample which is the same as the page length you set in View Options. Then in the left panel click on Sort Node. To answer your question about the things that people are open to, click on Sort Right.

---

[46] ske.li/bnc_bound_to_det
[47] ske.li/bnc_be_bound_to_freq
[48] ske.li/bnc_subj_be_bound_to

Question 51 **Does *at all* reinforce both positive and negative things? And where in the sentence is it typically found?**

Use the same procedures as in the previous question.

Is this a similar finding to *whatsoever* in Question 40?

Question 52 **Does *put* typically have the structure: someone puts something somewhere?**

Being such an extremely frequent verb, a sample will help you start to answer this question.

Filter

After performing a search, Filter allows you to exclude lines that contain recurring irrelevant elements.

Question 53 **Do we prefer *turkey breast* to *breast of turkey*?**

This could be an important question for someone translating a menu into English: such questions would be better investigated in a corpus of English menus. See DIY corpora (p.203). It is also possible that modern culinary trends were expressed differently in the BNC era.

Search for *turkey* in Simple Query. Then click filter in the left panel. Type *breast* into the field as in the screenshot and leave all other settings as they are.

Try a similar search for *Mother of God* vs. *God's mother* – the latter appeared on a label in an art gallery.

It is also instructive to compare *body parts* with *parts of the body*.

Question 54 **How often does *Ireland* occur in the context of *the troubles*?**

Search again for *the troubles*. Then click Filter. In its Simple Query field, type *Ireland*, and click the Filter Concordance button to make the subset. Such filtering may provide data for a more sophisticated question than *How many*?

Question 55 **Since when has *The Troubles* been a refere*nce* to a period in Irish history?**

To get back to the original "the troubles" concordance, click on the left thumbnail in red: *the troubles*.

Click on Filter, choose Text Types, select the Publication Date, 1960 – 1974, and *negative* at the top. Click *Filter concordance* – what do you find? It seems that "The Troubles" in an Irish context were not discussed during that period. This leads us to think that the term was coined after 1974.

Frequency

In language pedagogy, the role of frequency has of late been much trumpeted. The claim is that the more frequent a word is in the language, the more students will meet it and the more they should need it. This is true for core English up to approximately the most frequent 3,000 words, or lemmas, in fact. However, missing from such lists are multi-word lexemes, which a great deal of contemporary corpus research into lexis is addressing. Also missing from many of these lists are the patterns of normal usage in which the target vocabulary functions. Throughout this book, we investigate such patterns as collocation, colligation, chunks, patterns, lexical bundles and word templates for ourselves using Sketch Engine tools. We are also investigating patterns of "non-normal" usage, those linguistic exploitations that prevent language being bland.

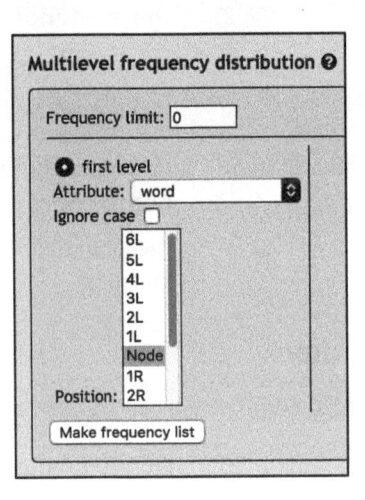

Multilevel Frequency Distribution

Multilevel Frequency Distribution is another tool that summarises data. It generates a variety of multi-word lists, depending on the Attributes selected. These lists reveal the horizontal, syntagmatic company that a Node keeps. We can generate:

Bundles — strings of word forms only

Syntagms — strings of POS only

WLTs — word form + lemma + POS tag (of the same word)

Hybrid Forms — strings of POS tags and words and/or lemmas

Question 56 **How do sentences start with *Given*?**

Enter *Given* into the Word Form field, rather than Simple Query, and select Match Case. Click Make Concordance, then Frequency.

To see *Given* plus one word, set Node as First Level. Then for the Second Level select 1R, i.e. one to the right. Click Make Frequency List.

You can see that Level, in fact, means Column. First Level refers to the column of data that appears on the left of the table generated.

To add the next word, select 2R in the Third Level, etc. And we find that sentences start with *Given* like this.

Given the nature of ...   *Given the fact that ...*

Given the importance of ...   *Given the choice, ...*

	word	word	word	Frequency	
P | N	Given	that	the	137	
P | N	Given	this	,	22	
P | N	Given	that	there	21	
P | N	Given	the	choice	17	
P | N	Given	that	this	17	
P | N	Given	that	it	17	
P | N	Given	the	nature	16	
P | N	Given	that	we	16	
P | N	Given	the	importance	14	
P | N	Given	the	current	14	

Click on the **P** on the left to see the actual concordances.

The question might also be answered with parts of speech instead of words. Select the Attribute, *tag*, in the second level to find that determiners are the most frequent item in the second slot. Tag in the third slot unsurprisingly reveals that nouns and adjectives follow determiners.

Selecting the appropriate attribute for each column is important for answering your question.

The level indicated by the radio button is the last column that will appear in your frequency list. Whenever you click on something in a column, its radio button is automatically selected. If, for example, you change Ignore case in the second level, its radio button will be selected, even if you have clicked on other elements in the third level. Check the radio button before clicking Make Frequency List.

Question 57   **Is *Given that* looking back to what has already been said, or forward to what is going to be said?**

These are two quite different functions of *Given that* and both are represented in these concordances.

When a word, often a pronoun, refers to something already mentioned, this is referred to as anaphora. The item of specific reference is referred to as the antecedent and the referring item itself is a pro-form: bold and underlined respectively in the following examples.

Corp ex.29   *The **petite blonde star** refused to go in his car and drove <u>her</u> own vehicle to his central London offices.*

When the pro-form precedes the antecedent, this is referred to as cataphora.

Corp ex.30   *Though <u>she</u> had no car of her own just now, **Charlotte** had been driving, and driving well, for more than four years.*

In the case of *Given that,* the anaphoric *that* is stressed when spoken and marked with a comma in the written form. This can be seen in Corp ex.31 and Corp ex.32. It is unstressed when cataphoric, as in Corp ex.33 and Corp ex.34.

Corp ex.31   *Well, it seems that taxis are considered "public transport" for the purposes of this exercise. **Given that,** as a group, taxi drivers are the most reckless, aggressive, and inconsiderate road users, they should have been the first, not the last, to be banned.*

Corp ex.32   *... so the increase in water storage will need to be somewhere between 10-15 percent. **Given that,** the debate looks set to intensify, not evaporate.*

Corp ex.33   ***Given that** the drive is very long, it is essential to spend a few days on this amazing journey.*

Corp ex.34   ***Given that** the number of different platforms that IE is not even available for is increasing as time passes ...*

Searching for *given that* in Simple Query reveals that it often occurs during sentences as well. Sort the concordance page left, and **Jump to** *a* to bypass the punctuation.

Question 58   **What patterns do other adjectives like *unthinkable* work in?**

Make a Simple Query search for *un*able*. We will now use the Frequency tool to investigate its colligation patterns.

To answer this question, it is not necessary to look at over 20,000 concordance lines. Click Frequency in the left panel and make a First level list only: node tags.

This list shows that the infinitive marker, *TO*, is the most frequent POS after these adjectives.

The second and third most frequent POS tags after these adjectives is NN and SENT. One of these suggests predicative adjectives and the other attributive. Which is which and why?

The fourth tag on the list, IN, i.e. preposition, does not include *to* as the infinitive marker. Click on the P beside IN. Make a two-level frequency list of the adjectives followed by prepositions as shown in this screenshot. Set the Frequency limit to 3. Then sort by clicking on the column headings: the left column heading to put the adjectives in alphabetical order, the right column heading to put the prepositions in order.

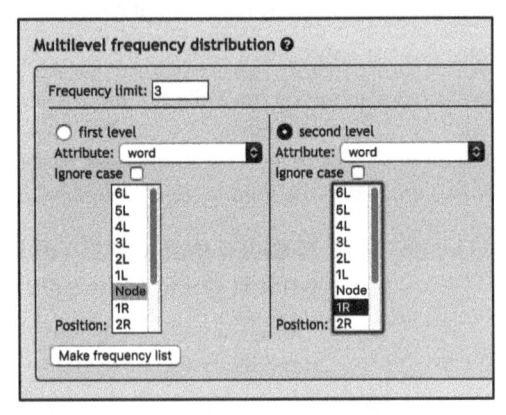

We have now made some observations about a set of adjectives formed with the affixes, *un-* and *–able*, concerning some of their colligation patterns. Perhaps the same patterns apply to all adjectives or other sets of adjectives. There's only one way to find out. In fact, this last sentence is a fixed phrase in English (with over 1,000 hits in enTenTen [49]) even if it is not strictly true.

Question 59   **How does the collocation *problem lie* work?**

We met this collocation in Question 4. Using frequency, we can now show what patterns follow it. It is quite instructive.

Question 60   **How does *arresting officer* come to have more than one meaning?**

It may be worth considering firstly, if *officer* refers to someone who works in an office. It is certainly worth observing the POS in compounds, as we saw with *open door*. The variety of combinations often needs to be borne in mind when interpreting meaning.

---

[49] ske.li/ett_onlyonewaytofindout

We can generate a word, lemma, tag (WLT) table by setting all of the levels at Node but with different Attributes.

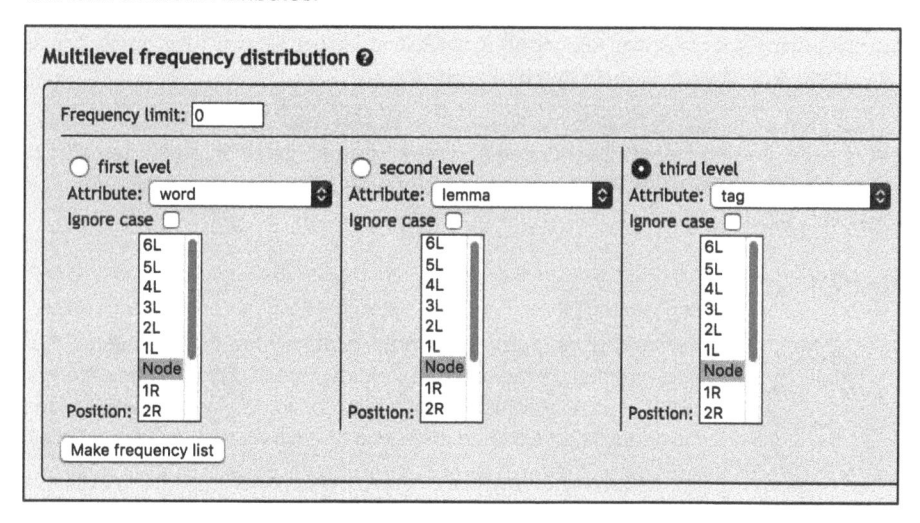

Here is the result of *arresting* as found through a Simple Query. It is interesting to see it almost as often an adjective (JJ) as an -ing verb (VVG) [50].

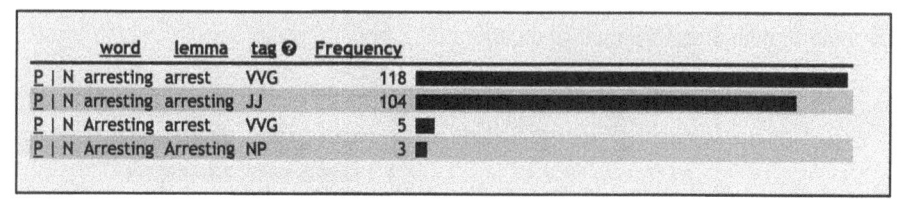

Click on the **P** to see the contexts. Here are five of the 104 adjective (JJ) sentences. The polysemy of this adjective is clear from these examples. These were selected using the check boxes, and Saved as a text file, and then imported into this Word document, complete with the angle brackets and spaces as shown.

Corp ex.35   *This area is the Coulin Forest, ... its mountains forming a compact group but individually having distinction of character and outline, some being of <**arresting**> appearance.*

Corp ex.36   *Mark usually achieved this by thinking out an <**arresting**> beginning, nearly always of the same type, asking his congregation to imagine themselves standing gazing at the Pyramids or the Acropolis ...*

Corp ex.37   *Ways of <**arresting**> decay also included covering eyes and mouth with carefully shaped pieces of jade and inserting jade plugs into other orifices of the body.*

Corp ex.38   *Mrs Spurling added: But this <**arresting**> image takes no account of the fact that Freya's was essentially an imaginative achievement. ...*

Corp ex.39   *She swung around and tapped the <**arresting**> officer on the breastplate.*

---

[50] ske.li/bnc_arresting_wlt

The word is closely related to the French, *arrêter*, meaning *to stop*. As a positive adjective, it suggests that something was impressive enough to make the viewer stop in their tracks[51] – at least metaphorically. What else does it suggest in these examples?

To see what immediately follows the Node, choose 1R under second level. 1R generates a list of items that occur one to the right of the node, e.g. words, lemmas, tags. 5L generates a list of items that occur five to the left of the node. Once you have determined the parameters for your columns, click Make Frequency List.

Zipf's law

As frequency graphs often show, relatively few items make up the bulk of the whole. This statistical phenomenon is known as Zipf's Law. George Kingsley Zipf (1902–1950), was an American linguist and philologist who studied statistical occurrences in various languages. In reference to corpora, his law essentially means that:

the frequency of any word is inversely proportional to its rank in a frequency table. Thus the most frequent word will occur approximately twice as often as the second most frequent word, which occurs twice as often as the fourth most frequent word, etc. (Johns 1991).

This screenshot demonstrates this tendency, as do many other such graphs in this book, regardless of the feature of language being investigated.

word	word	Frequency
P | N Given	the	960
P | N Given	that	470
P | N Given	this	121
P | N Given	a	121
P | N Given	these	54
P | N Given	his	33

In Sinclair's words,

The same tendency that we see in Zipf's Law is found in many other places in the numerical analyses of a corpus. Very often the main meaning or use or grammatical choice of a word is many times as frequent as the next one, and so on, so that twenty occurrences may be sufficient for the principal meaning of a word, while some quite familiar senses may occur only seldom (2004[52]).

For a clear and entertaining explanation of Zipf's law, see this video on Youtube[53]

---

[51] ske.li/ett_stopintracks_500
[52] http://icar.univ-lyon2.fr/ecole_thematique/contaci/documents/Baude/wynne.pdf p.16
[53] http://bit.ly/Zipf_mystery

Question 61	**Is the phrase *a long way* complete? Does it occur at the end of an information unit?**
	Search for the phrase, *a long way* and click on Frequency. Select the columns appropriate to your investigation. This screenshot shows the phrase, *a long way,* being most typically followed by (a) one of three prepositions, (b) a full stop indicating that it is common at the end of an information unit, and (c) it is also followed by *away*, which is not insignificant.

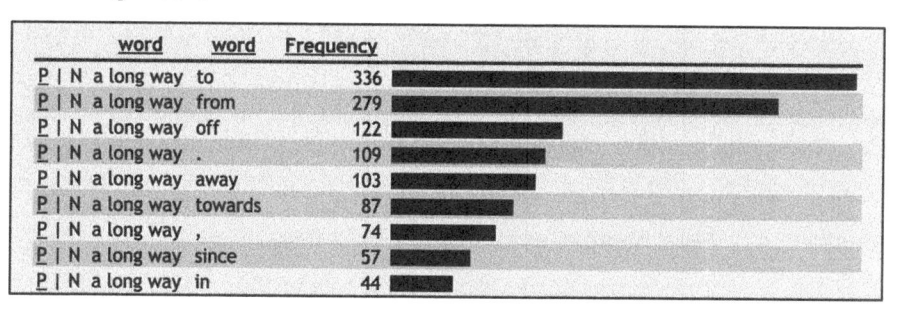

word	word	Frequency
P | N a long way	to	336
P | N a long way	from	279
P | N a long way	off	122
P | N a long way	.	109
P | N a long way	away	103
P | N a long way	towards	87
P | N a long way	,	74
P | N a long way	since	57
P | N a long way	in	44

We further find that *a long way away* is mostly followed by a full stop, comma or *and*, confirming its final-position status [54]. Click on the **P** beside *a long way to go*. And then Frequency again. This time, First level – 2L, Second level – 1L, Third level – node. The word *still* is particularly salient before this phrase [55].

Question 62	**According to everyone, *according to me* is wrong. Is it? According to whom?**
	Who decides what is right and wrong? Where do rules come from? Cambridge Dictionaries Online has a usage note about *according to me* here [56]. Where do they get their authority from? What is the difference between their authority and somebody else's?
	Perform a Simple Query for *according to*, then using Frequency, select R1 to find out what follows it. Does this answer the question? Or another question?

Question 63	**Is *thereby* always followed by –ing forms?**
	After performing a Simple Query search on *thereby,* click Frequency and make the first level the node and the second the tag as shown in the screenshot. This lists all the items that immediately follow *thereby*.

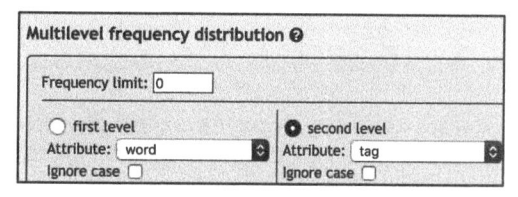

The result makes it quite clear that verbs are the most frequent elements after *thereby*, and the most frequent of these is in the –ing form. To learn more about the patterns of normal usage of *thereby*, use the Frequency listings, putting *thereby* in different columns (levels) and observing what goes before and after it.

---

[54] ske.li/bnc_a_long_way_freq
[55] ske.li/bnc_still_long_way_to_go
[56] See *according to* in the Cambridge Dictionary online.

Node Tags

In corpora, part of speech tags are codes that indicates a word's part of speech in the context in which it appears. *Word* here simply means a string of letters with a space either side, which in turn means that each word in a multi-word unit is tagged individually. See, for example, this sample of the phrasal verb, *go out with*[57].

In fact, tags indicate more than POS. In most cases, the first element of a tag identifies the POS. The following elements provide more specific categorisations. For example, VV indicates a lexical verb, VVZ indicates the third person singular of a lexical verb. VH is the verb *have* and VHG is the –ing form i.e. *having*.

Part of speech (POS) tags are used when we create searches for words functioning in a particular part of speech, and for identifying patterns in the grammatical company that words keep. They are used by concordancing software to group language phenomena in many revealing ways.

Question 64   **How context-sensitive are POS tags?**

The word *like* occurs over 150,000 times in the BNC, so it is helpful to be able to make searches more specific. It is also necessary for matching the specific word form in collocations and other constructions.

Undergoing considerable conversion, the word *like*, is tagged as a preposition (IN), a lexical verb (VV), an adjective (JJ) and a plural noun (NN) in the BNC, which the following four extracts show respectively.

Corp ex.40   *Europeans have turned whales into a sacred animal,* **like** *the Hindu cow.*

Corp ex.41   *Where appropriate, we* **like** *to take an active role.*

Corp ex.42   *Methinks it is* **like** *a weasel.*

Corp ex.43   *You give me anyone's phone line and mail for a month and I'll tell you exactly who he is, how old he is, his* **likes** *and dislikes, his character, his worries, what he had for breakfast and supper, what time he wakes up.*

The metadata in the BNC tells us that this last sentence is from Esquire, 1992, long before Edward Snowden's NSA revelations. It also seems to predate the preference for non-sexist language, as *anyone* here is assumed to be *he*. Nowadays we are more likely to use *they*.

It is not usually necessary to show the tags, but Sketch Engine can be set to display the part of speech tags of every word if required. For example, when 'show all tags' is on (see p.42), it looks like this:

> He /PP not /RB only /RB looks /VVZ like /IN me /PP , /, he /PP feels /VVZ like /IN mine /NN . /SENT

If you are wondering about the context in which such a sentence could have appeared, search for it in the BNC and click on the blue metadata tag to reveal the full metadata, and on the red node word to reveal more of the context.

Tagging is almost always done computationally using man-made algorithms: it is therefore unreasonable to expect 100% accuracy. Language is a very complicated business and not even linguists always agree on the part of speech of words in context. For example, in the BNC, *broken* is never tagged as an adjective despite 150 occurrences of *broken glass*, 72 of *broken heart* and 26 of *broken promises*.

---

[57] http://ske.li/bnc_go_out_with

See the 'broken' screenshot on p.42. The Penn Treetagger does not tag it as a lemma in its own right, which means that some searches do not work as you might expect. Also, if it not considered a lemma, Sketch Engine cannot generate a word sketch for it. Another example appears when studying the verb *cause* followed by a *to infinitive*. Most of the *causes* are in the phrase, *have cause to,* where it is a noun [58].

Corp ex.44   Later we shall **have cause to** doubt its accuracy and validity.

Corp ex.45   Well, I wish he did **have cause to** be jealous of me.

The 18 examples of *likest* are tagged as superlative adjectives in the LEXMCI corpus. They are, in fact, all 2nd person singular forms from an earlier period before English verbs shed most of their inflections.

Corp ex.46   Out of my doors, knave, if thou **likest** it not.

This could be a useful sentence to learn from memory – it is far more elegant than today's, *If you don't like it, piss off, prat.* It comes from *Thomas Lord Cromwell*, a play bearing Shakespeare's name but generally considered apocryphal.

The BNC was originally tagged with a tagset called CLAWS and was retagged by the University of Lancaster using an extended CLAWS tagset. This is known as BNC2, information about which is available on their website[59]: it describes related activities such as other tagsets, tokenisation, ambiguity – everything except when BNC2 was released.

However, most corpora use another tagset called the Penn Treebank Tagset, using software called the Tree Tagger (TT). The Sketch Engine team recently retagged the BNC with PTB, which is the only version used in this book. See the last pages of this book for a list of PTB tags.

Using the Node tags button

Clicking on the Node Tags button in the left panel shows a table of the POS tags for the search items.

Question 65   **I thought *lend* was the verb and *loan* was the noun.**

But I hear *loan* as a verb more and more often these days. After searching for *loan* in Simple Query, click Node Tags. Try this in both the BNC (1994) and enTenTen to see if any change of usage might be in evidence.

Question 66   **What is the difference between *be interested* and *be interesting*?**

Beware the flawed question: there is no 'one' difference between pairs of words, as the question implies. *What is the difference between* is a functional phrase used in many situations, as we observed on p.35.

In Simple Query, type *be interest**. Click Node tags to see the combinations of POS tags that result. Click on the P beside the most frequent ones to see their concordances.

See this link[60] for an investigation into the lexicogrammar of *be interested* Gabrielatos (2015).

Question 67   **Is *friend* used as a verb?**

In the BNC, try a Simple Query on *friend* then click Node Tags or Show Tags in View

---

[58] ske.li/bnc_have_cause_to
[59] http://ucrel.lancs.ac.uk/bnc2/bnc2postag_manual.htm
[60] http://bit.ly/Gabrielatos_interested

Options. Open new tabs in your browser and repeat these steps using more contemporary corpora. The following examples all come from enTenTen.

Corp ex.47 *Come for food, drinks and to meet all the people you've tweeted, **friended** or (gasp!) emailed who are in town for the conference.*

Corp ex.48 *… you want to be actively **friending** and directly connecting with 3-5 people a week that have influence in your industry.*

The following examples are not verbs, but are derived from the new usage of *to friend*. This is another example of the word formation process, conversion. Corp ex.50 goes one step further using a negative prefix as well.

Corp ex.49 *The Host Community on LiveJournal was hosting a **friending** meme.*

Corp ex.50 *Perhaps this will help us develop a theory of the entire cycle of **friending** and unfriending.*

The next example seems to say it all, really.

Corp ex.51 *Researchers flew under Facebook's radar, automated **friending** random strangers and THEN **friended** friends of those that **friended** the socialbots.*

Question 68 **Is *will* a lexical verb in addition to being a marker of futurity?**

Search for *will* in Simple Query. Then click Node tags: MD indicates its modal status, while tags starting with V indicate its status as a lexical verb. Having found that it is a lexical verb, how does it work? Is there one dominant V tag? Why? What are its typical subjects, objects, complements and its typical grammar patterns?

Question 69 **Does Penn Treebank distinguish between *to* as a preposition and *to* as an infinitive marker?**

Search for *to* in Simple Query and make a node tags list.

We could also ask if *for* is tagged separately: (a) as an indirect object (dative) marker, (b) as a preposition e.g. *for a long time*, and (c) as a phrasal verb particle. It is not.

We could similarly ask if *by, with* and *through* are tagged when they are used as instrument markers in passive constructions, but they are not.

If these words were tagged as particles as well as prepositions, searches could be made much more specific. Thinking about the roles of prepositions and particles in these ways would be a valuable step in a systematic approach to studying and teaching them.

Question 70 **Are the typical subjects of *couldn't bear to* nouns or pronouns?**

Remember to separate *could n't*. Note any typical verbs following *to*.

Here is one of many examples of this chunk in the BNC.

Corp ex.52 *Jessamy prized her privacy far too much, she **couldn't bear to** have a pack of journalists prying into every corner of her life.*

Question 71 **Who apart from journalists *pry*?**

Search for this word in the BNC and use a simple webpage search (CTRL F) to find *journalist* on the page. A left sort will indicate other subjects of this verb, and much more, as certain phrases appear.

Question 72 **Is *pry* only followed by *into*?**

Can it be followed by an object instead? i.e. somebody pries something.

Could it be a phrasal verb, and/or a transitive verb? As it is such an infrequent verb in the BNC, a simple right sort will answer these questions.

In the process of answering these *prying* questions, the connotations of the word appear from its context. David Lee's Classification (View Options) reveals the one text type in which this word is most significant.

Question 73 **What does *pry into* express that similar expressions do not?**

The author could have chosen *look into, investigate* or *put under the microscope* instead of *prying into*. Or could they? Give some thought to the constraints on such a choice.

Use Simple Query and Frequency to observe its negative prosody [61].

Question 74 **Pack of? When *pack* is not a short form of *packet*, what are the most common things that come in packs?**

Search for *pack of* in Simple Query and use Frequency to investigate the 1R column.

Do you think the author of the 'Jessamy sentence' associates journalists with *lies*, *wolves*, and other such nasties?

The cumulative effect of *couldn't bear, pack* and *pry,* is an example of lexical support. When speaking and writing, one of the criteria we apply to selecting a word from among its synonyms is its connotations: words with similar connotations lend support to each other to create the desired rhetorical effect. See the string of negative adjectives in Corp ex.31 for another example.

Serendipity

Serendipity is finding something valuable unintentionally. Many people are familiar with finding something of great interest in a dictionary when looking for something else. In Question 70 we were looking at the objects of *couldn't bear* and within four or five questions, we ended up discovering some rather unrelated but valuable features of English and language in general. These serendipitous findings are as common in corpus work as they are in dictionary searches, and other areas of life, e.g. the things you find when moving house! See Bernadini's 2000 article, *Systematising serendipity*.

Node forms

Moving on now from Node Tags, the next questions use the Node forms tool to work with prefixes and suffixes.

Question 75 **Which words employ these meaning-laden suffixes?**

-cide, -phobia, -phyte, -dactyl , -mania, -proof, -gate, -esque

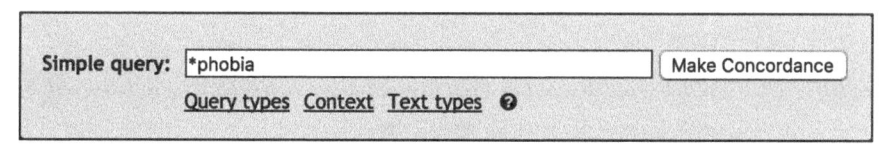

[61] ske.li/LEXMCI_pryinto_freq4r

After a Simple Query search in a enTenTen, involving operators (p.36), click on Node Forms to produce the list of word forms.

It is worth observing if they look as if someone is playing with, or exploiting, language, and what proportion of the word forms occurs once only. A word that only occurs once in a corpus is referred to as a hapax legomenon.

Question 76   **What are the differences between the prefixes *anti* and *ante*?**

They are best searched for in separate browser tabs, and as a lemma search with dot-asterisk. The lists are a good data set to answer such question as:

What do you notice about their relative frequencies? The answer to this probably relates to how often you encounter them.

Click node forms to generate the lists: What do you notice about the use of hyphens?

Are either of them words in their own right (free morphemes)? If so, what part(s) of speech are they and how do function in their contexts?

While these observations do not lead us directly to understanding their meanings, any hunches you might have had have probably been strengthened.

Doc IDs

After performing a search, click on Doc IDs. Click on **P** beside one of them and then click on the blue reference at the left of the concordance. The yellow metadata detail frame pops up.

Text Types

Chapter 7 is dedicated to Text Types, so this is a brief introduction.

Clicking on the Text Types button shows a summary of the metadata for a particular search. For example, the text types of the above searches for *anti* and *ante* are quite revealing.

On the main query page at the bottom of Text Types, you can specify David Lee's Classification categories, which reveal the domains and sub-domains more specifically. To select more than one of David Lee's Classifications, type a vertical bar | as shown in this screenshot.

> DAVID LEE'S CLASSIFICATION
> W_fict_prose|W_fict_poetry
> *Documentation*

Question 77   ***Harmony* is mostly a technical term in music. How do we use it elsewhere?**

Find *harmony* via Simple Query. Click Text Types and see that according to David Lee's Classification it mostly occurs in the humanities. Clicking on **P** (positive) shows that it is mostly used in music contexts. To answer the question, click on **N** (negative) beside W_humanities_arts. This will show the examples of *harmony* that are not in this domain. There are still references to music, but it also answers the 'elsewhere' question.

Question 78   ***Blench* may seem like a perfectly normal English word, but one does not come across it very often.**

How often does it occur in the BNC? According to text types, in what sort of texts does it appear?

By looking at the subject of *blench* it is obviously some sort of physical reaction. And a little bit more context suggests that it is one of surprise or shock, but not in life-threatening situations. Can you glean anything else by looking at the contexts?

Collocation

Although the Sketch Engine collocation tool is the subject of Chapter 8, the nature of collocation is introduced here as the concept is frequently referred to before that chapter.

'A pair of words that frequently co-occur' lies at the heart of most definitions of collocation. One of the two words is the *node* and the other is the *collocate*, as in *gauge interest, plausible explanation, emotionally satisfying.* Collocation is a paradigmatic feature of language.

The Lexical Approach (Lewis 1993, 2000) gave a new pedagogical impetus to lexis, and attempted to displace sentence grammar with collocation as the organising unit for language teaching. In various guises, this was at the heart of much of the Neo-Firthian linguistics being carried out at this time by Halliday, Sinclair and Hoey, to name but a few.

> The first of Hoey's ten priming hypotheses (2005:13) reads:
> Every word is primed to occur with particular other words; these are its **collocates**.

The following two paragraphs are from my *Stealing a March on Collocation* (Thomas 2015:90).

Collocation is defined variously, with some linguists lumping general co-occurrence phenomena together, thus making the term available for a wide variety of uses from morphology to discourse studies. At the top end of the hierarchy of language, Halliday and Hasan (1976:284) referred to the use of topic-related words running through a text as collocation. The BBI Combinatory Dictionary of English (Benson et al. 1986), distinguished 'grammatical collocations' from 'lexical collocations'. They define the former thus:

> A grammatical collocation is a phrase consisting of a dominant word (noun, adjective, verb) and a preposition or grammatical structure such as an infinitive or clause (p.xv).

However, the preferred term for this is colligation, which Stefanowitsch & Gries (2003: 210) define as "the linear co-occurrence preferences and restrictions holding between specific lexical items and the word-class of the items that precede or follow them". Thus pairings that consist of a lexical word plus a preposition (e.g. *damaging for*) or a lexical word plus a particle, (e.g. *necessary to, agreement that*) will not be counted here as collocations.

> The fourth of Hoey's priming hypotheses (2005:13) reads:
> Every word is primed to occur in (or avoid) certain grammatical positions, and to occur in (or avoid) certain grammatical functions; these are its **colligations**.

Other pairings which are not accepted here as collocations are multi-word lexemes (see Löbner's textbox). Multi-word lexemes include phrasal verbs (e.g. *pair off, fuss over, wimp out*), delexical verbs (e.g. *give a lecture, take a risk, do damage*), compound nouns (e.g. *case study, word list, mother tongue*) and combinations such as *nothing but* and *let alone, state of the art*. See *English as a Lingua Franca* by Prodromou (2008:46-7) for a list of 42 types of multi-word units with examples.

> Those linguistic units which carry lexical meanings are called lexemes. Typically, lexemes are single words, but there are also composite expressions with a special lexicalized meaning. Therefore, lexemes cannot be equated with words.
> Löbner (2013: 41)

The notion of collocation develops as we move through this book: Chapters 8 and 9 deal with the subject in considerable detail.

Question 79 **What roles do verbs and adjectives play with nouns?**

As nouns are the most frequent part of speech in text and in the lexicon, it is important to know the company they keep, especially their adjectives and verbs. We will explore some interesting pairings of rare words with common words. Together they express quite common meanings.

Search for each word in Simple Query. It is not necessary to study the concordance pages, rather click the Collocations button. Do not change any of the parameters in the form – simply click Make candidate list. Then look down the lists for the most frequent lexical words. The high frequency grammar/function words are elements in colligation, which will be investigated later.

Adjectives	Verbs
avid	allay
sheer	pique
abject	wreak
dulcet	prick up
abiding	hold down

In the process, you might also notice that the lists contain words in similar semantic fields and/or with similar connotations. These combinations create semantic prosody.

Question 80 **Would you consider *well within* a collocation?**

If *well within* is not in your active vocabulary, the little piece of research we undertake here is bound to raise your awareness of it.

A Simple Query search returns a fairly small number of hits. Sorting to the left and again to the right gives some idea of how this pair of words works. Does it match your understanding of *collocation*?

Using Frequency, however, reveals bundles that indicate that it is a semi-fixed phrase: the elements are finite but they mix and match in a variety of non-random ways.

Click on Collocations in the left panel, and without changing anything in the form, click Make candidate list. One word is even more frequent than the function words that are almost always more frequent than lexical words. Click on the P beside this word to see the constructions.

Visualize

The visualization graph divides a whole corpus, or subcorpus, into 100 blocks of equal size. These chunks are not related to specific documents, domains, genres, etc. Rather, it is necessary to think of the corpus not as a collection of documents but as millions of words that have been drawn from the documents of the corpus. In the BNC, the word *eagle* occurs 1,000 times (according to Word List[62]) and the graph of its distribution, as seen in this screenshot, indicates that it occurs significantly at about 42% and very significantly at 100%. Its other occurrences across the corpus are trivial.

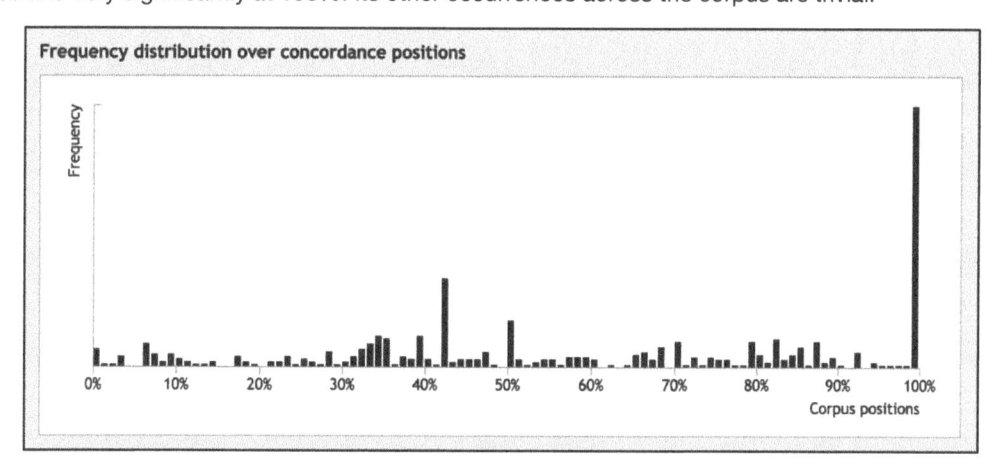

By contrast, this second graph depicts the word *shared,* which also occurs 1,000 times – it is evenly distributed across the whole corpus.

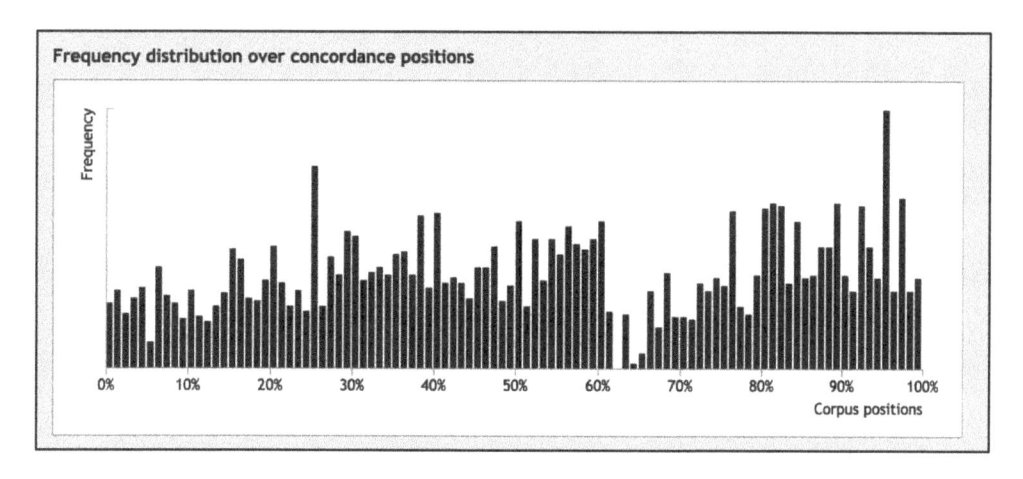

Visualize reveals that some parts of a corpus are quite specific. It is usually caused by the fact that in these parts there are some specific documents in which specific words are used. The Visualize tool makes several more appearances in this book, demonstrating further applications of this data representation. See the Index.

---

[62] ske.li/bnc_lemma_1000

Question 81   **Compare the distributions of *frame* and other words that also occur with a similar frequency.**

The Word list tool (p.195) is able to generate lists that contain all the lemmas that occur between 5000 and 5001 times in the BNC, for example[63].

---

[63] http://ske.li/bnc_lemmas_5000_5100

Chapter 4   Thesaurus

If *thesaurus* is a new word for you, where better to look than a corpus? Some might say a dictionary, but to stay in the spirit of *inferring meaning*, let us stay with the corpus for this exercise. Here are two sentences from the BNC that provide a lead into this word.

Corp ex.53   *Now spend some time, if possible with a dictionary or a **thesaurus**, making out a chart for yourself, exploring some of the feelings you experience.*

Corp ex.54   *No-one writing a report should be without a Roget's **Thesaurus**.*

In the first example, we see that *thesaurus* is a common noun and that it can be used as a source of words for making a chart. Secondly, it is an **and/or relationship** with *dictionary*, which tells us that the speaker differentiates these two items.

In the second sentence, it is a proper noun being recommended for report writing. It is an interesting, observable and perhaps inevitable feature of text that words from the same semantic fields co-occur – this is how Topic Trails in text manifest.

Just two sentences have provided some clues. How much more can be gleaned from multiple contexts? Enter *thesaurus* into Simple Query and try various operations to identify revealing company: various sortings, collocation and frequency lists. The name *Roget* is commonly associated with *thesaurus*, as indeed, *Roget's Thesaurus* is the name of a book. Other collocates reveal its relationship with words and other aspects of reference books.

Roget's Thesaurus is a book of semantically related words. It was compiled by Peter Mark Roget (1779-1869), pictured here, and was first published in 1852. He said it was designed to help the user to find the word, or words by which an idea may be most fitly and aptly expressed. Words are not arranged in alphabetical order, rather they appear under hypernym headings. For example, the word *compare*, can be found under *greatness, superiority, comparison, advice*. The entries contain synonyms, collocates, phrases and other compounds, as well as some quotations. It is available online[64].

This is also different from a synonym dictionary, which lists words alphabetically along with several synonyms. A very long page of such data can be found here[65].

However, the Thesaurus tool in Sketch Engine is not exactly a synonym dictionary nor a thesaurus à la Roget. Rather, it is a so-called *distributional thesaurus*. The words listed are the most salient words in the corpus which occur in the same context, where context means the same collocations in the same grammatical relationships as the search word.

---

[64] http://machaut.uchicago.edu/rogets
[65] http://bit.ly/mit_oldthesaurus

It is important to see the list as containing words in various semantic relationships, not just potential synonyms. The two items in an and/or relationship are often co-hyponyms (see p.179).

Question 82 **What semantic relationships hold between a hypernym and the words in the Thesaurus list?**

Click on Thesaurus in the left panel. Enter your search word, e.g. *colour*, and choose the part of speech. Try to predict the content of the lists in advance.

Do you see co-hypernyms of *colour*, hypernyms, hyponyms, antonyms, other? Synonyms of *colour* are not listed. As mentioned above, the list contains words which occur in the same lexical and grammatical contexts.

Question 83 **What words are listed when you search for a hypernym, *e.g. blue*?**

Can you imagine any context in which *blue* could be replaced by some of the words listed, without a dramatic change in the meaning? These reflect paradigmatic choices as mentioned on p.14.

Question 84 **How does the data reflect different meanings of polysemous words?**

Words are usually listed in score order. However, by turning on **Clustering** in Advanced Options, a very different picture emerges. *Orange, driver* and *seal* exemplify this beautifully. Compare different corpora.

> The sixth of Hoey's priming hypotheses (2005:13) reads:
> When a word is polysemous, the collocations, semantic associations and colligations of one sense of the word differ from those of its other senses.

Question 85 **What are some adjectives suitable for giving feedback to students?**

Ask the Thesaurus tool to create lists of some positive adjectives like *excellent* and *wonderful*, some neutral words like *satisfactory, acceptable* and some negative words like *terrible, hopeless, unsatisfactory, unacceptable*.

Antonyms are hardly synonyms, yet they do appear in the thesaurus lists. This is for the above-stated reason: they are among the salient words in the corpus which occur in the same context. This can be clearly seen with *gain, accept, exhale*, for example.

Word Cloud

You can't help but notice the **word cloud.** The sizes of the words reflect their score. Clicking on a word in the list or in the word cloud is a back door into another tool, Sketch Differences (Chapter 12). Which word is this the word cloud of?

Word clouds do not include the node word by default. To include the headword, open Advanced options, select Headword in cloud. With Advanced options open, you can also change the number of words that included.

While a thesaurus tool may seem redundant when English has such a plethora of published and online resources, it is very valuable to languages that are not so well served, and to specialised corpora as well. In Chapter 14 , we make our own Environment corpus and a Pride and Prejudice corpus. When these DIY corpora are compiled, Sketch Engine pre-computers its thesaurus.

Your Notes

Chapter 5   Top Level Queries continued

We interrupted Top Level Queries to provide some important information about the roles of the Left Panel buttons. We prefer Simple Query to the other top level search fields when we don't have or need specific information about a word. It is often a good starting point. Via Simple Query we have also learnt about customising our View Options and working with the Menu Items.

We now return to the rest of the top level queries, as shown in this screenshot. We will work through each of these fields and discover how they enable different types of searches, which in turn enable many different types of language discoveries.

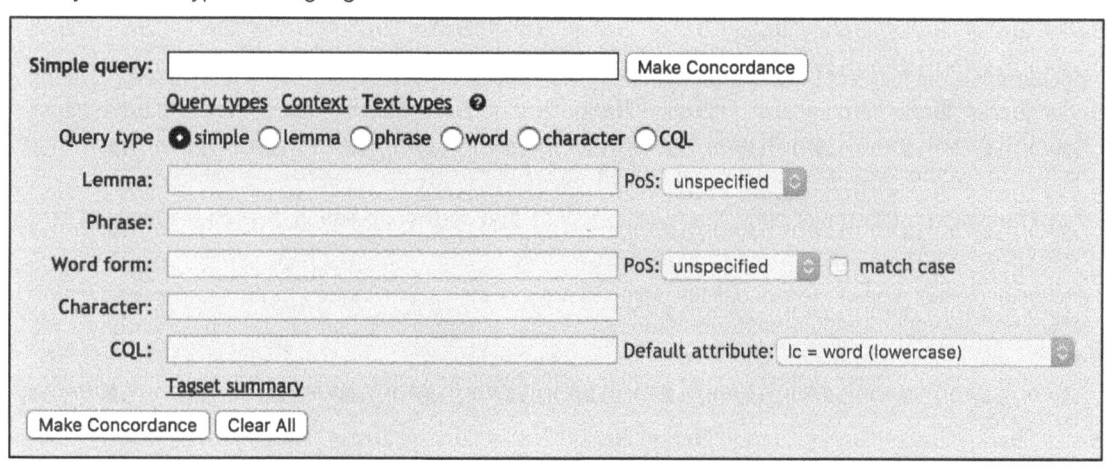

Before we begin, we need to clarify the terminology of the lower branches of the Hierarchy of Language which come under the heading of morphology.

Morphology

The taxonomy of morphology (depicted on the following page) accounts for the processes that words undergo grammatically and lexically, as can be seen in the left and right sections of the taxonomy respectively. Its metalanguage is used extensively in this book, as many types of searches and post-processing involve these concepts. The word *morpheme* refers to the minimal unit capable of expressing meaning of its own. Free morphemes can stand on their own, e.g. *curious*, while bound morphemes, e.g. *–er*, require a free morpheme to attach to. Free morphemes are commonly referred to as the *base* while bound morphemes are *affixes* (Mair 2008: 39-40).

Inflection refers to changes made to the form of a lemma that effect grammatical distinctions. Conjugation is the name of the process that verbs undergo when they change their forms to express person,

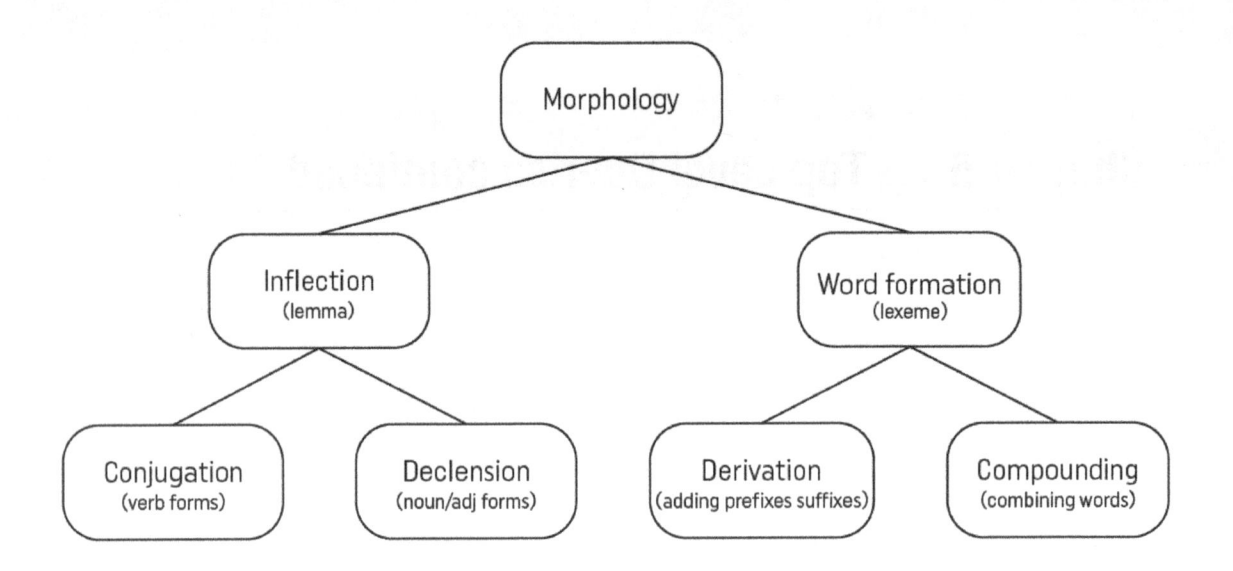

```
                    ┌──────────────┐
                    │  Morphology  │
                    └──────┬───────┘
                ┌──────────┴──────────┐
        ┌───────┴────────┐    ┌───────┴────────┐
        │   Inflection   │    │ Word formation │
        │    (lemma)     │    │    (lexeme)    │
        └───┬────────┬───┘    └───┬────────┬───┘
    ┌───────┴──┐  ┌──┴───────┐ ┌──┴──────┐ ┌┴──────────┐
    │Conjugation│ │Declension│ │Derivation│ │Compounding│
    │(verb forms)│ │(noun/adj │ │(adding   │ │(combining │
    │           │ │ forms)   │ │prefixes  │ │ words)    │
    │           │ │          │ │suffixes) │ │           │
    └───────────┘ └──────────┘ └──────────┘ └───────────┘
```

number, tense, aspect, e.g. *compute, computes, computed, computing*. Technically speaking, *–ed, -er, -s* etc. are *endings*, not suffixes.

Declension is the name of the process that nouns, adjectives, adverbs and determiners undergo. Nouns change their forms for number (*computer – computers; corpus – corpora*), adjectives and adverbs for degree (comparative and superlative) and determiners such as *this, those, his, their* for various combinations of number and person. The change from *who* to *whom* is also regarded as declension.

Word formation on the other hand is a lexical process that sees the creation of words to express new concepts.

Derivation is the name of the process that involves adding affixes (prefixes and suffixes) to words. Unlike inflection, derivation creates different meanings and/or changes the part of speech which gives the word a different syntactic role. Some common prefixes include *dis-, un-, re-, il-* and suffixes *-ness, -ity, -hood*. Some more recent and colourful and humorously exploited affixes include *-athon, -gate, -monger, -aholic*.

Compounding sees the combination of two or more words to make a new meaning. They can appear as one word, hyphenated or as two words, e.g. *homework, home-based, house work,* each of which express a single concept. These are variously referred to as multi-word units/expressions/lexemes.

Question 86   **Does the asterisk operator yield inflected forms as well as derivations?**

Search for *court* in Simple Query and note the number of hits. Click Node forms to see if there are derivations as well as inflections.

Search now for *court** and make the same observations.

Conversion, Polysemy and Homonymy

There is another word formation process which involves the derivation of one lexeme from another (e.g. the verb *father* from the noun *father*) without any overt morphological change. There are also many adjectives in English which have the same form as past participles, e.g. *broken, limited, unexpected,* and there are many adjectives with the same form as present participles, e.g. *working, forthcoming, arresting*. This phenomenon is labelled variously: conversion, zero-derivation and zero-affixation (See Carstairs-McCarthy 2002).

When a lexeme has several meanings that are in some way related, e.g. *perfect* as in *perfect example, be perfect for sth,* and *to perfect a technique,* this is polysemy. Homonymy, is the same lexeme with unrelated meanings, e.g. *bark* (of a tree, of a dog), *bat* (the 'flying mouse' and the sporting equipment). It is not always a clear-cut distinction, e.g. in the COBUILD Dictionary online, there are 17 meaning of the noun *frame* some of which are subdivided as can be seen here[66].

The creators of this dictionary had to *divide up the semantic space* (Hanks 2013: 70) that the word occupies. What might motivate a lexicographer to give many separate meanings when the first part of the first definition encompasses many of them?

> frame: an open structure that gives shape and support to something.

The senses of a word can be lumped together or fine distinctions can be isolated. The many meanings of *frame* demonstrate the adoption of the word in specific domains, which the lexicographers have deemed necessary to define. Of particular interest to readers of this book is #13:

> frame: (in language teaching, etc) a syntactic construction with a gap in it, used for assigning words to syntactic classes by seeing which words may fill the gap.

One approach to determining the number of a senses a word has is to cluster its collocates into lexical sets. See the polysemous phrasal verb, *blow up* in Question 302.

Here are some more examples of conversion, some of which might be regarded as polysemy, others as homonymy, sometimes both when the word has multiple meanings: *dog, address, count, mushroom, hamper, peer, bark, elbow*. Learners need to pay attention to such features of English vocabulary (Schmitt 2010), and anyone studying concordances needs to bear this in mind. The example of *broken* (p.42) has already demonstrated that even tagging algorithms can be confused by these features. A frequency list of many thousands of instances of participles used as adjectives, yet tagged as verbs, can be seen here[67].

Word Family

A set of words with the same stem or root that are the product of both inflectional and word formation processes is known as a **Word Family**. The 570 word families of the Academic Word List (Coxhead 2000) illustrated the efficacy of this term.

Question 87   **How can a word family be derived from a corpus?**

> Using the asterisk operator in Simple Query, we can derive most, if not the whole word family of *advantage*: *advantag*
>
> This yields not only words that have *advantag* in the middle, but also at the beginning and end. Click Node forms, to generate the list of all the word forms. Use the Frequency tool with lempos as the Attribute to generate a list that shows the results of conversion as well, i.e. *advantage* as a noun and as a verb are listed separately.
>
> See Corp ex.19 for a rare member of the *advantage* family.

Lemma

Having already been introduced, the concept of *lemma* will be developed both technically and linguistically in this section. When a corpus is compiled, among the main machine processing tasks are *tagging* and *lemmatizing* – this involves putting every word in every text on a separate line accompanied

---

[66] http://www.collinsdictionary.com/dictionary/english/frame
[67] ske.li/bnc_the_verb

by its lemma and POS tag. In this book, these 'triads' are referred to as WLT as we saw in the *arresting* example on p.57.

When you search for a lemma, it returns all of its declined or conjugated word forms that are represented in that corpus. It is a stratum of data that serves as a valuable criterion when creating a query.

The declension of nouns is not a particularly salient feature of English – it mostly marks singular, plural and possessive forms with an *s* e.g. *sound, sounds, sound's*.

Apart from the standard plural *s*, English has also preserved the classical plurals of words such as those underlined above. The plural of lemma is usually lemmas, but *lemmata* is also still used. We have seen the plural of *corpus, corpora* many times. *Stratum* is the singular, *strata* the plural. We will explore the use of *data* in Question 205.

Question 88   **Are these words forms of classical nouns used in the singular or plural?**

In the lemma field, it is necessary to enter the base form of your search word. Even though *criteria, bacteria* and *media* are far more frequently used in modern English than their base forms, lemma searches require base forms.

Using the LEXCMI corpus, enter some of these nouns and similar ones that you know, into the lemma field and make your observations. The Node forms button can be put to good use here.

bacteria, media, millennia, hypotheses, analyses, algae,
fungus, lemma, corpus, conundrum, forum

Because such words have lost or are losing their singular-plural distinction, the plural forms are sometimes treated as singular nouns. When in the role of subject, the verb must agree, so use this opportunity to investigate the contexts. For example, do we find *bacteria is* or *bacteria are*, and in what text types?

Question 89   **Which words that end in –*sis* form their plural with –*ses*?**

Once you have generated a list of nouns ending in -ses, use the Frequency tool to make a WLT list to find the –sis and –ses pairs.

It is also worth paying attention to the pronunciation of these words.

Question 90   **What are the plural forms of Germanic irregular English nouns?**

English has also preserved a small number of plural forms from its Germanic roots, e.g. *man, woman, child, tooth, wolf, ox, mouse*. Many of these irregular forms in English are the result of I-mutation, which is discussed at Online Etymology[68].

Of Mouse and Man If John Steinbeck had only been content to work in the singular, he would not have had to deal with word forms such as *mice* and *men*.

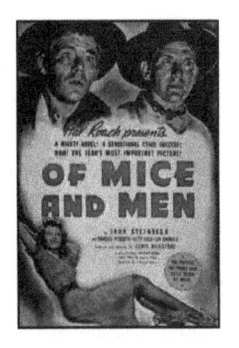

---

[68] http://www.etymonline.com/imutate.php

Morphology

Question 91 **Are possessive forms of English nouns included in the list of word forms of a lemma search?**

Perform some lemma-noun searches for common nouns (e.g. *brick, light*), proper nouns (e.g. *Australia, Google*), abstract nouns (e.g. *sanity, favouritism*), collective nouns (e.g. *committee, middle class*), mass nouns (e.g. *shampoo, lava*) and singular nouns (e.g. *gloom, pity*)[69]. Then search for them again with the apostrophe *s*, e.g. *sanity 's*, remembering to put a space before the apostrophe.

What do your findings tell you about the definition of *lemma* according to the rules of automatic lemmatisation?

In contrast to English, nouns in highly inflected languages have many word forms that express number and case. Czech, for example, has seven cases, singular and plural, and some historical relics, such as *pluralia tantum* and dual. Czech nouns have potentially fourteen word forms. Lemmatisation is particularly important to such languages.

Verbs, however, are a different story. The lemma *go* consists of the five word forms, *go, goes, going, went, gone*. Perhaps more curious (or *curiouser*) is the noun *go* and its plural *goes*, both of which appear in this sentence:

Corp ex.55   *Choddo had a **go** at a few and scored wins after just two **goes**.*

This screenshot shows the word forms of *go*, and their frequencies in the BNC resulting from a lemma search not limited to the verb.

Such data might pique your curiosity as to whether the base form of verbs is always significantly more frequent than the other word forms. On finding that it is, the data needs to be interpreted to account for why this might be the case.

The Lemma field is case-sensitive. For example, in the BNC *grant* (n) (6,121 hits) vs. *Grant* (2,412 hits); *centre* (22,250) vs. *Centre* (6,930). Capitalisation does not guarantee a proper noun due to sentence capitalisation. Proper nouns can be specified using tags in CQL, as we see on p.139.

word	Frequency
P | N go	82,713
P | N going	62,387
P | N went	45,631
P | N gone	18,000
P | N goes	14,414
P | N Go	3,939
P | N Going	1,061
P | N Gone	250
P | N Went	145
P | N Goes	128
P | N GOING	41
P | N GO	15
P | N goest	5
P | N GONE	3
P | N goer	2
P | N gOing	1
P | N gO	1
P | N WENT	1
P | N GOES	1

Question 92   **Is *holiday* used as a verb more today than in the BNC days?**

In the Lemma field, type *holiday* and select **verb** from the POS droplist. Try this in both BNC and enTenTen. Because of the very different sizes of these two corpora, compare your findings using **per million**. What do you find?

Furthermore, Node forms reveals a preference for one form, doesn't it?

The Visualize tool reveals its quite equal distribution across the corpus. Do any of these observations shed further light on Question 7?

---

[69] See COBUILD Grammar Patterns 2, Part 1 for many more examples.

Question 93 What do you notice about the company that *grant* and *Grant* or *centre* and *Centre* keep in the BNC?

You will notice that some of them form compounds, which you can classify according to the morphology diagram above. You will also notice that their patterns of collocation and colligation are quite different.

Inferring meaning

Inferring meaning of unknown words in a text is much discussed in language teaching literature. Language learners are often tasked with inferring the meaning of a word which occurs once in a text, and even in an isolated sentence. Compare this with what we have been inferring from multiple examples in short extracts from hundreds if not thousands of native speakers.

Question 94 If you are not familiar with the common noun, *thatcher*, can you infer its meaning from multiple contexts?

Given the period in English history that the BNC covers, it is not surprising that the Iron Lady is well represented, not that she will be included in this investigation.

Can you deduce the verb from the noun *thatcher*? Searching for *thatch** and right sorting should take you some way to answering the original question.

Question 95 What observations can we make about the word *slouch*?

If you do not know this word, resist the temptation to look it up before doing the following. Inferring its meanings and uses is an interesting voyage of discovery.

Do a lemma search without specifying part of speech. Then …

1. Click on Node Forms and see if all the word forms are represented.
2. Click on Node Tags and make some other useful observations.
3. Click on Doc IDs and check that the word is not used disproportionately in one document, which does happen, especially with uncommon words.
4. See what Visualize offers in terms of spread across the corpus.
5. Click on Text Types to see in what domains *slouch* is most common?

> Remember that if the page length is set to at least the number of hits, sorted pages show quite a few patterns at once. See p.44.

What other patterns of normal usage can we infer about *slouch* from a left sort?

1. Is there anything of interest about the subject when *slouch* is a verb?
2. Do only people slouch? Do both males and females *slouch*?
3. Does *slouch* ever start a sentence?
4. Is it used in both positive and negative contexts?

If *being no slouch* is a positive thing, what does this tell us about *slouch* itself? Do any patterns of normal usage emerge from right sorting the concordance of *slouch*?

The following corpus ex., is from an editorial in the Independent, 1989.

Corp ex.56   *since the picture of the human mind has to be radically reconstrued following the work of von Neumann, Turing, Shannon and Wiener, it is hard to understand how none of these people received a mention. Chomsky is no slouch either.* (BNC)

1. Is it followed by any particular prepositions?
2. Are there prepositional phrases indicating where, when, why, etc. people *slouch*?
3. Are any of the prepositions part of a phrasal verb with *slouch*?
4. What is a *slouch hat*?
5. Is the verb a troponym of (a) standing, (b) sitting or (c) moving?

Now summarise what you know about this word and comment on the discovery process.

Question 96   **Do we *elaborate* something, or *elaborate on/about/over* something?**

In the process of answering these questions, it is worth observing how the structures influence meaning. The use of passive is also important in this context

Search for the lemma and specify *verb*. Sort to the right as that is where the patterns in this data need to be observed[70]. Beware of the tagging errors here – this word is also an adjective, in which case its pronunciation is different[71].

To answer the question about *elaborating something*, it is necessary to look for Subject-Verb-Object (S V O) patterns: who elaborates what? It is worth noting all of the objects and to see if they form lexical sets. In the section on Clustering (p.184) we look into this idea of grouping words into lexical sets that occur in a particular syntactic slot.

Left sorting does a similar job. Verbs are preceded by other elements of the verb phrase, such as modals and auxiliaries. This grouping of the auxiliaries reveals the word's use in passive voice, perfect aspect, to-infinitive form, thanks to the periphrastic nature of English, as elaborated on p.97.

The following corpus examples also express the polysemy of this verb. Examining its collocations and colligations even in this tiny sample, the patterns associated with each meaning can be gleaned. These lexicogrammatical patterns are at the core of word templates as we explore later.

Corp ex.57   *To **elaborate** a little on the definition I gave earlier, an 'edition' is any number of books, small or large printed from one setting of type.*

Corp ex.58   *Her answer was crisp, and she did not **elaborate** any further.*

Corp ex.59   *This point will be **elaborated** further in the discussion of 'crime' in the next section.*

Corp ex.60   *Although he discusses and exemplifies the other maxims, Grice does not **elaborate** on the simple instruction 'Be relevant'.*

Corp ex.61   *William Stukeley further **elaborated** the legend in the eighteenth century when he proposed that ...*

---

[70] ske.li/bnc_elaborate_vb_colls_r
[71] http://bit.ly/howjsay_elaborate

In the full concordance, *and* occurs frequently linking *elaborate* to another verb, e.g. *developed and elaborated* occurs four times. The and/or relationship is another type of pattern of normal usage that emerges very clearly from word sketches as we shall see in Ch.9.

Question 97   **Is there anything noteworthy about parts of the body used as verbs?**

Before searching for the following words as verbs and before looking in a dictionary, what does your intuition tell you?

shoulder, toe, stomach, thumb, knuckle.

The default position to take is S V O, with a person performing the verb. We ask, for example, *Who shoulders what?* We then need to ask *under what circumstances?*

Verbs of Motion

Verbs of motion, such as *go* and its troponyms, are intransitive, i.e. subject + verb, so when investigating the patterns of these verbs, we are firstly interested in their subjects. This information is part of the semantics of the verbs and it provides a structure for using them.

Here are some more words for *ways of walking*:

tramp, tiptoe, lope, wander, swan, mince, step, tread, trudge, meander.

Such a list raises further questions:

- What are the differences between them?
- Why are there so many ways of walking?
- What use are they?
- Who uses them and when?
- Are there as many ways of doing other things?

We will try other approaches to answering these questions under componential analysis (p.83), word templates (p.117 and p.185) and sketch differences (p.191).

Question 98   **Do only people lope, meander, tread and mince?**

If such verbs have other subjects, do they mean something quite different, or are there common elements of meaning? This is an example of the need to reconcile homonymy and polysemy.

Under what circumstances are these verbs performed?

Also of interest to verbs of motion are the adverbs that describe **how** they are performed, and the **spatial adverbials** that express where the verb takes place – its range and destination.

Corp ex.62   *Beneath the viewing deck a few chimps dropped from the branches and **loped** off **towards** their night quarters.*

Corp ex.63   *...from where the Blue Nile **meanders gently towards** Sudan's capital, Khartoum...*

Corp ex.64   *As China **treads cautiously** along the path to internationalization of the yuan, will ...*

Tread cautiously is not typically used as a verb of motion. See these examples from the FeedCorpus[72].

---

[72] http://ske.li/feed_tread_cautiously

Many verbs of motion are also used transitively, which means that the pattern is S V O. To find some examples, search for some of these verbs followed by *the*, e.g. *walk the*. Any S V O findings are unlikely to be verbs of motion. They will therefore have a different meaning and/or usage, perhaps quite idiomatic. See this frequency list [73].

These verbs also occur in idiomatic phrases, e.g. *walk tall, walk the plank, walk the beat.* Match these three phrases with these three glosses: (a) a form of execution, (b) patrolling, (c) pride. Now find some examples of their usages.

These verbs often combine with adverbs and prepositions to make phrasal verbs. Many verbs of motion also occur in delexical structures, such as *take a stroll*, in which the verb is 'nouned'. Many of the noun forms of these verbs are used in various compounds and expressions such as a *walkover, strollathon, bush walk, protest march.* Search in the lemma field with the verb plus a dot-asterisk, e.g. *stroll.**

Can you think of some other series of troponyms that start with *go*, but not in a walking sense? Series of troponyms and other semantic relationships are given at Wordnet [74].

Question 99　**Is there any regularity in the adverbs that describe different semantic groups of verbs?**

Compare the adverbs used with verbs of *walking* with those of *travelling*. Or those of Body-Internal Motion (Levin 1993), such as:

fidget, gyrate, rock, squirm, twitch, wriggle.

There are hundreds of verbs of motion, classified famously by Levin. See this webpage [75].

By now we have arrived at some answers to the undersung topic of verbs of motion. They have their own features semantically and syntactically. Let us move on.

Phrase

According to Oxford Dictionaries [76], a phrase is:

> 1. A small group of words standing together as a conceptual unit, typically forming a component of a clause.
> 1.1 An idiomatic or short pithy expression.

The following definition comes from the *Glossary of Linguistic Terms* [77]:

> A phrase is a syntactic structure that consists of more than one word but lacks the subject-predicate organization of a clause.

This is the definition that linguists use to distinguish phrases from clauses. However, the definition of *phrase* for Sketch Engine's search field is 'a group of adjacent (a.k.a. *contiguous*) *word forms* in a fixed order'. For proper use of this search field, this quite narrow definition must be borne in mind.

For example, a search for *go fish* in the Phrase field returns four lines only in NMC.

Corp ex.65　*I had to laugh at your comment,* **go fish**. *Yes, we were a happy bunch in the 70's weren't we?*

Given that the Phrase field is also case-sensitive, *Go fish* returns seven lines, while *Go Fish* returns four.

---

[73] http://ske.li/bnc_walk_the_freq
[74] http://wordnet.princeton.edu. Click on *Use Wordnet Online* in the left panel.
[75]: http://elies.rediris.es/elies11/cap61.htm
[76] http://bit.ly/oxdict_phrase
[77] http://bit.ly/ling_glossary

We know that searching in the Simple Query field returns the inflected forms of both items. With *go* conjugating and *fish* declining, we get 20 hits, most of which are not the fixed phrase, *go fish*.

By the way, is the apostrophe correct with 70's, as we investigated earlier? It is important to remember that incorrect, non-standard, deviant, erroneous forms, mistakes – call them what you will – do occur in the language that native speakers produce.

Question 100 **I wonder if *I had to laugh* is a fixed phrase in English.**

Corp ex.65 opens with the phrase, *I had to laugh.* This could arouse one's suspicions, pique one's curiosity. The BNC seems to think that it might be, but only in a few text types. It usually stands alone. What else can you find out about this phrase?

Question 101 ***I wonder if* or *I wonder whether*?**

Both of these are bountiful in the BNC but not equally so. Can you identify any systematic usage in one over the other? Remember that we are always looking for criteria according to which we make our linguistic choices.

Question 102 **Does *I wonder* open an indirect question that requires subject-verb inversion?**

For example, *What time is it?* inverts after an introductory clause: *I don't know what time it is*. Look in the BNC at *I wonder* and see if this inversion is standard. A sample of 1,000 right sorted lines is quite revealing.

Question 103 **Do the subject and verb typically change places in indirect questions?**

To answer this question convincingly, study the different *wh-* words and the word order of their clauses.

Search in the Phrase field with: *Do you know wh.**

Here is just one example exhibiting this inverted word order.

Corp ex.66 *Do you know **whose** button this is?*

After performing the search, use the Frequency tool. Set First level as node. Change the attribute in the Second and Third levels to Tag[78]. Which tags dominate?

Click on the **P** beside any of the lines to see sentence examples.

Wh- words:
who
whose
what
when
where
why
which
how

Question 104 **Is the phrase *in mixed company* a euphemism, oblique or a cultural reference?**

Mixed company was referred to earlier in the context of fig-leafed language (p.12):

> *Victorians and vicars birdwatching in mixed company blushed when they spotted one.*

Search the BNC for this phrase. The small number of hits is indicative of its limited use in English. Reading either side of the node may lead to recognising its reference to social acceptability.

[78] ske.li/bnc_doyouknow_tag_tag

Question 105   **Is the 'way how to do something', a structure in English?**

Before considering the structure, consider how frequent the two words are individually? Search for them and write their frequencies here.

      Word 1: *way* _____ Word 2: *how* _____

Now try to predict how frequently you would expect the two words to co-occur.

Type *way how* into the Phrase field and see how often this pair co-occurs. Then see how often it is followed by a *to infinitive*. Is this a pattern of normal usage in English?

It is worth noting that other 'way-like' words do not occur in front of *how* either. Try some of the following: *strategy how, system how, approach how, plan how, method how, technique how*. Nouns that do precede *how* can be seen here[79].

Question 106   **In what contexts is *more than likely* used?**

In what sort of texts is it used?

Is it used as a reaction as well as in running text?

What does it express the speaker's attitude towards?

Question 107   **Can we say *more than unlikely*?**

We can say anything. But do we? Significantly? In specific contexts? If not, what are some alternative wordings?

Multi-word units

The explosion of interest among linguists in multi-word units in the last twenty years has seen not only an explosion of research, but of terminology. As Cobb wrote in 2006, "If vocabulary was flavour of the month in last-decade applied linguistics, in this one it is the multiword unit (MWU)."

Innovating linguists sometimes use a known term in their own specific way or they create a new one. The following componential analysis of four of these terms is unlikely to meet with unanimous acceptance among linguists: it can be seen as an attempt to distinguish them as a basis for further work, and to clarify how they are used in this book. Some of these distinctions are elaborated on p.120.

Question 108   **Does the phrase *once in a lifetime* function as an adjective?**

It occurs 23 times in the BNC, followed by nouns such as *affair, event, find, holiday, opportunity.* How is it tagged?

Are there any other adjectives with a similar meaning that are used with these nouns? Why use one instead of another?

[79] ske.li/bnc_1_n_how

MULTI-WORD UNITS	Collocation	Phrase	Chunk	Bundle
semantically whole	not necessarily	yes	yes	not required to be
flexibility of word forms	open to conversion and inflection	permits variation	fixed	word forms only
length	2 lexemes	not fixed	not fixed	fixed (n-gram)
storage	holistic	holistic	holistic	not stored
phonology	not pronounced as units	usually one nucleus	usually one nucleus	not pronounced as units
order	A – B or B - A	fixed	fixed	fixed

Question 109 **How do we use the chunks we acquire?**

Native speakers of any language have vast stores of multi-word units and using them contributes significantly to FASI. However, since they are not tagged as MWUs in corpora, they cannot be automatically retrieved. Rather, most corpus searches reveal them as patterns that hover around specific words.

What we need to know about chunks is how they fit into streams of language and the types of text that they are typically used in.

When they appear in KWIC format, and sorted left and/or right, the company they keep emerges quite clearly. Furthermore, when observed in the BNC, the metadata indicates the domains and mediums in which they occur.

Some of these will be more fruitfully sought in larger corpora such as enTenTen.

every so often	if truth be told	only a matter of time
age before beauty	never walk alone	alive and well
by and large	all very well	be it on your own head
once in a lifetime	gloom and doom	from cradle to grave
crux of the matter	food for thought	given half a chance

Learners of English would do well to prioritize such chunks in their study plans. This involves observing them in their contexts and getting a feeling for how they might meet a need, especially when there is no direct equivalent in the first language.

Linear Unit Grammar

Two units in sentences and utterances.

Linear Unit Grammar (Sinclair and Mauranen 2006), henceforth LUG, divides stretches of language into (a) Message units and (b) Organisation/Orientation units. In the following example, the sections in italics express the sentence's proposition or message ('M' language), while the rest ('O' language) organises the relationships between Messages across different levels of context, and with the reader.

> Indeed, *every sentence is idiosyncratic*, as indeed *it is systematic*, too.
> (Ellis 2008:396)

This structural division applies equally to written and spoken language, although the focus of most studies that have pursued LUG is on the spoken. Here are two examples from LEXMCI tagged as conversation using some of the chunks above. The M language is in italics.

Corp ex.67   Now I mean that's ah *that's all very well if you equate litigation to something like window cleaning* you know *the more of it the better* ...

Corp ex.68   But { * Well *, do you think, would you think, by and large, *the times are better now * than they were *?* }

These two examples of conversation justify using *utterances* as a separate term for spoken sentences.

Working from a LUG perspective, we will now focus on one aspect of Organisation/Orientation language.

Organisation/Orientation language consists largely of single and multi-word adverbials, e.g. *although, be that as it may, surprisingly,* that express various relationships within and between utterances. These are variously known as discourse markers, conjuncts, disjuncts, stance markers, signposts, sentence adverbials and sentence stems. The different labels represent their different roles. The important thing is that they are not a part of the message bearing clause structure.

One type of Organisation/Orientation language is sentence stems. They make important contributions to text on the levels of discourse, stylistics and pragmatics. These are often chunks expressing temporal and causal relationships in the discourse.

Apart from single word items, they are mostly prefabricated chunks, which guarantees that they are well-attested in corpora and easily processed by people familiar with the genre. With Sketch Engine's Phrase field being case sensitive, these sentence-initial chunks can easily be found. For example,

Remember that	Given that
It may be the case that	It should be noted that
There is no doubt that	It is clear [and other adjectives] that
It appears/seems that	It has been suggested that
Having said that	This does not mean that
Despite the fact that	It was agreed that

Procedures for finding your own sentence stems is discussed on p.136.

Question 110   **What happens after a sentence stem?**

It is valuable to have such sentence stems at your fingertips, but knowing how they are typically followed up in their genres is also part of knowing them. Look them up in the Phrase field and use Frequency to observe what follows them. It is sometimes surprising to find that even the most general of these are followed by quite a limited range of options.

When using the BNC, make sure you are showing David Lee's Classification as well – there are observations to be made.

We will return to LUG when we study the structures of M language in the section on word templates.

Word Form

Unlike Simple Query and Lemma searches, which search for lemmas as well as word forms, words sought via the Word Form field are returned precisely as entered. This is particularly useful when investigating the use of a word form that is also part of a lemma.

Question 111 **How different are the words *hair* and *hairs* in English?**

While most singular-plural pairs are used simply as a real world indication of number, some word forms have quite different usages.

Use the Word form field to search for both *hair* and *hairs* using separate browser tabs. The first thing to notice is the difference in the number of hits. Make a sample of *hairs*, the same size as the number of *hair*. Sort both concordance pages to the left and the right and compare their patterning. Can you answer the question from these observations?

Question 112 **Are both *though* and *although* used to start sentences? Equally?**

Perhaps you already know the answer to this through intuition, or through being taught it. If not, what do you think the answer might be? Match Case is useful for identifying words at the start a sentence.

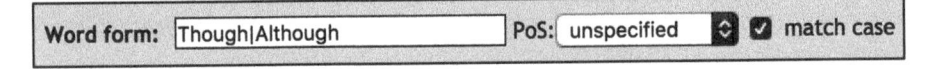

> Word form: Though|Although   PoS: unspecified   ☑ match case

You don't have to process tens of thousands of lines. Rather, click on **Node Forms** in the left panel to see which is significantly more frequent in sentence initial position. Click on the P beside either of them, then on Text types under Frequency.

Question 113 **Is it true that *and* and *but* cannot start sentences?**

These two questions deserve deeper answers than *yes* or *no* – check the text types as well. Also, compare the hits per million of those that start sentences with those that don't.

Question 114 **Which is the correct form of the discourse markers when listing things in prose, *first or firstly*?**

Search for both words in Word Form field using the vertical bar: First|Firstly, and select Match Case. Since we find both *first* and *firstly*, set David Lee's Classification as the References. Make a sample of say 1,000 and then use Multi-level sort.

it is difficult to arrive at a descriptive, data-driven decision. In fact, the preference for one over the other is a moot point among stylists, purists, prescriptivists and the like.

Question 115 **Have you ever wondered if some surnames are also common nouns?**

For example: Thatcher, Butcher, Baker, Barker, Teacher, Hooper, Cooper, Blower, Archer, Brewer, Crier. This must pique your curiosity about the origins of surnames. After searching for say, parker, in the word form field, click on node tags, where the proper noun and common noun tags indicate their relative usage. Click on P. The sorting shows any lexical patterns that might exist. What is a nosey/nosy parker?

Some readers may be familiar with Bill Posters. Open this link[80] and identify some of the patterns of normal usage around the node. You might wonder if Bill is even a person.

If the collocation *pique curiosity* piques your curiosity, open this permalink[81].

Countability

The issue of the countability of nouns looms large[82] in learning English as a foreign or second language, despite many a native speaker of English being unaware of it. In the first of the next two corpus sentences, *scholarship* refers to **academic pursuit** and has no plural form, whereas in the second, it is a **financial award** and there can be more than one of them. Both examples are from ukWaC.

Corp ex.69   *Fine art, architecture, **scholarship**, literature, music and piety jostled for attention alongside hunting, feasting, jousting, politics, diplomacy and war.*

Corp ex.70   *Lawrence won a **scholarship** to Nottingham High school, leaving at the age of 16 to work as a clerk in a local factory.*

Another example is the word *experience*. In the first of the next two sentences, it refers to knowledge of the world and has no plural form, whereas in the second it is an event of which there can be more than one.

Corp ex.71   *I am a political refugee with personal **experience** of being the target of hate speech.*

Corp ex.72   *British gay men reported having at least one **experience** of unprotected sex last year, ...*

Note that in other languages, these two notions have quite distinct forms, e.g. Czech has *zážitek* and *zkušenost*, and German has *Erfarhung* and *Erlebnis*.

Countability is an important factor in the use of determiners. Mass nouns such as *water, toothpaste, money, homework* and *coffee* only have plural forms when they refer to discrete entities; however, not all of them do. We use quantifying nouns that do take the plural if necessary, e.g. *tube of toothpaste, bar of soap, cup of coffee, piece of homework.*

Select some illustrative sentences in corpora that indicate the usage of *coffee, coffees* and *cup/mug (etc) of coffee*, and other such contrasts.

English also has expressions of quantity such as *array, bunch, group, heap, multitude* and *range*, which are typically followed by *of*.

All of these **nouns + of** can easily be sought in the Simple Query field and a frequency listing will show the items that follow them. It will show any items that meet the criteria, but human intuition, context and one's knowledge of the world will distinguish *bars of chocolate* and *soap* from *bars of music* and *bars of a cage*.

Question 116   **Are the quantity nouns that follow *of* in the singular or plural?**

Here are two examples. Note that in the first, *multitude are* (plural) and in the second *a multitude binds (singular)*. Which is more typical?

---

[80] ske.li/ett_bill_posters
[81] ske.li/bnc_pique_curiosity
[82] ske.li/bnc_loom_large

Corp ex.73   *A **multitude** of medical conditions **are** due to being overweight, which in many people may simply be the product of self-indulgence rather than food addiction.*

Corp ex.74   *..., yet a **multitude** of non-verbal signals **binds** them together in a group.*

Use the Word Form field to investigate some more examples of these words as they are used in the singular. They can also be used in the plural, but then agreement is not contentious. Some nouns are used mainly in the plural. To search for the plural form only, use Word Form.

Use the frequency tool to make bundles, e.g. 1L Node 1R, or 2L 1L Node 1R. We can expect to find *of* very frequently after the singular noun, and determiners and adjectives before it.

In the case of *array*, a wealth of positive adjectives precede it, lending the word positive connotations which in isolation it probably does not have for most speakers.

Question 117   **Are singular nouns always used with a determiner? Do they have singular verb agreement?**

Singular nouns are nouns which have no plural in at least one of their senses. For example, *ability, brainchild, crux, dearth, epitome, fray, grounding, heartbeat, impasse,* and etc. through the alphabet. For a longer list, see COBUILD Grammar Patterns 2: Nouns and Adjectives, p.13.

Choose some of the nouns listed above and search for them, one at a time, in the Word form field. Using the Frequency tool, choose the Attribute Tag in 1L and Word for the node. This answers the first question.

To answer the second question, use the Frequency tool again, but choose the Attribute Word for the node and Tag for 1R. In the case of *ability*, most of the verb tags end with Z, which indicates 3rd person singular, ergo, singular agreement.

VVP is the tag for verb, singular, present, non-3rd person. If these occur in the frequency lists, click the P to find out why.

Character

While this field is of particular relevance to languages such as Chinese and Japanese, it serves English in some useful ways, too.

Brackets and parentheses

Bracketed or parenthetic information is often an admission of irrelevance or downgrading: by putting a comment in brackets, the author is implying, *well it's not germane to my point, but it occurred to me while I was writing and I thought you might be interested ...*

In contemporary writing, therefore, there is less and less information in brackets (even footnotes rarely contain information). This makes reading a very smooth process indeed. It places a demand on authors to work everything germane into the regular syntax of well-crafted sentences, or to leave some material out. In the following sentence from the BNC, the author uses parentheses twice and for different purposes. Curiously, she gives some examples of parenthetic information in parentheses!

Corp ex.75   *His stimulus material was a film and he particularly noted the expression of parenthetic information (asides, or personal expression of feeling) in the recall of such events (something which does not appear in recall of verbally presented stories).*

> An **aside** is a dramatic device in which a character speaks to the audience. By convention the audience is to realize that the character's speech is unheard by the other characters on stage. (Wikipedia)

The second use is more of an aside, something that she mentions between the first parenthesis!

An aside: by looking at the metadata for this example, you can see the name of the author (B. Wolf), the title and year of publication. By searching for this on the internet, you can see that the author's name is Bernice. By doing an image search for Bernice, it is clear that this name is used for women. Then you can use the pronoun *she*.

Question 118   **How much information typically appears in brackets (parentheses)?**

Type a left bracket into the Character field. Make a sizeable Sample and Sort to the right. Use the browser's CTRL F to highlight the close bracket:).

What appears in brackets? How many words? Are there any phrases or clauses? Give some thought to the reasons an author might have put such things in brackets. And observe the text types of your findings.

Consider carefully the use of brackets in your own writing.

@ a.k.a. *at*

This symbol is best known today in email addresses but this was not always the case.

Question 119   **How early did people have email addresses?**

Starting with the BNC, enter @ into the Character field. Use the Select Lines check boxes to separate the email address from the other uses of @. Click Selected lines in the left panel and then in View Options, choose Publication Date.

Question 120   **How is the *at* symbol used when not in email addresses?**

Search for it in the BNC in the Character field. Make a three level Frequency list: 1L node 1R.

Question 121   **Are capital letters used after colons and semicolons?**

Type these punctuation marks into the Character field, perform searches and then use Frequency to make a list of at least 1R.

Question 122   **How do answers begin?**

Type a question mark into the Character field. This contrasts with Question 27: Do you love me, where we could not use a question mark in the Simple Query field.

To answer the question, make a frequency list of three or four word bundles after the question mark.

> March 6th, 2016 (BBC News)
>
> Internet pioneer Ray Tomlinson, who is credited with the invention of email, has died at the age of 74.
>
> The US computer programmer came up with the idea of electronic messages that could be sent from one network to another in 1971. His invention included the ground-breaking use of the @ symbol in email addresses, which is now standard.

To answer a better question, click on Text Types in the left panel under frequency. Click on the P beside W_fict_prose in David Lee's Classification and create the bundles using the frequency tool: the first level will be 2R. Repeat with S_conv.

What was the better question?

From the Text Types list, we can also observe how relatively infrequent direct questions occur in academic prose.

Task: After studying the following table, write the number of hits that each of the following return. Use the same corpus.

Simple Query	?pine _____	does not work with a full stop
Lemma	.pine _____	does not work with a question mark
CQL	".pine" _____ lemma attribute	does not work with a question mark

The following operators work in these fields: Lemma, Phrase, Word form. Some of them behave differently in CQL, as we will investigate later (p.139 ff).

Operators used in fields other than Simple Query

Full stop	Before, during or after a word, a full stop stands for any one character in the search, not necessarily in the results. It depends on the field you choose. For example, searching for oper. in Word form returns opera/Opera. Searching for it in the Lemma field returns opera/operas, etc, This is the normal behaviour of these fields.
	In the Word Form field, b.g gives *big bag beg bog bug*. Click on Node Forms to obtain the list. This is useful for pronunciation teaching in generating lists of words that can be used in minimal pairs activities.
	In the Lemma field, .rick gives all word forms of the lemmas that have these four letters starting in second place, e.g. *brick, tricks, pricked, tricking*. This typically offers words that rhyme. Note that in Simple Query, a question mark gives this list.
Asterisk	After a full stop the asterisk permits any number of letters, including zero, in place of the full stop. In the BNC Lemma field, b.*g gives over 153,000 hits[83], including *broadcasting, brainstorming, bing, beg*. In the Word Form field, it returns well over 250,000.
	.*ship finds words ending with *ship*
	oxy.* finds words beginning with *oxy*
	.*advantag.* finds words containing *advantag* of which there are 27 different ones in the BNC. Use Node Forms to create this list.
Backslash	To search for a full stop, use the backslash and the full stop. In computing, this is referred to as *escaping,* see. p.150.
	Dr\. finds *Dr.* only. Without the backslash, you also get Dr., along with hundreds of other three-letter combinations starting with dr.

[83] http://ske.li/bnc_b.*g

Working with Affixes

Affix is the superordinate for *prefix* and *suffix*. The full stop operator is like a blank tile in Scrabble – it can stand in for any letter. Used alone it is particularly useful for s/z alternative spellings. In combination with the asterisk, however, we discover what prefixes and suffixes attach to stems. And as we have already seen many times, some things will be very typical and others less so. Given our creative use of language, we coin many words in this way, as we see among the less frequent ones. Here, for example, are six of the dozens of recent coinages, a.k.a. neologisms, starting with *faux* that occur once only in enTenTen. What parts of speech are they?

faux-modest, faux-sarcasm, faux-sophistication,
faux-patriotic, faux-lesbian, faux-deferential

Question 123 **Which of these *faux* words were in use in the late 20th century?**

Search *faux** in Simple Query or *faux.** in other fields. What does the BNC data indicate about the recent history of this prefix?

To find out if any of these BNC *faux* words caught on and entered the language, look for other examples in more recent corpora.

By the way, do **words** *catch on*? Is this a collocation? What other things *catch on*?

Nonce words are words, often multi-word units, that are created for a specific communicative situation and cannot be expected to be met again – they often go unrecorded. Many new words in a language start their lives as nonce words. For example, *chortle*, invented by Lewis Carroll for his poem Jabberwocky (1872) is a fixture in English, isn't it? Its Text Types are quite telling.

In Hanks' words, Joyce's *Finnegans Wake* is an exuberant, scatological and richly comic outpouring of invented words, portmanteau words, puns and intertextual references. He estimates that it contains 80,000 lexical inventions in its 608 pages (2013:275-6).

In corpus terms, many nonce words are also *hapax legomena*, that is, they occur only once in a corpus. According to Zipf's Law, this applies to between 40% and 60% of words. We will use the Word List tool to search for words that occur once only on p.195.

Question 124 **What are some words with the suffix *–ity* indicating the state or quality of the adjective it is attached to?**

Try .*ity. This gives all the words that end in *-ity*. Those which are the abstractions of adjectives are typically singular nouns (see also Question 117). Nevertheless, performing this search in the Lemma field returns plural forms as well, e.g. *opportunities, eccentricities*. Are these also abstract forms of adjectives?

LGSWE (p.232ff) has a comprehensive list of noun suffixes with their functions.

Question 125 **Is *dis-* the only prefix taken by *cover*, as in the title of this book?**

Search for .*cover in the Word Form field. What are the differences between the words that you find? Do their contexts and co-texts provide any clues?

Who *discovers* what under what circumstances?

Question 126 **How do other prefixes fare?**

Try mega.* in the Word Form field in the BNC. Click on Node Forms – the list has *Megan* at the top while the following occur only once:

megafirm, megafabulously, megamoney, megamum, megamouth

Question 127 **Given *that Megan* is a fairly uncommon name, how did it get such a high score?**

How many *Megans* do you know or know of? Wikipedia's list of *Notable Megans* might jog your memory.

Click on P beside Megan in the Node forms list.

Click on Text Types. David Lee's Classification shows that more than half come from W_fict_prose. Click on its **P**.

To find out what books they come from, select bnc.doc title in View Options' References as shown in this screenshot.

This use of *Megan* says more about the BNC than about English.

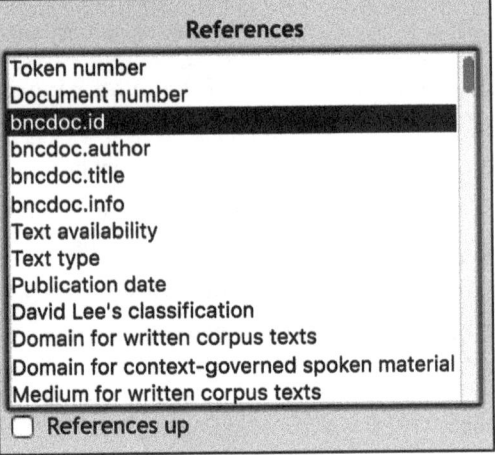

Question 128 **Are there any affixes making verb forms out of *friend*?**

In the BNC, put *.*friend.** in the Lemma field and choose verb from the POS droplist. Then click on Node Forms.

Repeat this search in the enTenTen corpus. How do the node form lists compare? Do you find that the standard form still has a strong place in contemporary English?

Question 129 **It emerges that *be-* is often used as a prefix. Does it have meaning or a function? Is it limited to any particular parts of speech?**

In the BNC, search for be.* and make a list of Node Tags to see which parts of speech have words starting with *be*. In the Node tags frequency list, click on the heading *tag* to group the parts of speech.

It will be more efficient to focus on a particular parts of speech, than deal with them all. Having established that there are many, search again for be.* in the lemma field and choose verb. Make a frequency list with lemma as the attribute.

The words of interest are those which are obviously be + free morpheme, e.g. *befriend, bewitch, bejewel.*

The data is not the answer – it is a starting point, as we have seen in many questions so far. Remember that the question asks about the meaning and function of the prefix.

Question 130 **Why do people say things like *not uninteresting*? Is it not enough to say *is interesting*?**

We find that *not uninteresting* occurs once only in the BNC and 162 times[84] in enTenTen. Using .*, however, we find that *not un...* is quite well represented, even in the BNC[85]. Is this negative particle + negative prefix a pattern of normal usage? Does it belong to any particular text types? If not, can any other explanation be found in the data?

This is an example of the literary figure *litotes*, often inverting the sense of a positive attribute by preceding it with a negative, and very often employing double negatives e.g. *no oil painting, far from hygienic, not infrequently, not bad looking*. It goes back as a literary device to classical literature and can be found operating in many languages (Pulverness 2015).

We will now observe how this operator can be used between words.

Question 131 **Is it true that more English words have *k* as the third letter than as the first?**

This may seem like a bizarre question, but it concerns a finding by psychologists Kahneman and Tversky (1973) about the way humans process information. Before we investigate it, what do you think the answer is?

To find words with k as their third letter, type ..k.* into the lemma field.

To find words that start with k, type k.* into the lemma filed.

With the results of both, use Frequency: choose attribute lemma, Ignore case and set the Frequency limit to 1. The first thing we notice is the Zipfian tendency for a small number of words to have a great number of occurrences.

To find out how many such words there are, it is necessary to keep clicking Next till you get to the end, and multiply the number of pages by the number of lines per page. There are 79 pages of lemmas with k as their third letter[86].

There is no 'Go Last' button that would jump to the end of the list in a single click – this means that along the way you will observe some interesting words and non-words.

To exclude hapax legomena, make the Frequency limit 2. In the case of words starting with k, this reduces the number of pages from 43 to 20[87], in accordance with Zipf's Law.

The answer to the actual question is *yes*, contrary to the intuition of most of their subjects. See a description of Kahneman and Tversky's research at Psychwiki[88].

Remember that computers process information differently from people, as noted by Baker (2006:11 & 19) in relation to corpora.

---

[84] ske.li/ett_not_uninteresting
[85] ske.li/bnc_not_un_freq
[86] ske.li/bnc_k3_lastpage
[87] See where the *hapax legomena* begin: ske.li/bnc_k_words_p20
[88] http://www.psychwiki.com/wiki/Availability_Heuristic

Question 132 **I've heard something that sounds ironic:** *in the looks department.* **Apart from actual departments, what** *departments* **are referred to?**

Corp ex.76 *I mean, Emma's no slouch in the looks department, as you know, but this Cindy of yours is like - well, like something turned out by a machine*

Try a Simple Query search for **in the * department**, then click on Node Forms.

As we have already noted a number of times, patterns of normal usage emerge at the top of the lists and graphs, while the exploitations of the language are inevitably lower down. Some examples in the BNC: *the brain department, the butchering department* are at the bottom in terms of frequency. There is even one hit in the NMC of *in the irony department*!

Question 133 **What semantic prosody emerges when the phrase** *or just plain* **is used?**

Search for this in the Phrase field, and make a Frequency list of the words 1R. They are either nouns or adjectives. To find out how it has been tagged, click on Node tags or use lempos as an attribute. Alternatively, make a Frequency list with 1R Word in the first level and 1R Tag in the second. This allows you to click the Tag column heading to sort the list alphabetically.

What do you notice about the nouns and adjectives in terms of their prosody or connotations?

Vertical bar

The vertical bar can be placed between items so that the concordancer searches for them at the same time. In regular expressions it means OR.

Question 134 **Can** *amid* **and** *amidst* **be used interchangeably?**

In any field but Simple Query, you can use the vertical bar between words: **amid|amidst**. Make a Sample, investigate their text types, etc. Can you find any systematic difference between them? Whatever answer you arrive at will influence how you choose to use one or the other.

Whilst investigating this pair, observe their semantic prosody. It is of surprising interest. This list of collocates[89] is revealing.

Question 135 **Is there any pattern in the use of prepositions with synonyms?**

Using the vertical bar in *struggle|battle|fight* searches for all of these items. This particular search reveals interesting patterns in preposition use. Since all three are both nouns and verbs, choosing PoS when making the query will make it more focussed. Various frequency listings are useful here. To find other candidates for similar searches, click on Thesaurus in the left panel, and type in a word.

Question 136 **Can the vertical bar be used to look up British and American spellings at the same time?**

Try color|colour and centre|center, for example. Try such searches in both the BNC and LEXMCI and see which corpus is the more British. This may be a useful test when creating your own corpora in Chapter 14 , DIY corpora.

---

[89] ske.li/bnc_amid_colls

Corpus Query Language – a brief introduction

Until now, we have been searching corpora by typing into the Simple Query, Lemma, Phrase and Character fields. In the background, Sketch Engine converts these into Corpus Query Language (CQL) queries, which you can see by clicking on ConcDesc at the bottom of the left panel. This screenshot shows the CQL that was generated for Question 136.

CQL is not only an alternative way of forming searches, but it has many features that enable very specific searches. In many cases there is no alternative to a CQL query. Here are some questions that simple CQL queries can provide data for.

Before we start, check that you are using BNC TreeTagger. The BNC without TreeTagger uses CLAWS with which the following steps are incompatible. See the Penn Treebank Tags on the last pages of this book.

Concordance description

Corpus: **British National Corpus (TreeTagger)**

Operation	Parameters	Hits
Query	lc,"color|colour"	11490
GDEX	100	11490

Question 137 **How many sentences are there in a corpus?**

The Penn Treebank tag, "SENT", which marks full stops, question marks and exclamation marks, invites a wide range of questions, as we are about to see.

Knowing the number of sentences in a corpus, especially in a specialised corpus or subcorpus, allows calculations of average sentence length, which is an important stylistic feature.

Type the query, as shown in this screenshot: the tag is in capital letters and is between non-curly quotation marks. Choose tag as the Default attribute. Then use some of the tools to check the reliability of the tagging. For example, are decimal points counted as full stops?

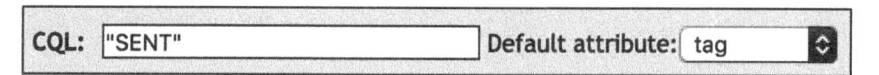

CQL:	"SENT"	Default attribute:	tag

Question 138 **Does English permit numbers at the beginning of sentences?**

In other words, are sentence initial numbers written as words as the style manuals tell us? After the sentence punctuation tag, we add the tag for cardinal numbers "CD", and select TAG as the default attribute.

"SENT" "CD"

Then make a node forms list. To use the data to answer the question, it is necessary to click on some of the "P"s in the list to see why some of the numbers are not written as words.

Question 139 **Is it true that past participles are only used in compound forms?**

In this context, compound forms refers to verb structures that require auxiliaries. This question surprises a lot of people and a lot of people benefit from knowing the answer. To search for past participles, enter **"VVN"** in the CQL Field. Set the Default Attribute to *tag*. Note that VVN searches for lexical verbs, not auxiliary verbs.

We are looking to see if there are any instances of VVN without *be* forming passive voice and progressive aspect, or without *have* forming perfect aspect and causative. A by-product of this analysis is finding out if the past participle performs any other function(s).

Top Level Queries continued

Use the Filter button to exclude *be* and *have* from left of the node. Choose Negative at the top, enter *be* in the Simple Query field and set the range 5L and 0R. Click Filter concordance button. Repeat the procedure with *have*. This reduces the number of lines to c.30% of the VVN hits.

This should not be a difficult question to answer, but with so many of the words masquerading under VVN being wrongly tagged, it is necessary to approach this differently.

- The Sample button can be put to good use.
- Read some concordance pages to answer the question.
- Select Lines check boxes are useful in such situations.
- Use the Frequency tool to generate columns (levels) to the left of the past participles.

What uses of past participles emerge from this data?

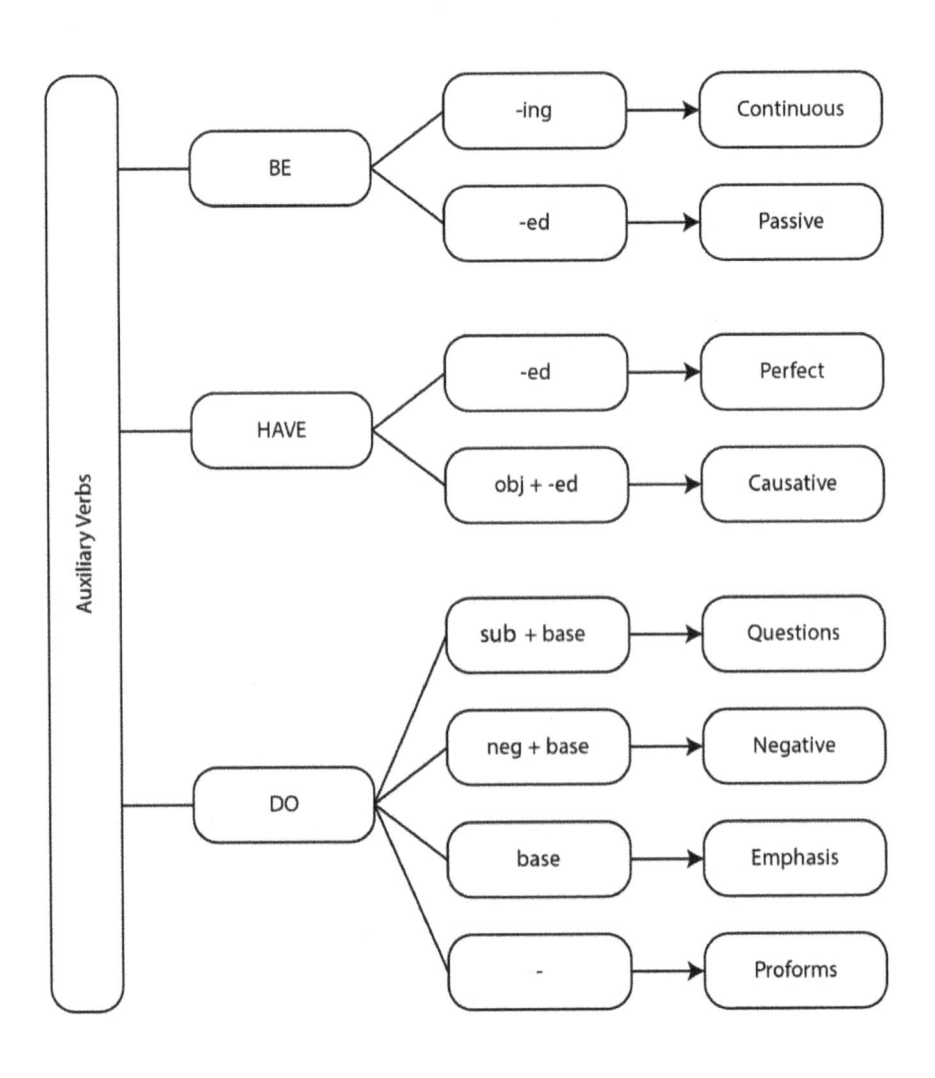

```
Auxiliary Verbs
├── BE
│   ├── -ing      → Continuous
│   └── -ed      → Passive
├── HAVE
│   ├── -ed      → Perfect
│   └── obj + -ed → Causative
└── DO
    ├── sub + base → Questions
    ├── neg + base → Negative
    ├── base       → Emphasis
    └── -          → Proforms
```

Periphrasis

Periphrasis is when grammatical functions are expressed by auxiliary words in combination with lexical words, as is the case in analytic languages. Chinese is a prime example as it has no verb forms other than the base form and nouns do not have plural or possessive forms – these features are expressed by particles or understood from context. In contrast, synthetic languages express grammatical function such as tense and aspect with inflections. See the Italian example in the table below. However, as Crystal points out, most languages have features of analytic and synthetic languages (2006:370).

The comparative and superlative forms of adjectives and adverbs are mostly the product of inflection, i.e. *-er, -est*, while the use of *more* and *most* are examples of periphrasis. Delexical verb structures also exemplify the periphrastic nature of English because the verbs are semantically light or even empty. We investigate this structure on p.99.

From a linguistic standpoint, English has two tenses only, past and present, as we have already noted. From a pedagogical standpoint, however, the term 'tense' is used to refer to all of the expressions of TIME including **progressive** and **perfect**, which linguists refer to as *aspect*. Unmarked aspect is referred to as **simple**, e.g. simple present, simple past.

The diagram opposite depicts the use of the two verbs that are used as auxiliaries to form aspect and voice. It also shows the periphrastic role of *do* in creating other language constructions.

In Italian, the *passato prossimo* is formed with the verb *avere* (italicized in the table below). This periphrastic structure is quite similar, though not equivalent, in both meaning and form to English present perfect. Italian's *imperfetto* however, is formed with endings (underlined) and expresses the periphrastic English *used to / would always*.

> Time is a game played beautifully by children.
> Heraclitus

Future time in English is expressed in ways that reflect or respect our uncertainty about things which have not yet happened. Because there is no inflection to indicate the future, it is expressed periphrastically with *will, shall, going to* and *be to,* as well as with the present progressive; for fixed schedules we use present tense. Italian has a set of endings (in bold) to mark the future.

scrivere to write

Pronouns	Presente	Passato prossimo	Imperfetto	Futuro semplice
io	scrivo	*ho* scritto	scriv<u>evo</u>	scriv**erò**
tu	scrivi	*hai* scritto	scriv<u>evi</u>	scriv**erai**
egli	scrive	*ha* scritto	scriv<u>eva</u>	scriv**erà**
noi	scriviamo	*abbiamo* scritto	scriv<u>evamo</u>	scriv**eremo**
voi	scrivete	*avete* scritto	scriv<u>evate</u>	scriv**erete**
essi	scrivono	*hanno* scritto	scriv<u>evano</u>	scriv**eranno**

Understanding the systematic use of auxiliary verbs helps teachers teach and learners learn. For conducting CQL searches, it is necessary to know how elements combine and co-operate to form the compound forms that grammatize vocabulary.

The following chapters will develop this linguistic knowledge and introduce more Sketch Engine tools that can answer more and more language questions.

Discovering English

Does English need discovering? Many linguists, of the armchair and empirical varieties alike, have been writing for over a century about *English as she is spoke* [90] and writ. Now that English has achieved lingua franca status, describing her every curve and nuance has become something of an industry. This serves as a great impetus to linguistics departments in universities – their findings are filtered down to a vast community of language professionals by a relatively small band of journal and book publishers. Since the work of teachers is above all to teach, and that of translators is to translate, such language professionals are very glad of the work that linguists do. As Gleiser wrote in defence of scientists:

> Behind the scientist's complicated formulas, the tables of data obtained from experiments, and the technical jargon, you will find a person eagerly trying to transcend the immediate boundaries of life, driven by an unstoppable desire to reach some deeper truth (2005).

Nevertheless, of great interest to the current book is treating "the learner as a research worker whose learning needs to be driven by access to linguistic data and whose role is to identify, classify and generalize that data," as Tim Johns wrote almost a quarter of a century ago. For this he coined the term, data-driven learning, as discussed in the Introduction. Thus, we are less interested in the findings of linguists for the wholesale consumption of teachers, learners and translators than in the process of discovery which allows learners to create knowledge for themselves. This statement by Piaget was also quoted in the Introduction and is worth repeating here:

> Each time one prematurely teaches a child something he could have discovered for himself, the child is kept from inventing it and consequently from understanding it completely.

This does not suggest throwing a child to the wolves, but rather that there is an element of guidance from a "more knowledgeable other" as Vygotsky has it. After all, the support of a teacher enables leaners to achieve things that they never would alone, which is the thrust of Vygotsky's Zone of Proximal Development, and Bruner's scaffolding. Guided discovery is a logical consequence of this co-operation between the teacher as *the guide on the side* (King 1993)*,* and the learners. Teachers facilitate learning rather than transmit information. As Tom Cobb wrote,

> Lexicographers use a corpus and concordance to assemble in moments and force the patterns out of data that would otherwise require years, and it is not inconceivable that learners might be able to do some scaffolded version of this too (2005).

To return to our question: Does English need discovering? In our work so far, *Discovering English with Sketch Engine* has been enabling the reader to obtain language data that can be interpreted to answer set questions with the help of instructions for Sketch Engine tools as they are introduced step by step. The process is intended to develop awareness of language as a linguistic object, furnish information about English that may be new, and above all to provide skills training in finding answers to one's own questions. It is hoped that knowledge is being created every step of the way. This is what needs discovering.

On with the show!

---

[90] See the Wikipedia: English As She Is Spoke

Chapter 6   It depends on the context

> Context is relevant to the study of almost anything.
>
> Clark & Ivanič 1997

Context was discussed in the Introduction: context of culture, context of situation. We will explore these in Chapter 7 . In this chapter, we are concerned with syntagmatic contexts, i.e. words and phrases in the context of other words (collocation), and other parts of speech (colligation). As we see in this screenshot from the BNC, context depends on some things and some things depend on context.

Hanks (e.g. 2013) takes the view that words in isolation, instead of having meaning, have **meaning potential**. Actual meanings are realised when people use words in specific contexts, whether verbal (linguistic) or situational (real world). As Cameron and Kulick point out, It is in discourse – the use of language in specific contexts – that words acquire meaning (2003:29).

In our daily lives, we rarely meet words in isolation, but when asked what the first thing we think of is when we hear the word, *bar,* for example, several things come to mind.

```
third parties. This depends upon the context of the cla
e present context depends on the statements of princi
ttitudinal positions depends upon the wider context of
in a given context depends on how it fits into its surrou
matical sense of it depends on context and the knowle
roper title to print depends on the linear context , a m
ibid.). Oral speech depends on context to communicate
is `real' but that it depends exquisitely on the context
earby context ... it depends for its success on having fai
rge in this context depends also on which of the asset's
rocess is folding. It depends on contexts in parse trees,
```

What context do you instantly create for this word? What is your first association?

People have different responses according to their previous real world encounters with a word, although as Meara points out, "the most striking thing about associations is that they are actually extremely boring and predictable" (2009:21). This psychological data about what a sample of the population associates with words is not available in corpora, but it is available in word association lists (see p.167). One such is the Edinburgh Associations Thesaurus which is publicly accessible online [91]. Search for *bar* in the Stimulus field, and click Associate words as in this screenshot.

There is inevitably a considerable overlap with the words we associate with other words and the words we actually use. As the responses to *bar* indicate, this is a highly polysemous word, out of context. In context however, the word's meaning

> **Interactive Associative Thesaurus**
> Enter a word in one or both boxes.
>
> [_____] Stimulus (Find associations produced from the given word)
>
> [_____] Response (Word which was produced as an association to what)
>
> [Associate words] [Reset form]

---

[91] http://www.eat.rl.ac.uk

potential is immediately realised. Consider why each of the many meanings of *bar* in the following chunks are not ambiguous:

> *bar of chocolate, drinks at the bar, a bar of music, behind bars, navigation bar, bar chart, bar association, scroll bar, handlebar, toolbar, raise the bar*.

In addition to lexical company, grammatical context is also involved in realising a word's meaning potential, as we saw in *bound to* in Question 47.

In Sketch Engine, the **Context** level lets us filter a top level query. *Filter* is an important word here – it refers to searching for something in the context of something else, e.g. find *house* in the context of *dwelling*, find *impact* with the prepositions that follow it.

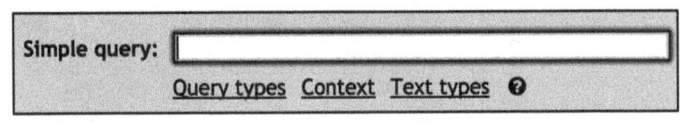

To open the Context part of the window, click the underlined Context button. It toggles open-closed. Once you have entered something in any of the fields in the top section, you can filter or constrain the search by words (lemmas) and by parts of speech (POS), and by both.

Lemma Filter

Question 140   **Is *seize control* a fixed phrase?**

If not, it might be a collocation in which the words occur in both orders and other words appear in between them.

Putting *seize control* in Simple Query or Phrase cannot answer these questions. In the BNC with *seize* in Simple Query field, *control* in Lemma Filter, and the window set as in the screenshot, we find that the verb conjugates and in all but 6 of the 58 lines the pair is together. Most of them are followed by *of the*.

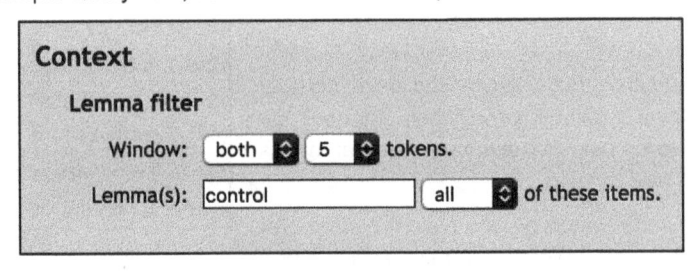

Corp ex.77   *McLaren's conviction that Branson wanted revenge, to find a way to **seize control** of the Pistols for good, 'and cut me off at the pass', now became an obsession.*

Question 141   **Is there a standard order in which we say the three items of cutlery?**

Type one of them (*fork* or *spoon* or *knife*) into Simple Query and another one into Lemma filter. Sort them. Even though this order differs in British and American English, it is fixed in those varieties.

This type of fixed string of three words is referred to as a trinomial, of which there are many in English. Some others are *cool, calm and collected; deaf, dumb and blind; healthy, wealthy and wise; hook, line and sinker*. Their word order is fixed. Recognising these chunks is valuable for interpreting language, but for generating language more is required, of course. For example, there are two quite different verbs significantly preceding *hook, line and sinker*, namely, *swallow* and *fall*. What syntactic relationship do these verbs have with the chunk?

English also abounds in binomials. For lists of binomials and trinomials, see the Versatile Glossary.

Question 142 **Does *only* at the beginning of a clause predict the emphatic *do*?**

As we saw in the periphrasis diagram (p.93), *do* is an auxiliary verb. It is a lexical verb as well.

In the following three examples, *do* is an auxiliary but it is not forming questions or negatives.

To perform this search, enter *Only* into the Word Form field and select Match Case. Enter *do* into the Lemma Filter, 5R. There are c.50 selected examples here[92].

Corp ex.78 *Only* after Pericles' death **did** the rot set in ...

Corp ex.79 *Only* in the nineteenth century **did** it begin to include the unfair management of people or things.

Corp ex.80 *Only* then **did** he zip himself up and reach for the telephone.

Would you conclude this a pattern of normal usage?

Question 143 **Do sentence *structures* have their own meanings or semantics?**

This question asks if the meaning of a sentence results not from the interplay of words alone, but also from the structure in which they are used. By analogy, we could compare the roles of materials and the structure of a building, or the elements of a piece of music (e.g. harmony, rhythm, melody) and its structure (sonata, symphony, concerto, etc), or the effect of words used to describe an emotion in a poem vs. a play vs. a novel. Is structure part of the meaning? Does structure contribute to the effect the words have on a reader or listener – its perlocutionary effect?

Starting small, let's take sentences which begin with *While*. Try to ignore the lexical elements in these sentences and focus on *While* and the comma.

Corp ex.81 *While development was slow, the effort paid off.*

Corp ex.82 *While this is sound advice, the fact is that `Revocable' Credits are very rare.*

Corp ex.83 *While chancellors were usually cardinals, the notaries were not.*

So, does the structure *While A B, C D* convey a meaning? Can you describe it?

To find more examples and counter-examples to test the *while* hypothesis, use the BNC: search for *While* in the Word Form field and match case. In the Lemma filter, put a comma and choose, say, 5 tokens to the Right.

To reduce the number of concordance lines, use the 1st Hit in Doc button. Having all the results of a search eliminated except for the first one that appears in a document reduces a bias that might result from an author's stylistic preferences or idiolect. Click Sentence under View Options[93].

Unsurprisingly, many of the sentences start with the temporal use of *while;* we are interested in its concessive use. According to LGSWE (p.849), *while* almost always

---

[92] http://ske.li/bnc_only_do
[93] ske.li/bnc_while_comma_1st

expresses time in spoken English, while in academic prose 80% of its use is concessive.

Clicking on Text Types will confirm LGSWE's finding. Click on P beside anything marked academic.

After performing the above search, the grey bar across the top of the concordance page ends with what you see in this screenshot.

> Filter all but first hit in document 733 (6.5 per million)

Phrasal verbs

Phrasal verbs have had a number of mentions in this book already: see *Verb – phrasal* in the Index. *Phrasal verb* is defined variously, but in this book at least, a phrasal verb consists of a verb and one or two particles, which can be prepositions or adverbs [94]. It forms a single semantic and syntactic unit.

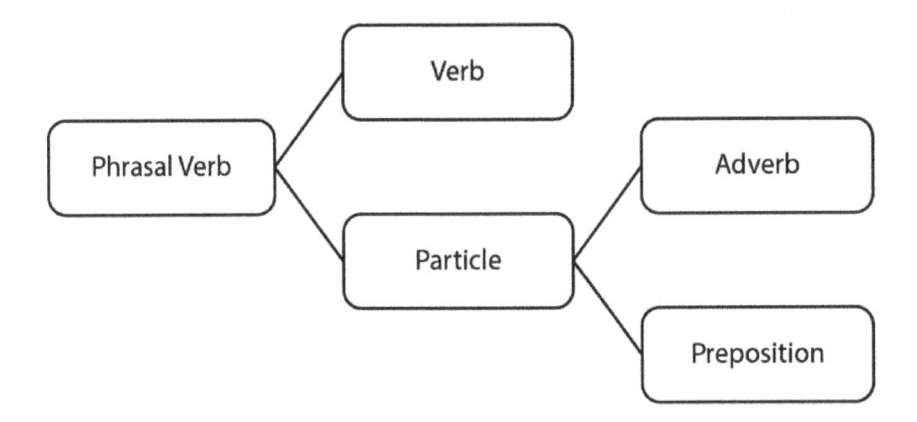

Unlike collocations, the meaning of the group is not usually a combination of the meanings of the words. In phrasal verbs, the particles often express a function or metaphorical meaning. For example, *Collins Cobuild Phrasal Verbs Dictionary* (2002:35) gives twelve meaning/functions for *out*.

Here are five of the twelve.

    1. leaving e.g. *want out, clock out*

    3. searching, finding, obtaining e.g. *pry out, work out*

    9. duration and resisting e.g. *brave out, tough out*

    11. arranging, dividing, selecting, distributing e.g. *dish out, tease out*

    14. attacking, criticizing, protesting e.g. *punch out, dish out*

This systematic pairing of a verb and a particle, whose meaning or function is describable is evidence

---

[94] http://bit.ly/ling_gloss_phrasal_verb

that phrasal verbs are not random, and explains how new ones are frequently coined. For native speakers, the meaning of a newly-coined phrasal verb is usually understood on first hearing through a complex network of analogies. And of course, context.

To observe this particle at work, search for some of the above phrasal verbs in Simple Query in LEXMCI, and observe their subjects, objects and any other salient company. With References set to Language Variety, *am* (US) and *br* (UK) may give a surprising first impression of their geographical spread. Or you might prefer to observe their genre, medium etc.

In Simple Query verbs are conjugated, but it does not permit anything to appear between the two words, and the separable nature of phrasal verbs is an important aspect of their syntax. The results you obtain in Simple Query will be quite different from those that emerge using Lemma (verb) + Lemma filter, as we are about to see. This simple tool allows a search to be quite focussed – instead of thousands of concordance lines being returned for a search, a well-constructed query will return many fewer and far more relevant results.

Question 144 **Is the phrasal verb *put down* separable?**

Since phrasal verb particles are always *after* their verbs, we set the Window drop list to Right and the number of tokens to, say, 3. See this link [95] for the results of this search, sampled and sorted to the right. The number of lines was set to the page length setting (in View Options). The answer to the 'separable question' is clear. Try this with some other phrasal verbs.

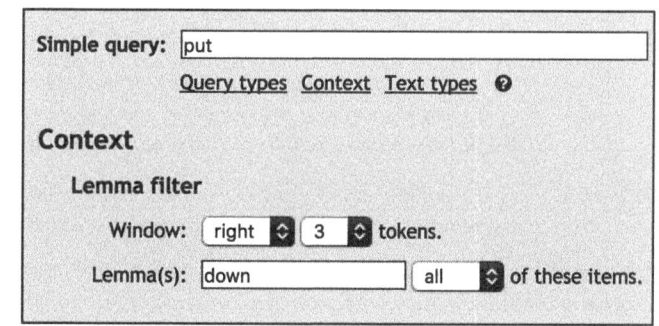

An important note about sorting Context search results: the Sort Left and Right buttons in the left panel sort to the left and right of the *node*, not of the context. To sort the concordance after *down*, in this case, it is necessary to use the Sort dialogue box, as described on p.50.

Question 145 **How do the objects between *put* and *down* realise the various meaning potentials of this phrasal verb?**

Now that we have some data, we can explore the relationships between form and meaning: What do we put down? Where do we put it? Who does the putting? Do we put something down or put down something?

The following sentences contain different types of intervening objects.

Corp ex.84   *Personally I'm optimistic about life in Britain but most people round here are emigrating and **putting** Britain **down**.*

Corp ex.85   *She just **put** the phone **down**, and I knew, he drew a shaky breath, 'that it was all over.'*

Corp ex.86   *He might have had the last word, but he hadn't really forgiven her for her temerity in trying to **put** him **down**.*

Corp ex.87   *Yeah right I'll **put** him **down** with a question mark.*

Corp ex.88   *But a vet who examined the dog at the Halewood RSPCA home said he was too ill to be rehoused with a new family and it was kinder to **put** him **down**.*

---

[95] ske.li/bnc_put_down_500_right

Corp ex.89   *The men holding Gabriel **put** him **down** again. "In bloody credible," Lambert said.*

There is clearly a difference between *putting people down* and *putting things down*. What things? And what about putting your *head* or *hand* down or even your *foot*? Who does these things in what circumstances? Create more specific queries to answer these questions.

In the Context Lemma field, you can type both *foot* and *down*. Right sort the list and see what the object of *put* is.

Question 146   **Is someone *putting their foot down* a reflexive structure?**

Corp ex.90   *… the only one in this house to **put** their foot **down**, is me! Every time.*

This example invokes a domestic discipline schema. Can you imagine what goes before and after this statement? And who says it?

Question 147   **Excuse me, did you just say *someone put their* … ? Isn't *someone* singular and *their* plural?**

Enter *someone* in Simple Query and *their* in the Context Lemma field.

This is a good opportunity to use the Select Lines feature as we saw in View Options (p.45). Remember that you can use the Permalink button to save this set for a follow-up exploration or to use in a presentation, etc.

Corp ex.91   *How times changed – now **someone** would express **their** concern over whether the thing had been cooked long enough to annihilate any salmonella!*

This use of 3rd person plural for non-gender specific 3rd person singular is frequently used in English to avoid indicating the gender of the referent, for example. Facebook uses this construction: *Anne updated their status.* In the following sentences, it is implied that students and users in general are male.

> Remember that as you explore this concordance page, clicking on various sorting options changes the breadcrumb trail, where the red items are clickable.

When we say that a **student** knows 2,000 words, we mean that he has learned 2,000 lemmas (Stubbs, 2002, p.26).

And in this attested exchange, the interviewee chose the 3rd person plural to obscure the gender of someone special:

*Is there **someone** special in your life?*

There is, but they don't live in this country.

If you are wondering how new this might be in English, repeat the search in the Brown Family corpus, with the references set to year. It has texts from 1931 to 2006. For an even more historical enquiry, ask the EEBO corpus, which is introduced on p.130.

We have digressed somewhat from phrasal verbs. They make various appearances in later sections.

Excluding items

Only after conducting a search do we sometimes find that the results contain something irrelevant. Assuming the search was well constructed, the irrelevant hits are referred to as false positives. For example, searching for *grant* returns a lot of *Hugh*. Searching for *rather* returns a lot of *would*.

Question 148 **How is *rather* used, apart from in the phrase *would rather*?**

Search for *rather* in Simple Query and exclude *would* in the lemma filter by selecting "none of these items". A frequency list of the node and 1R is a good start to answering the question. Also revealing is 1L. Explore!

Question 149 **I want to study *concern* as a transitive verb, not in the phrase *be concerned with*.**

Put *concern* in the top Lemma field and choose verb. Enter *be* and *with* into the Lemma Filter and select *None of these items*.

Now that we can use the negative filter, it can be applied to Question 139 to 'uninclude'[96] *be* and *have* from the left context of the past participle.

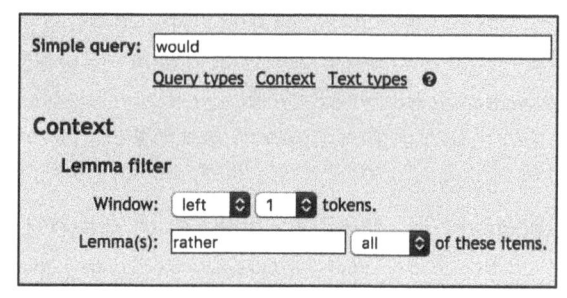

Reconstructing phrases

Sometimes we recall the salient words of a phrase but are not sure of the exact wording. This is often caused by the fact that our focus is on lexical words when interpreting language. Sometimes we recall phrases but are not sure of the exact meaning or usage. And as the phrases below indicate, their meanings are not always transparent. They are chunks which have their own meanings. While the meanings may be obvious, the usage is not. For example, why is *Oops* or *Sorry* the response to *Were you born in a barn?* It is therefore important that chunks be studied as wholes, and in their various levels of context.

In this section, we will use the Context fields to help us jog our memories and to provide data to explore contexts.

Question 150 **What was that phrase I heard somewhere with *use* and *ornament*?**

Type *use* into Simple Query and *ornament* into the Lemma Filter: right context. There are 24 hits in the BNC. Left Sort them and you'll find the four-word phrase. Even though it only occurs four times, this is the answer to the question.

Question 151 **What's that phrase with *could bother*?**

Type the first word into Simple Query and the second into the Lemma filter. And set the Window Right 5. When you right sort the list, several phrases emerge.

A *phrase*, in the sense of both Oxford definitions we saw on p. 81, mostly consists of one or two lexical words plus function words. Here are some salient words from fixed phrases you could complete. You might like to test your intuition first. Once you identify each phrase, check its text type(s) as well. If there are any that you would consider adding to your productive vocabulary, note the company they keep.

age … beauty, … cradle … grave, if truth…, world … fire; slip … tongue; contrary … popular; last … least; believe … ears; lead … horse; bark … tree; rock … place; faint … blood; meat … sandwich, stamp … approval.

---

[96] ske.li/ett_uninclude

The combinations of lexical and function words that constitute these phrases are no less true of language at large. As we observe throughout this book, every word keeps very close company with a small set of best friends, and close company with a wider circle of words, and quite irregular company with vague acquaintances. Words form relationships as people do. They even fall out!

Question 152 **What's the phrase that has *whole, sum, parts*?**

Search for *sum* in Simple Query and *whole* and *part* (not *parts*) in the Lemma Filter. Sort to the right and observe the phrase [97] in all its variety. If you find that there is no single canonical form of this expression, then this is another fact about language to bear in mind.

Similarly, *born in a tent* or *born in a barn*? Both wordings are used with the same illocutionary force with the same intended perlocutionary effect.

Question 153 **Does the collocation catch⇔ virus apply to computer viruses?**

Use a more recent corpus than the BNC for this search.

Question 154 **Is *not only* always completed with *but also*?**

The following screenshot provides some examples where it does, but is this the whole story? Look at more of the concordances and observe where this is not the case.

```
s area. Not only that, but we also offer unbeatab
  them. Not only the model, but also any accessor
re sold not only in Palembang but also smuggled
d were not only male but also older. She recalls t
ion for not only women, but also men and childre
paratus not only threatens our rights but also mis
people not only attended but also gave workshop
omes. Not only this, but also each sex's different
proved not only of Ahmadinejad, but also of his s
```

POS Filter

The POS filter allows us to filter any Top level query by one or more parts of speech.

Note that this is a completely separate filter from the Lemma filter. Do not make the mistake of using the POS here to specify the POS of a word you enter in the Lemma filter. This is a common misunderstanding. Read this paragraph again.

Question 155 **How do we *elaborate*?**

To find the adverbs that describe how we *elaborate*, use a Context POS Filter: adverb 1L (one token to the left), then Left sort. It is unfortunate that English grammar does not distinguish lexical and functional adverbs more overtly. There are better ways to approach this question, as we will see later.

[97] ske.li/LEXMCI_whole_sum_part

Question 156 **Is *up* necessary in the structure with *look* and *dictionary*?**

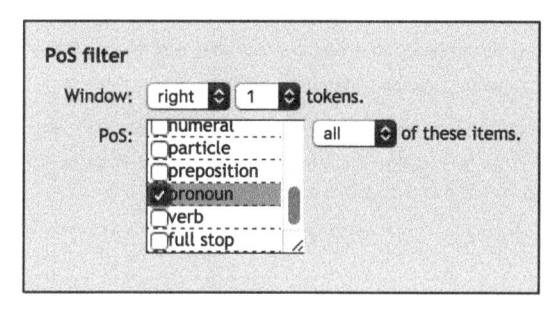

With *dictionary* in the top section, *look* in the left lemma context and *preposition* in the left POS Context filter, the answer emerges quite clearly, especially when left sorted.

Fronting

In English, the unmarked word order of clauses is Subject Verb Object. Although an object can precede the subject, O S V , e.g. *that book I would never read*, this is a marked choice. It is often made under the influence of what has gone before, which makes it a discourse level choice, not a clause level choice.

In unmarked English syntax, new information occurs late in a clause – moving it to the beginning is a marked choice. This movement is referred to as fronting. None of the English corpora currently available in Sketch Engine have tags indicating such syntactic features.

However, complement clauses such as those underlined in the following examples, are searchable. They have a finite set of words that start them, so the following examples turned up when the these "Wh" words were put in the Word Form field with Match Case selected, and in the POS Filter, put Pronoun 1R as in the screenshot.

Corp ex.92 *Why we're worrying about them, I don't know.*

Corp ex.93 *How you do it, is entirely up to you.*

Question 157 **What other words would you use to find more examples of this type of fronting?**

Would you restrict the following word to pronouns?

In the process of experimenting with various combinations, do other patterns emerge that make this worth investigating, or that you can learn something valuable from?

Bound and Free Morphemes

This linguistic phenomenon was introduced on p.73.

Question 158 **Which two-syllable adjectives form their comparatives with *more*?**

The comparative and superlative forms of regular adjectives are formed using the endings, *-er* and *-est*, respectively. This is true for adjectives with one or two syllables. Longer adjectives form their comparatives and superlatives with *more* and *most*.

So says the standard, prescriptive statement of this grammar rule. But some adjectives, regardless of their length, form their comparative with *more* and some with *–er*, and some do both.

Type *more* into Simple Query and choose *adjective* in the POS filter 1R, and then create a frequency list. Neither dictionaries nor corpora indicate the number of syllables in words, so it is necessary to select them manually.

We now find that there are many two-syllable adjectives on the list, which need not surprise us, given that this frequency list has more than 100 pages.

The next step is to find which adjectives that form the comparative periphrastically, also do so using the *–er* inflection. For example, do these two-syllable adjectives which are preceded by *more*, also form their comparatives with *–er*?

lonely, sullen, fishy, sorry, dreamy, handsome, solid, profound,

Each of these words can be sought using the Lemma field and then listed using the node forms button. Here is one such result.

word	Frequency
P | N lonely	99,650
P | N Lonely	2,665
P | N loneliest	1,222
P | N lonelier	805
P | N LONELY	47
P | N Lonelier	9
P | N Loneliest	8

To generate a list of all adjectives ending in –er, type .*er into the Word Form field and specify the part of speech. Create a node forms list – in the BNC it has 26 pages. The last 10 pages contain hapax logomena, which is almost 40%. Very Zipfian!

Question 159 **How productive is the suffix –er with nouns?**

A productive morpheme is one that allows the formation of new words.

Type .*er into the Word Form field, choose Noun, create the list, then click the Node Forms button. The task now is to find words that contain a stem + er.

In this case, –er is a derivational morpheme, i.e. on the right side of the taxonomy of morphology, whereas when used with adjectives to form the comparative, it is an inflectional morpheme, as represented on the left of the taxonomy.

There are many words on the list that are obviously not a base + er, e.g. *member, chapter, corner*. These are free morphemes in their own right. In some cases, the etymology[98] of words accounts for these combinations.

Question 160 **Think big! Shouldn't an adverb complement a verb?**

Let's look for *think* + adjective. Type *think* into the Word form field and select adjective in the POS filter. Among the almost 1,000 hits, *think big* can be clearly seen when the concordance page is right sorted.. This does not mean **how** to think, in which case it might be *think* adj + *ly* or *in a ADJ way*. *Think pinkly* (See Potts 2013).

Think Christmas. We'd better look for this, too.

---

[98] http://www.etymonline.com

What does *think* mean in this structure? Does it just mean use your brain, or put yourself into the noun's frame of mind, or use it as your reference point?

Question 161 **When is a passive structure used to convey active meaning?**

I couldn't believe my ears when I heard a Yorkshireman say, quite some years ago, *I was sat watching TV*. I found no reference to this in my grammar books and my access to corpora was a thing of the future.

In Simple Query, *be sat*. In POS filter, Verb: 1 token to the right.

Sort by references to see the text types (David Lee's Classification) in which this uncommon but well-attested structure occurs.

The BNC does not distinguish regional variation; nowadays this structure is quite widespread throughout the UK. Another verb that works similarly is *stood*.

Open this link [99] which is a LEXMCI search for be + sat | stood + VVG. Can anyone or anything be the subject? Is it limited to first person singular? A frequency list of L2 L1 node R1 is revealing.

Do the –ing verbs belong to any semantic domains? LGSWE (p.365) offers these: activity, mental, communication, existence, occurrence, causative aspectual. Make a Frequency list of 1R.

To develop the question concerning the passive, bear in mind that the agent is usually expressed by *by*. This turns up in a related phrasal verb construction, *be sat down by*, as in:

Corp ex.94 *Before ultimately being sat down by my primary physician to tell me the worst.*

In a hospitality context (restaurant, airline) this is more commonly expressed by *be seated by*.

In your searches, is American English represented?

Question 162 **What structures follow *be said*?**

Forming bundles around a word or phrase furnishes data that can be used to answer such questions. See the notes in this text box.

Use the Frequency tool with *be said* in the first column and the words that follow in the second column. Is there anything of interest? Repeat, adding a third column. Repeat adding a fourth column. They reveal different patterns. Consider how useful this information is.

> When creating **bundles** around a specific word, it is important to start the search in the **Word Form** field, as bundles are by definition, strings of words, not lemmas. If the bundle is being created around a phrase, use the Phrase field, not **Simple Query** for the same reason.
>
> Because so many English word forms are used in more than one POS (conversion), choose the POS from the drop list beside the Word Form field.

Broaden your investigation to include other speech act verbs.

---

[99] ske.li/lexmci_sat_stood_vvg

Question 163 **It would be reasonable to expect the words that follow *positively* to be positive, would it not?**

Search for *positively* using Simple Query and set the POS filter to Adjective 1R. Click on Frequency and ask for Node and 1R to summarise the findings [100].

Do you get the feeling that *positively* is expressing a degree of the adjective? The adverb probably does so in these collocations:

abundantly clear, directly responsible, fundamentally different, generally available, physically capable.

In these collocations, however, the adverb seems to be expressing the speaker's attitude:

relatively small, absolutely necessary, virtually impossible, completely new, potentially dangerous.

The use of *probably* and *seems* in the previous two sentences exemplifies the author's deliberate choice to hedge, as these interpretations are subjective.

The most frequent adjective after *positively* is *dangerous*. What other adverbs describe it? To answer this question, create a Simple Query search for *dangerous* and make a positive filter for adverbs 1L, then make your frequency list [101]. What does *positively* do that the other intensifiers don't? In other words, why would an author choose *positively* over the other intensifiers?

What precedes *positively* + adjective? To answer this question, make a frequency list that has 1L (lempos) as the first column, and then *positively* in the second level and the adjectives in the third. Is it of interest that all the verbs (-v) are copular verbs?

Does the adjective *positive* describe nouns in a similar way [102]?

Positively is not the only word to behave like this. It would be reasonable to expect the words that follow *painfully* to be negative. You might also like to observe what adjectives are described as *fiercely* and *obscenely*.

Repeat the '*positively* procedure' and investigate. A set of negatively-charged adjectives, e.g. *dangerous, vicious, painful*, can be regarded as a Semantic Type which collocates with *positively*. As the denotations and connotations of both words bleed into each other, the combination conveys more than the sum of its parts.

Combining both filters

We can also search for something in any of the top level query fields and constrain the search with both the lemma filter and the part of speech filter.

---

[100] ske.li/bnc_positively_adj
[101] ske.li/bnc_adv_dangerous
[102] ske.li/bnc_positive_noun

Question 164 **What verbs are used in the context of *word* with *dictionary*?**

Type *word* in the top Lemma and in the context filter use the settings as in this screenshot.

```
Context
  Lemma filter                              PoS filter
    Window: [both] [5] tokens.                Window: [right] [5] tokens.
    Lemma(s): [dictionary]  [all] of these items.   PoS:  ☐ particle        [all] of these items.
                                                          ☐ preposition
                                                          ☐ pronoun
                                                          ☑ verb
                                                          ☐ full stop
```

Delexical verb structures

This common, yet seriously under-represented structure in English language teaching material, consists of a semantically light verb followed by a noun phrase. However, it functions as a multi-word lexeme, i.e. the group expresses a single meaning. Some common examples of delexical verb structures are *take a photo, have a dream, give a smile.* Many of them have single-word verb equivalents, which is possible because of conversion. The syntax in the single verb structure is inevitably different from a delexical one, as can bee seen in this pair of examples:

Corp ex.95   Travis **gave a wry smile** of acknowledgement.

Corp ex.96   Lord John **smiled** at the Duchess from the sideboard.

The verb is referred to as 'light' because it carries little meaning in delexical structures – the meaning of the construction derives from the noun, e.g. *photo, dream, smile.* This differs from a verb-noun collocation where both words retain their separate meanings, e.g. *develop a photo, fulfil a dream, force a smile.* Some sources use the term *light verbs* instead of *delexical.* See Leech et.al. (2010) for even more terms.

To search for delexical verbs, we put the verb in Simple Query or Lemma, and the noun in the Lemma Filter, with the Window set to Right. See the screenshot below.

Question 165 **What are some features of delexical verbs?**

Firstly ensure that David Lee's Classification is showing to the left of the concordance.

In the BNC, search for *make* (verb) and then make a frequency list: node (lemma), 1R (lempos), 2R (lempos). List (or make a list of) those which look like candidate delexical verbs.

Convert this list to *take* by replacing "make" in the URL with "take" to save repeating this process from scratch. The underlined *make* here is the first of two that need to be replaced.

> https://the.sketchengine.co.uk/bonito/run.cgi/freqml?q=alc%2C%5Blempos%3D%22%28make%29-v …

Using CTRL F in the browser to search for –n will helps identify candidates.

This excludes chunks such as *make sure that, make it possible, take over from*, etc. It does not exclude multi-word lexemes or collocations such as:

take advantage of, take part in, take care of,
make way for, make love to, make room for.

Note the use of articles in this structure: are zero, definite and indefinite articles used? In equal proportions?

Make new frequency lists with the verb (lemma) in the last level. What occurs before the verb? Subjects?

Question 166 **What differences can you identify between delexical structures and their single word 'equivalents'?**

For example, *photograph* vs. *take a photo(graph)*, *guess* vs. *make a guess*, *smile* vs. *give a smile*.

Are the non-delexical constructions of the verbs *photo*, *guess* and *smile*, transitive? If so, what are their typical subjects and objects, and if not, how do they work? In the delexical structure, the verb and the noun are the V O.

Question 167 **What adjectives are used before the nouns in delexical verb structures?**

With search parameters set according to the screenshot below, *dream* will occur anywhere up to three tokens to the right of *have*, and an adjective will be somewhere in between. Right sort the results to group the adjectives [103].

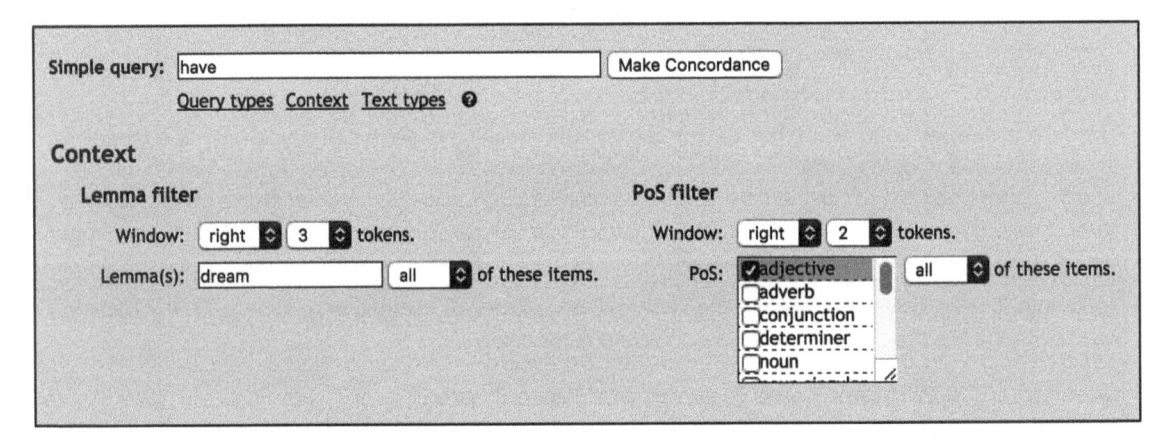

An important feature of delexical verb structures is the role that adjectives play. In fact, adverbs do not describe verbs in non-delexical structures as adjectives describe nouns, e.g. *make a separate list* means something quite different from *list things separately*, likewise *take a good photo* and *to photograph well* mean quite different things. And *to photograph goodly* recalls Question 160: *bigly, pinkly* etc. Although *goodly* is rare in English, it has its place, hasn't it?

Here are some more delexical verbs worthy of investigation:

make a friend, give a smile, give preference to, give something a try, have a break/rest, make a guess, make a start, take a bow, take a breath, have a look, give a nod.

---

[103] ske.li/bnc_have_adj_dream

Question 168   **Can you identify any differences between *take a look* and *have a look*?**

Consider if there are different adjectives, different articles, if the construction is followed by different types of things, and if they occur in different text types.

Question 169   **Do any of the words preceding the nouns form compound nouns with them?**

Consider if these these examples from the BNC contain compound nouns or adjective + noun.

Corp ex.97   *If you have to make a **selection decision**, for example, what information do you require and how do you research it?*

Corp ex.98   *John Edmonds, give a **keynote speech** under the monumental shadow of …*

Question 170   **Is choosing a delexical verb structure over a single verb structure a matter of stylistic variation?**

To answer this question, perform some of the searches again and use the Text Types button and text types in Frequency to see what the BNC metadata reveals.

Searches could also be conducted in other corpora, depending on what you want to explore. Try the Brown Family, LEXMCI, the London English Corpus and CHILDES.

Question 171   **Is *having a liking* for something the same as *liking* something?**

In most delexical verb structures, the noun has the same word form as the verb, e.g. *profit, risk*, and this is the result of conversion. However, this is not the case for *like*. The delexical structure is made with *liking*.

Type *liking* into the word form field. Then click on node tags to see the extent to which this word form is used in various parts of speech. Click the P beside the noun tag. Sort the resulting concordance page to the right groups *liking for*. Do you think that this can be replaced with the single verb *like* without changing the meaning?

Sorting the page to the left shows quite a few other structures that *liking* operates in.

For more on delexical verbs, see Leech et al., 2010, Chapter 8.

Negative filter

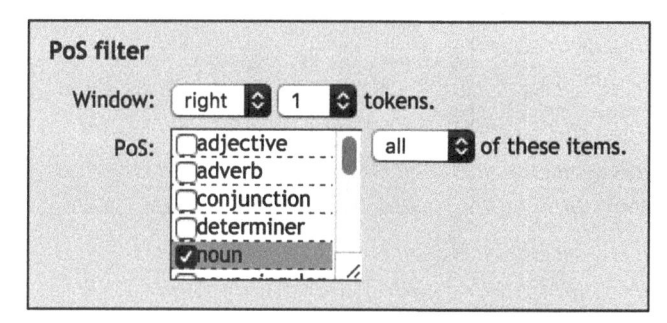

We have already looked at the phrase *once in a lifetime*, and found that it was sometimes followed immediately by nouns. To look for the lines which do not contain a noun straight after the phrase, we use the drop list beside the POS filter. This is where "none of these items" comes in handy.

Hypernyms

There are, for example, many types of dwellings. People live in houses, flats, apartments, palaces, tents, tree-houses, quonset huts, and igloos. None of these words are synonyms despite sharing some key features. They are hyponyms of *dwelling* and are co-hyponyms with each other. The umbrella term [104] is referred to as a hypernym [105] or superordinate.

Question 172   **What is the relationship between *dwelling* and *house* in these sentences?**

Corp ex.99   *The building contains two dwellings, the main house and a renting apartment located on the highest module.*

Corp ex.100   *The house was the most pretentious dwelling in the village ...*

Hypernyms serve a textual function: it often feels clunky repeating a word when writing and speaking. The strategy of using co-hyponyms and synonyms cannot work because they mean different things. For example, none of the co-hyponyms of *house* can substitute for it. However, being more general than a hyponym (e.g. *hut, igloo*), a hypernym gives more semantic space to the idea being expressed. Try a web image search for "is that really a house?" and consider which pictures might be better discussed using a hypernym.

This space also permits hedging. When we do not know the name given to a specific type of house, event, illness, psychological state, game, etc., or if its features stretch our prototypical understanding of a word, e.g. the Longaberger Basked Building in Ohio pictured here, we might embed a hypernym in some other vague language, as in these examples using *some sort of*.

Corp ex.101   *Dude, she's either super confused or playing some sort of weird **game**.*

Corp ex.102   *In France you are allowed to pitch a tent, a caravan or a yurt or some sort of temporary **building** for at least 2 years after you have been given permission to build your own house.*

A neat way of looking for hypernyms is to search for *and other* in the Phrase field: it yields many thousands of hits. Avoid Simple Query as it also searches for *and others* which gives quite different results. Use Frequency, 1L and 1R of the node to find such things as *pensions and other benefits, leaves and other debris*. Extend the frequency listings to 2R or 3R to see a variety of noun phrases.

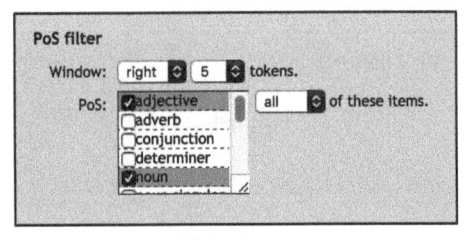

---

[104] ske.li/bnc_umbrella_term
[105] ske.li/deske_hypernym

Use the POS Filter as shown in this screenshot, to make the search quite specific. Use Frequency to generate the lists with the Levels set to L1-Node-R1-R2. See here[106] for the resulting frequency list.

	word	word	word	word	Frequency
P | N	banks	and other	financial	institutions	15
P | N	gender	and other	social	relations	8
P | N	aircraft	and other	aerial	devices	8
P | N	polytechnics	and other	further	education	5
P | N	listed	and other	public	interest	4
P | N	copyright	and other	intellectual	property	4
P | N	causal	and other	nomic	connections	4
P | N	action	and other	intangible	property	4
P | N	London	and other	major	cities	4
P | N	London	and other	large	cities	4

Question 173 **Does *include ... such as ...* also find hyponyms in context?**

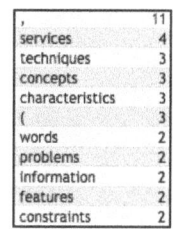

,	11
services	4
techniques	3
concepts	3
characteristics	3
(	3
words	2
problems	2
information	2
features	2
constraints	2

Search for *such as* in Simple Query and *include* in the Lemma Context field. Left sorting the concordance page gives hypernyms and **general nouns** (see Mahlberg, 2005). The Frequency tool generates an impressive list of hypernyms, with nothing more than 1L in the First Level. The screenshot shows the result of this process when generated from my students' *Informatics Reading Corpus* of c.7 million words. Once you make your own corpora, (see p.203), it is possible to generate lists of hypernyms that are more relevant to its field, tenor and mode.

Question 174 **What things come under the umbrella of *device* nowadays?**

Using the search techniques described above that indicate and locate hypernyms, compare the use of *device* in old and new corpora. The Brown Family offers a diachronic perspective[107].

Hypernyms are useful in vocabulary teaching because they can be used as the headings of lexical sets. They also used in as semantic type labels and are thus employed in word templates.

About lexical bundles

We have worked with bundles a number of times up to this point (see Index). Let us now take a closer look at them.

A bundle is a string of consecutive word forms that occur in a text or a genre/domain specific collection of texts. They are extracted by taking words 1, 2, 3, 4 then 2, 3, 4, 5, then 3, 4, 5, 6 etc in the case of 4-grams from a whole text or whole collection of texts. Such strings are also known as n-grams, and they are declared bundles if they meet an established frequency threshold, which in the case of LGSWE (p.990), is ten times per million for four word bundles.

It is statistically inevitable that the relatively finite set of Organisation/Orientation language units, in Linear Unit Grammar (LUG) terms, turns up in bundles, sometimes whole but more often as fragments. For example, the bundles in the Academic Formulas List (AFL) of Simpson-Vlach and Ellis (2010), which occur in both spoken and written academic genres, are presented in their appendix in order of significance and are of varying lengths. Here are the first ten.

---

[106] ske.li/bnc_andother_freq
[107] http://ske.li/bf_device

in terms of, at the same time, from the point of view, in order to, as well as, part of the, the fact that, in other words, the point of view of, there is a

Each of these bundles consists of one lexical word and some function words. In the three AFL sets each containing 200 bundles, there are almost no two-lexeme collocations (a.k.a. TLC, see p. 164), *total number, present study, important role*, being exceptions. The lexical words are almost exclusively factotum, i.e. words which do not belong to any specific domain.

Bundles are by and large semantically transparent, structurally incomplete fragments of used language, and are not required to have any psychological unity as chunks and templates do (See Conrad and Biber, 2005).

As Organisation/Orientation language, they are particularly suited to genres analysis, e.g. the O language bundles of journalism, fiction, scripted sitcoms and classroom interactions vary greatly. Biber found that lexical bundles are a reliable indicator of register variation. For example, in conversation, nearly 90% of lexical bundles are declarative or interrogative clause segments, while the lexical bundles of prose are basically phrasal rather than clausal (quoted in McEnery et.al.2006:89). In Csomay's words (2005), lexical bundle functions correspond well to the communicative functions in discourse structure found through linguistic variation.

It is also statistically inevitable that Message bearing key words in a text do not turn up in highly frequent or statistically significant bundles in a corpus.

Question 175 **What similarities and differences emerge from the bundles of similar words?**

Let us delve into some of these academic nouns: *potential, importance, advantage, benefit, contribution, strength*. Choose at least three of them and use the Frequency tool to make bundles that have the same parameters. For example, set all four columns in the Frequency table as word forms, with the second level (column) as the node. If your target word functions in more than one POS, start the search in the word form field and choose noun.

The most frequent four-word bundle of *potential* is *the potential of the*, sometimes in the role of subject, other times object. Then comes *the potential for a, the potential to become, the potential for conflict, the potential to generate*, etc.

The bundles that emerge are clear indications of the similarities and differences between these semantically related words. They provide some reason to suspect why a speaker might choose one over another. As Stubbs says, "Because one way is selected (often subconsciously), it follows that utterances always encode a point of view" (1996:197).

About patterns

Whereas bundles are machine-generated data for linguists to study, grammar patterns and word templates are the result of computer-aided human analysis.

COBUILD Grammar Patterns 1: Verbs (Francis, Hunston and Manning 1998a) start with a basic structure such as **V from n** (i.e. verb + a prepositional phrase starting with *from*). This is then sub-divided into Structures, which in the case of this pattern includes:

Structure 1: **Verbs in phase** which includes *abstain, shirk, withdraw*.

Structure 2: **Verb with prepositional object**. This is subdivided semantically into, for example,

> **Result Group** includes *arise, follow, spring*
>
> **Differ Group** includes *diverge, standout*.

Structure 3: **Verb with Adjunct** and includes *defect, recoil, transfer, vanish*.

There is also a second book COBUILD Grammar Patterns 2: Nouns and Adjectives (1998b). The important finding from this extensive linguistic analysis, is the relationship between pattern and meaning: the words in Groups with the same patterns also have similar semantics.

Hanks's verb patterns are quite different and my word templates owe a great debt to them. They show the typical arguments of verbs, expressed as semantic types, and present their lexical and grammatical company in unmarked word order. They demonstrate how a verb's meaning potentials emerge in concert with their structures. They contain the Message element of sentences and utterances. They are created using corpus data in combination with a considerable amount of human processing, especially of the lexical sets. This ongoing work is published online and is publicly available as the **Pattern Dictionary of English Verbs**.[108]

About Word templates (1)

Cambridge Dictionaries Online[109] defines *template* In general English as 'something that is used as a pattern for producing other similar things'. This captures one of the key aspects of word templates – they enable the production of other similar things, which is valuable in foreign language learning.

A word template realises one meaning potential of a word by arranging its lexical (collocation) and grammatical (colligation) company in unmarked word order. For example, here are several word templates for *clothes* derived from the BNC.

- sb changes their clothes
- sb brings | takes a change of clothes
- sb goes clothes shopping
- sb changes their clothes (when they get dirty or for a new situation)
- sb changes into their dry | work | party | riding | normal clothes
- sb takes off their clothes
- sb removes their clothes (fiction)
- expensive | elegant clothes make [impression]

These templates display a range of collocations and colligations. They are the structures in which the given collocates of *clothes* function. They are a distillation of used language. They can be read and understood. Reading a word template gives a satisfying experience of completeness. *Somebody* is the most typical subject of the verbs when *clothes* is the object. This is less likely to be the case with verbs such as *operate, burst, sentence* and *spoil*. When someone is interpreting language, they realise the meanings and uses of specific words. When someone is generating language, templates provide the speaker or writer with the possibilities for and restrictions on word usage. As the skeletons of clauses, the language user fleshes them out with grammar elements to situate them in the real world of the discourse.

Let us look at several examples, starting from the analytic end.

---

[108] http://www.pdev.org.uk
[109] http://bit.ly/cambdict_template

Question 176 **What company does *join* keep?**

Join (verb) occurs over 17,000 times in the BNC and has numerous collocates. In this section we are targeting one particular pattern.

In the lemma field, search for *join* as a verb and in the POS filter, set pronoun 1R.

Make a frequency list of Node as lemma, R1 and R2. Click on the P beside *join me in*, as this will be our target structure [110]. David Lee's Classification reveals the text types in which this most frequently occurs, which in turn reveals its Context of Situation. Left sorting reveals a particularly frequent modal verb and pronoun, while right sorting reveals not only several frequent verbs but also the verb form that typically follows prepositions, in any context as we will see in Question 224.

> Hansard is the traditional name of the transcripts of Parliamentary Debates in Britain and many Commonwealth countries. In David Lee's Classification, they are tagged as Written texts.

The basic pattern that emerges is *someone joins someone in doing something*. This does not, however, express the illocutionary effect that emerges from the corpus examples. This is why we replace the vague placeholders such as *someone, something* and *doing* with representative items in the guise of semantic type labels. These are shown in square brackets.

Will [colleague(s)] join me in [congratulating] [someone]?

Hypernyms are particularly suitable candidates for these labels. *Congratulating* was chosen because it is the most frequent and because it expresses the typical positive prosody. But it is a moot point if it adequately represents the 'parliamentary speech acts' that are in the concordance: *wishing, welcoming, expressing sympathy, extending, paying tribute to, sending, thanking, supporting, saluting*.

The object of the -ing verb depends on the template of the 'doing' word. For example, there are 19 hits in the BNC for *join ... pay*, 9 of which include *tribute*, as can be seen here [111].

Question 177 **Who or what *blows their top* and why?**

Let us now turn to the productive use of a prepared word template.

[sb.] blows [their] top at a [person | annoyance]

It shows:

people blow their top

the 'their' slot is a possessive adjective

top is followed by the preposition *at*

at either the person who has done something annoying or a negative abstraction.

Open this permalink [112] and observe the use of *the* in place of the possessive adjective – a different templates realises a different meaning. Similarly, when the subject changes from *somebody* to *mountain | volcano*, we have a new template with quite a different meaning, albeit more literal. And rare.

Corp ex.103   When Mount Pinatubo **blew its top** in 1991, it shot 15 million tons of sulfur dioxide into the stratosphere,

The word template does not overtly state that the prepositional phrase is optional. When it is not used,

---

[110] ske.li/bnc_join_me_in
[111] ske.li/bnc_join_5pay
[112] http://ske.li/bnc_blow_top

which is more often the case, the cause of the angry outburst is recoverable from the context. Highlight the word *at* using CTRL F. Read some of the concordances and identify the cause of somebody blowing their top.

We also hinted at Word templates in the discussion of Question 161:

> sb. is | was sat | stood + [passing the time | leisure activity]

Open the link [113] and consider if the –ing activities represent abstract, academic, physical, cognitive processes or activities? They are a constrained set which lends further weight to the view that grammar patterns have their own semantics. This is a basic tenet of Construction Grammar.

Click on P beside some of the verbs and observe what follows them. Each of these verbs has its own templates, which means that in the process of producing language linearly, the templates cascade one into the next.

> watching sth, waiting for | to ..., talking to ... etc.

The related construction, *be seated by* (introduced on p.109), uses *by* not only as a particle for the passive agent, but as a preposition with time expressions, meaning *next to* and *according to*. Such are the roles that *by* plays. Here is one example of each, taken from enTenTen [114].

Corp ex.104   *After being seated by your dive master, watch in amazement as ...*

Corp ex.105   *Participants are asked to be seated by 1:45 p.m.*

Corp ex.106   *... but unfortunately we were seated by the toilets, which grew more and more annoying throughout the meal.*

Corp ex.107   *... men are seated by birth order of our spirits in the feast of LOVE above!*

In order to turn a target word into language that conveys the nuanced message that we intend, we have to *grammatize* it.

> Step One: select the collocating words and colligating structures to generate the template that realises the word's meaning potential.
>
> Step Two: select auxiliaries and particles for tense and aspect, determiners and adverbials, and any other necessary elements.

The incipient patterns of these very general verbs are stepping stones to word templates.

> someone goes somewhere
>
> someone puts something somewhere
>
> someone gives something to someone
>
> someone makes something from something
>
> someone does something

The first four are from Goldberg (2006:93) in a discussion of first language acquisition: "the categorisation of attested instances leads learners to generalise constructions beyond their original contexts." Here she is referring to children hearing these general verbs often enough to acquire their patterns, which are reinforced as they hear other words with similar meanings in the same patterns. Thus they acquire lexicogrammar in context.

These five are *general* verbs because each of them has many troponyms. i.e. verbs that are more specific ways of doing them. They are also general because their arguments, i.e. their subjects, objects

---

[113] ske.li/lexmci_satstood_verbs
[114] http://ske.li/ett_be_seated_by

and adverbials, are not nearly as constrained as in the following examples of semantically richer verbs, for example,

> something (but not any something) **bursts**
>
> someone (but not any someone) **sentences** someone (not any someone) to a period of time
>
> someone (but not any someone) **spoils** someone (but not any someone)
>
> someone has an **ability** to do something
>
> someone is **capable** of doing something

Most of the examples so far have been motivated by verbs, but the key words in a text are typically nouns (Scott & Tribble 2006: 70). Here are the six semantically similar nouns we saw in Question 175. A speaker will choose one at any given moment and will have to grammatize it:

> *potential, importance, advantage, benefit, contribution, strength.*

Given that they have similar semantics, it should not by now surprise us that their word templates are similar. The choice of a noun and its role as subject or object influences the choice of verb.

In language teaching, learners build word templates by studying key words and their company in a text. These are then sought in corpora to determine their typicality, which is a valuable language learning procedure. In addition to the words' collocating arguments, focus is also placed on their order, i.e. syntax. As a teaching and learning activity, this procedure draws students' attention not only to a number of linguistic features at the same time, but to the interdependence of grammar and vocabulary. This brings us back to Halliday's term, *lexicogrammar,* which refers to the unity of lexis and grammar, or a continuum from one to the other.

Once we have acquired some more Sketch Engine skills, we will develop the notion of word templates further (p.187).

Distinguishing bundles, patterns and word templates

The following table attempts to summarise the similarities and differences between these units.

	bundle	pattern	word template
elements	n-gram (string of word forms)	syntactic elements belonging to groups of words	syntactic elements with semantic types
form	fragment (complete or not)	e.g. V n for n	node and [semantic types] and lexical words in order
collocation	no	no	yes
sources	full text or collection	word list	a text
procedures	extract n-grams from source	corpus analysis of words	observation of collocation and colligation of key words
uses	stylistic analysis	writing teaching materials	to be grammatized
LUG	mainly Organisation/ Orientation language	M language	M language

Chapter 7   Text Types

Corpora are designed for specific purposes which dictate the ground rules for the selection of texts. For example,

> Who were the authors or speakers? Native speakers?
> Gender?
> Age?
> How well do the interlocutors know each other?
> What regional variety(s) of English do they speak?
> In a letter, email or interview?
> What are they talking about?
> What should their communication achieve?
> At what point in history?
> Where was the text obtained?

> These are precisely the questions that learners need to be encouraged to pose in order to read and respond *critically* to texts, which they need to realise are *never* neutral, *never* unproblematic, but which always proceed from a particular perspective. (Pulverness 2015).

In order to understand the full meaning of a text, "one needs to relate the text externally to the conditions of its production and reception" (Widdowson 2004:123). Each of these conditions has some general characteristics which can be added to a corpus as metadata. In Sketch Engine, they appear as Structures and Attributes.

In addition to grammatical and pragmatic constraints, the text type metadata under discussion here identifies linguistic layers that have determined other linguistic choices that language users have made. Part of one's linguistic competence is making choices that are appropriate to the Context of Situation.

Much of the work undertaken in this book so far has dealt with language as system, which in Stubbs' terms is inter-subjective, social and public. He contrasts this with linguistic competence which is individual, mental and private (2007:149). Searching a large cross-section of the primed idiolects of individual's language identifies trends in the public language. Hopper had previously pointed out that each individual's speech is 'a vast collection of hand-me-downs that reaches back to the beginnings of the language' (1998:159). Thus, our choices not only concern *how* to word our communicative intentions, but *what* pre-existing norms of language can be brought into service.

In this chapter, we will explore some features of public and private language that can be identified using Sketch Engine's text types tools. This is heavily dependent on the metadata available.

Question 178   Can you answer any of the bullet point questions above, or glean any other information about the context of situation of Corp ex.108?

Corp ex.108   *As I say Knobson. Will this mean Hughes buggering off 'cos he didn't play? Eric attempting to find a new spiritual home? What makes it even more sweet is the fact that they crapped on about us only getting to the 2nd round last year and how they were going to get to the final. Bollocks.*

This BNC extract is from a Leeds United email list (1985-1993), a rare text type in this corpus. This comes from a It is unlikely that this person, probably male, would have expressed himself this indelicately in an interview with the press or in their autobiography. To check what you gleaned from the corpus example, find this sentence in the BNC. Click on the red node and use *the expand left, expand right* buttons and read more of the text. To see the metadata, click on whatever appears in blue at the left of the concordance page.

The relationships that hold between idiolect, dialect and the whole language are illustrated in the following diagram. Compare this with the floral diagram on p.12, which depicts **core** language. The language each individual uses is influenced by the speaker's unique and individual experiences with the language. Everyday language is not a collection of freely constructed novel sentences but is instead built up out of combinations of ready-made regularities previously experienced by the speaker and pre-existing in the discourse (O'Grady: 2010:90).

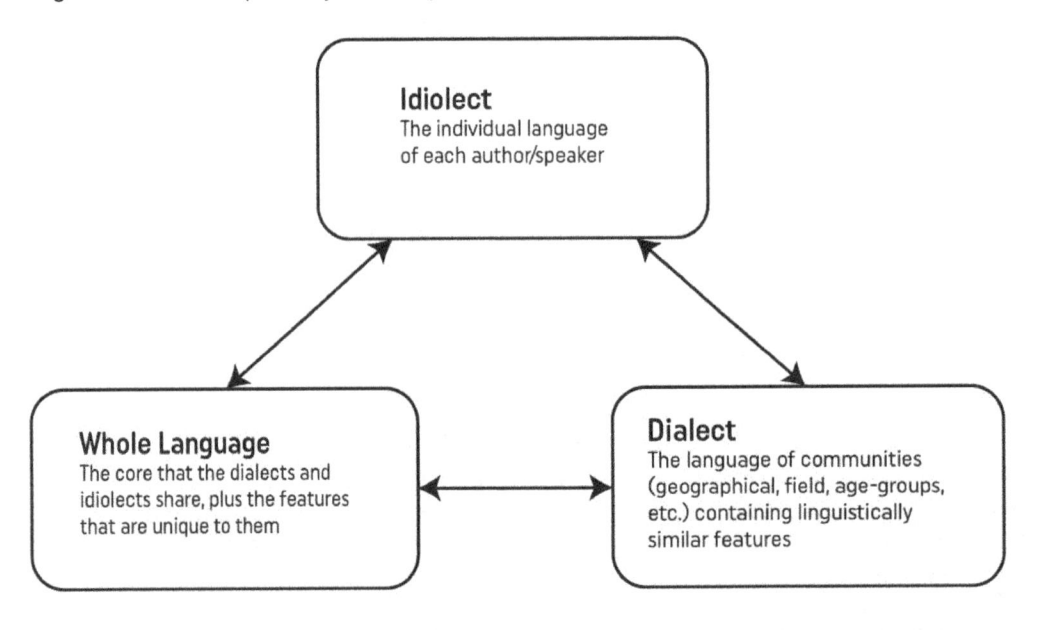

Idiolect
The individual language of each author/speaker

Whole Language
The core that the dialects and idiolects share, plus the features that are unique to them

Dialect
The language of communities (geographical, field, age-groups, etc.) containing linguistically similar features

Sketch Engine's Text Types filter allows us to investigate what individual varieties have in common with each other, distinct from the core language and the whole language. This, in turn, allows us to observe not only what is said, but in which contexts. A search that specifies text types will return many fewer results, which simplifies manual data processing.

Text Types in the BNC and in Sketch Engine

The original metadata in the BNC has approximately 30 categories for each text, e.g. Text type, Domain, Publication Date and Medium. A list of genres

bncdoc.id	KCW
bncdoc.info	19 conversations recorded by `Kathleen' (PS0H8) between 15 and 17 January 1992 with 10 interlocutors, totalling 4977 s-units, 23839 words (duration not recorded).

and the number of texts for each one can be found on the BNC website[115]. In some cases, the metadata is quite detailed. Here is an example from someone identified as PS12C.

The information in the Structures and Attributes screenshot below is available from Corpus Info in the left panel. Clicking on chevrons expands them to reveal sub-classes.

Structures and attributes	
bncdoc	4,054
text	3
s	6,052,192
p	1,514,906
align	2,779
caption	89,990
hi	210,715
lb	169
bibl	1,037
body	55
div	3,783

Because Sketch Engine is designed to handle many different corpora, each with its own metadata structure, it adjusts interfaces that display metadata accordingly. This is why some of the features exemplified in this book appear differently when you use other corpora.

Because our Sketch Engine searches focus on usage, this chapter does not delve into general features of discourse and text such as the political stance of a collection of texts or the language of advertising. Such work can, however, be undertaken to some extent, using Sketch Engine's Word list function, collocation and frequency listings in combination with subcorpora, as we see in later chapters.

Filtering Text Types

It is a truth universally acknowledged that a single search in possession of a good filter must be in the running for a focussed concordance.

If you do not recognise the allusion in the above sentence, can you identify which one is the original in this screenshot (ukWaC)? It is clearly another template that has been exploited (see notes accompanying Question 18). To explore it further, open it here[116].

It is a truth universally acknowledged , that a single man in possession of a good fortune
It is a truth universally acknowledged that free coffee and chocolate biscuits are our unique
It is a truth universally acknowledged that every writer in possession of a novel longs
It is a truth universally acknowledged that a sharing of information, and thus a continuum
It is a truth universally acknowledged that most security products lack usability. In fact
It is a truth universally acknowledged that wealthy, single men were pursued by women or
It is a truth universally acknowledged that portly "personality vocalists" of a certain
It is a truth universally acknowledged that a person in possession of a good, few hundred

In this section, we start using Sketch Engine's third and final level of constraining a search, namely Text Type. Under Simple Query, click on the Text types button to open out the sets of mainly check boxes.

Question 179   **What things are *proven* and who *proves* them?**

> The word *prove* is often misused, as it is in this sentence: *The assumption that the learners may choose the higher level to **prove** their progress to the teacher.*

---

[115] http://bit.ly/bnc_class_codes
[116] ske.li/ukwac_universally_acknowl

Firstly, let us consider the verb pattern of *prove* in its transitive use:

sb | sth proves sth

A Simple Query for *prove* yields many thousands of hits. To make the search more focussed, enter *proves | proved* into the Word form field and set the POS Context filter as in this screenshot. With the page length set to 1,000 lines and a Sample of 1,000, the page should look resemble this [117].

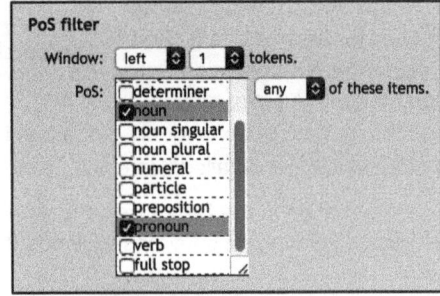

Sorting it left and right reveals valuable patterns of collocation and colligation. Sort by References reveals something else entirely.

Question 180 **What things does science claim to *prove*?**

And what things are said to be *proven* in the name of science?

Give some thought to this question before consulting the BNC: who proves what in science? Repeat the above search, but this time select some of the Science domains. Make some notes in this table.

Who (S)	proves (V)	what (O)

Proving something entails finality. Since the late 20th century, academic humility prefers to leave the door open or at least ajar: research papers tend to conclude with questions for further investigation rather than trumpet incontestable conclusions.

Might we therefore conclude that the word *prove* has fallen out of use in academic prose? Can you find any evidence of this?

Question 181 **Why does *prove* have so many adjective complements?**

Using the results of the previous search, make a Frequency list with *proves|proved* in the first level and tag in the second. Not only is JJ (adjective) significant, but so is TO (to infinitive). Click on the **P**, to observe how both of these function, then sort the concordance pages and note the patterns.

For example,

NP prove to be Adj
as in this example:

Corp ex.109 *the use of existing parsers should **prove** to be beneficial.*

In which text types is this usage frequent? Note also how the pattern is grammatized.

---

[117] http://ske.li/bnc_proved_s_1000

Question 182 **When *prove* is used in the passive, what are the agents?**

Agents are mostly expressed by *by* or *with*, sometimes *through* as we will see in Question 227. Search for *prove* in Simple Query, and select the sciences in Text Types. Limit the search dto agents by using the vertical bar (p.85) as in this screenshot.

What follows these particles?

Question 183 **Is there any difference in the use of *prove* in the domains of research and of maths?**

To search for something within David Lee's Classification, start typing in the field and a droplist of options appears. Note that W is the first letter for written texts and S for transcripts of spoken language. The Word list tool (Chapter 13) provides the full set[118].

Question 184 **What differences can you identify in the uses of *prove* and the noun form, *proof*, in law compared with scientific research?**

Admittedly, this is a lot of delving into one word. But this discovery process provides opportunities to combine the skills gained so far with the knowledge you already have about language and linguistics. Furthermore, such observations of lexicogrammatical patterns help convert receptive (passive) vocabulary into productive (active).

There are many words in general English that have specialised uses in certain fields. For example,

Music: *bar, note, key, rest*

Computer science: *bucket, tree, packet*

Linguistics: *hedge, move, chunk, particle*

To use field-specific terms correctly, it is worth observing them on their home turf. This can be best achieved in general corpora which have the necessary metadata. We will make field-specific corpora (p.179), where the data will belong to the domains, fields, etc. you specify.

Question 185 **How do sentences start in different genres?**

We have already seen that the tag, "SENT", can be used in combination with Frequency to list the beginnings of sentences. It can be both interesting and instructive to compare how sentences start in different genres. We might, for example, compare how sentences start in interviews[119] with what happens in advertising language[120], using the SENT tag in combination with David Lee's Classification. This is a fascinating study.

Mode: spoken and written

Are there more differences than similarities between spoken and written English? Give some thought to how this could be demonstrated empirically.

---

[118] http://ske.li/bnc_dlcs
[119] ske.li/bnc_bundle_sentstarts_s_interv
[120] ske.li/bnc_bundle_sentstarts_w_adv

In both modes of **core** English, there are no significant differences in morphemes, or in words and their collocation and colligation patterns, as we have observed many times already. Thus, the elements and structures of clauses, as word templates testify, would appear to be quite stable.

There is, however, an important role that discourse and pragmatics play in Message bearing clauses. The choice of tense (past/present), aspect (progressive/perfect), voice (active/passive) and modality depends on such factors as what has already been referred to in the text, and on what the author/speaker expects the reader/interlocutor to already know about the topics (field) and the relationships between the parties (tenor). In addition to the verb phrase, these factors also influence the use of articles (definite/indefinite/zero) and pronouns. This is the grammatization of word templates discussed on p.119. As early as p.31 we saw some other real-world factors that influence the wording of clauses.

Furthermore, many of the phrases we use to organise spoken language do not appear in written language because of their references to here and now, who and what – this is referred to as deixis. Orienting a listener in real time (synchronous), face-to-face communication requires different linguistic resources from orienting a reader: a list of three-word bundles comparing spoken and written English can be seen at this permalink[121]. Click on some of the **frequency counts** to see them in action. This very telling list was created with the Word List tool.

Question 186 **Are *moreover* and *whereas* used in speech or do they belong to the written language?**

Is this the right question? Perhaps it is more to do with the level of formality, regardless of the medium. What can you discover?

Question 187 **In what domains does the collocation *clench teeth* most commonly occur?**

Search for the collocation with *clench* in Simple Query and *tooth* in the Lemma filter – not *teeth* because this is not a lemma.

David Lee's Classification shows the genres/domains in which this collocation occurs in the BNC. Click the Sort References button[122].

Click Right Sort and be prepared to identify some other important features.

Question 188 **When are words spelled with hyphens?**

The use of hyphens is unstable in English orthography. Many compounds are written as two words, as pairs of hyphenated words, and as single words.

In ukWaC, *well pleased* occurs over 800 times, while *well-pleased* occurs less than 50 times. The results are very different in the BNC and the Brown Family which indicates language change.

The ukWac figures do not tell us how many of these occurrences are in spoken texts, where spelling may be at the whim of the transcriber. Nor do they tell us how they are dispersed across different written texts, where orthography may be standardised by authors or publishers (Aston 1988). It is therefore helpful to refine searches using Text Types. Remember that lists generated using Frequency are more flexible than the simple "node forms".

---

[121] ske.li/bnc_3grams_spokvswrit. Note that this is a huge processing task and can take some minutes.
[122] ske.li/bnc_clench_teeth_refs

In the BNC, search for the hyphen in the Character field. Generating a Node forms list will provide you with a list of the uses of hyphens [123]. Once you have a credible list, you can compare some of the hyphenated items with non-hyphenated forms, e.g.

>Are *one-day* and *one day* used differently?

>Are centuries typically hyphenated?

>Are fractions typically hyphenated when written as words?

>Do hyphenated words tend to belong to a particular part of speech or text types, and is there anything noteworthy about their collocates? Lempos will come in handy.

Question 189   **Who says or writes *to be well pleased*?**

There are plenty of *be well + adjective* in the BNC. Use the permalink below [124] to see how many lines down *pleased* is.

Search now for *be well pleased* in Simple Query. Sorting by References reveals the domains in which this phrase occurs. An interesting example of classroom language is copied here:

Corp ex.110   *Yeah so as you say it's a it's a developing thing and the only a life-form it's growing it's spreading. Yeah new words words come in erm you know I **'m well pleased** Yeah. That's wicked. Yeah. It's really wicked, Oh like a lot of old slang words from you know like a hun fifty or so back years ago are now proper words now.*

This student is not only well pleased that words come and go from the language, but has declared the process *wicked, really wicked*. We will explore this adjective in on p.178.

Question 190   **Is it true that *above-mentioned* and *aforementioned* are used in written and spoken language respectively?**

It will be necessary to look for both of these words with and without hyphens. Choose a corpus that indicates spoken and written language.

Question 191   **How often does *see* mean *understand* and how often does it refer to sight?**

Observing this as a feature of spoken language would be a good start: use Text Types to restrict your search to Spoken language.

Do any noteworthy patterns emerge among the subjects of *see* in the 'understand' sense?

Is *see* in the 'understand' sense used only in the present simple?

As you look through the lines, use the Select Lines check boxes. When you have enough, click on Selected Lines in the left panel and examine your new set.

Text types in web-crawled corpora

Although research into the automatic classification of text types is well underway, it is not yet sophisticated enough to apply to web-crawled corpora, which include those whose names end *WaC* or *tenten*.

---

[123] ske.li/bnc_well_hyphen_pos_freq
[124] ske.li/bnc_be_well_adj_freq

Open enTenTen [2012] and click on Corpus info. Click on doc under Structures and Attributes to see the metadata available. It is quite limited when compared with the BNC. Note that this use of *domain* is not a linguistic term, rather an internet one.

The Top Level Domain (TLD) is the last part of a URL, e.g. com, eu. In a web-crawled corpus, these give a general idea of where the texts came from. The enTenTen list of TLDs is here [125]. Country internet codes can be found at many websites including Wikipedia [126].

The Second Level Domain (SLD) contains hundreds of URL endings, which may be considered the closet alternative to text type categorisation.

Question 192   **Which countries have the most TLDs in enTenTen?**

dot-com is obviously not a country, but having been established in the USA in 1985, it is now the most commonly used TLD, and a high proportion have US registrants. Most .us sites are used by state and local governments.

Question 193   **Which varieties of English use *the high street*?**

Search for this phrase in enTenTen. The SLD list indicates that it is extremely common in one variety. How do the other varieties of English express this notion?

Given that there are so many hits in this giga-corpus, it is worth making frequency lists to see bundles it operates in.

The items that appear in the lists that are generated from Structures and Attributes are used in the three Text types domain fields in an enTenTen search.

Synchronic and Diachronic Corpora

This book is essentially concerned with "English as she is spoke" in the last 30 years, which is why our research questions have mostly been asked of synchronic corpora, i.e. those representing language at a particular time. However, some research questions require observations of language variation through time, which is an inevitable outcome of a world in flux, as the well pleased student in the previous corpus example commented. Think about the changes that have taken place during your lifetime in the fields of transport, disease, employment, sexuality, technology, religion, language, environment, war, public art, etc. New vocabulary has come into being to service these worlds, e.g. *friendly fire, collateral damage, administrative detention, special rendition, quantitative easing, heterosexual marriage, female priest, digital native, key word in context, smart technology*.

Research into language change is typically conducted in diachronic corpora, which contain texts representing a wide time-span and tagged with dates. Baker (2006:29) defines a diachronic corpus as:

> simply a corpus which has been built in order to be representative of a language or language variety over a particular period of time, making it possible for researchers to track linguistic changes within it.

Some of the corpora we use in Sketch Engine do contain archaisms, i.e. the use of older forms to create an 'olde-worlde' allusion, often for humorous effect. The example of *doth* (p.29) is a simple demonstration of why contemporary uses of earlier usage are not particularly suitable for diachronic study. Interestingly, McEnery, Xiao and Tono (2006:96) point out that,

[125] ske.li/ett_top_domains
[126] https://en.wikipedia.org/wiki/List_of_Internet_top-level_domains

diachronic study is perhaps one of the few areas which can only be investigated using corpus data. This is because the intuitions of modern speakers have little to offer regarding the language used hundreds or even tens of years before.

Sketch Engine users interested in diachronic study have several options. We can follow the Leech et al. research (2009) that used the 1961 and 1991 Brown Family members to compare grammatical features. As described below, the Brown Family now contains corpora from 1931 and 2006 as well. Using Leech-like procedures, findings from the BNC can be compared with recent web-crawled corpora such as enTenTen (2012) and the New Model Corpus (NMC). The NMC has approximately the same number of words as the BNC and was built from web data in 2008. It contains genres such as blog, business, medical and speech (as it is created in subtitles). For more information see the Sketch Engine site [127]. A third option is to create your own corpora as we see in Ch.13. Further diachronic options within Sketch Engine are discussed below in Trends.

The Brown Family

The Brown Corpus was created in the period 1961 to 1964 by Nelson Francis and Henry Kučera at Brown University, Rhode Island (USA). It was originally entitled "The Standard Corpus of Present-Day Edited American English". Despite the respect it commands today as the first ever electronic corpus, in its time and place, its creation was regarded as a waste of time and money. After all, native speaker intuition was then and there regarded as an adequate source of sentences to prove any linguistic point. In fact, it pre-dated the first recorded use of the term *corpus linguistics* by 20 years.

By today's standards, it is a very small corpus with a modest sampling frame containing little more than one million words, the text types are limited to edited texts by native speakers of American English, and there is a rather limited set of categories represented by not very many texts. Despite these limitations it is nevertheless a small corpus that represents the language that it set out to do.

In the 1970s, the Lancaster-Oslo-Bergen (LOB) corpus was created with a similar sampling frame and is of a similar size. This "comparable" corpus differs in one major variable, namely that its texts are British.

The University of Freiburg created two more corpora that replicated Brown and LOB but drew their texts from 1991-2. The Frown Corpus contains American English and the FLOB Corpus contains British English.

These four corpora are thus referred to as the Brown Family, and permit comparisons of British and American English at two periods separated by a 30 year gap.

These four corpora are listed here [128] along with three more. AE06 is a comparable corpus of American English from 2006 and BE06 is the British counterpart (Lancaster University). This leaves the BLOB corpus of British English that uses texts from 1931 (±3 years).

These notes have been taken from *Change in Contemporary English* (Leech et.al. 2009) and supplemented with information from the Varieng website [129]. The book is subtitled *A Grammatical Study* and investigates changes evidenced by comparing data from 1961 and 1991. This fascinating study is not the focus of DESKE, however for anyone interested in diachronic studies, know that Sketch Engine has not only this seven member Brown Family tagged with CLAWS, but has recently retagged them with PTB. The metadata permits questions to be asked of each family member, US and UK English, from

---

[127] https://www.sketchengine.co.uk/new-model-corpus
[128] http://ske.li/brown_family (CLAWS)
[129] http://www.helsinki.fi/varieng

1931, 1961, 1991 and 2005, and of genres including fiction, learned, skills and hobbies.

In Question 7 we asked if anyone really says *while holidaying*. Open this permalink[130] and see what the Brown Family can contribute.

Question 194   **Can we identify sexist language through suffixes?**

The masculine form of words used to refer not only to men, but to mankind, and was therefore considered gender neutral. As Cameron and Kulick write (2003:97), "In patriarchal societies masculinity is culturally construed as 'unmarked' gender position...."

There has been a shift away from this and *person* has become the suffix replacing *man*. For example, *chairperson* or just *chair* is now preferred to *chairman*, regardless of the gender of the person occupying that position. Search various corpora to find both of these endings and compare them.

Search for chair* in Simple Query in the BNC and in ETT. Then make Frequency lists of Node, R1, R2 (ignore case) and compare your findings.

Question 195   **Is *man* still used as a verb?**

If so, who mans what and under what circumstances? Is this verb likely to be emasculated? To *person*?

Trends

Trends is a new Sketch Engine tool which at the time of writing has been implemented in three corpora, namely the BNC (not Treetagger) and two others not yet mentioned in DESKE.

FeedCorpus: This contains feeds from social media. It is dynamic and nearly up-to-date with language evolution. In one month it collected c.300 million words. At present, it has documents from 2006 to 2013.

Early English Books Online: This contains more than 800 million words from English books published between 1473 and 1820. Henceforth referred to as EEBO.

The Trends button is in the left panel of these three corpora. Click on it and click on Compute trends. This screenshot shows the top scorers in the EEBO.

In diachronic analysis, we usually want to start by finding the words that have changed most over time (Kilgarriff, Busta, Rychlý 2015). Let us see what trends Trends can identify in the EEBO. And how.

lemma	Trend		p-value	Freq	Graph
knowe	-3.7320	−	0.000000	41,199	
ende	-3.4874	−	0.000000	39,025	
whatever	3.4874	+	0.000000	62,249	
frequently	3.4874	+	0.000000	47,442	
reflect	3.4874	+	0.000000	29,277	
enquiry	3.4874	+	0.000000	16,295	
liable	3.4874	+	0.000000	14,994	
powerful	3.4874	+	0.000000	28,284	

Question 196   **When did English lose the final *e* in the spelling of many common words?**

In the screenshot, the only words to decline are words that we now spell without the final *e*. Create this list and look down it. Are there enough words like *knowe* and *ende* to develop a research question? Click on *next* at the bottom of the list.

---

[130] http://ske.li/bf_holidaying

Click on several words to see chronologically sorted frequency lists. Did the final *e* fade away around the same time?

Question 197 **When did *publish* enter the language?**

Click on Advanced options in the Trends form, and type the search item into the Regular expression filter. When you click on *publishe*, the list not only answers the question but relates to the previous one.

Question 198 **What are some words that have disappeared from English?**

Type *do* into the Regular expression filter. There are of course many words starting with do and the graphs indicate their various entries and exists from the language.

Do used to be spelt *doo*. In this concordance [131], *doo* is followed by a verb. It is a sample of 1,000 and ends in 1795. Can you identify any of its uses according to the Periphrasis diagram on p.96?

Question 199 **Can this diachronic corpus enrich our understanding of *does not a*?**

We made some preliminary forays into this in Question 10. Using EEBO type the phrase into Simple Query. Clicking Text types under Frequency returns the list of decades when it was used. Bearing in mind that this corpus has data from 1473 to 1820, it is interesting to observe how late the phrase entered the language. Could it be because this periphrastic use of *do* was a late arrival?

The FeedCorpus is a very different corpus. When we compute trends, words appear that are common even in EEBO. The words of interest to the FeedCorpus creators are those which have not occurred in any corpus before.

Here are a few words and phrases that you might find worth comparing in terms of their presence and usage in old and new corpora, as well as the BNC.

air kiss, bling, blogosphere, bromance, do the math, dumb down, chattering classes, killer app, lighten up, mankini, next big thing, no pressure, nuanced, on the same page, power dressing, recap, regift, rubbish, scare quotes, significant other, be so over, toxic shock, Twitterati, virtuous circle, win-win situation. And the adorable *shirkaholic*.

The Varieng website [132] contains a table of corpora that represent a variety of periods, genres and varieties of English, each of which has their own concordancing software.

Question 200 **Marriage equality for all?**

If *equality for all* is a tautology, what is Orwell's, *some animals are more equal than others*? In the 21st century, same-sex marriage is hotly discussed, and is unsurprisingly well represented in contemporary corpora.

What can you observe about *gay marriage, straight marriage, heterosexual marriage, homosexual marriage,* etc. as terms, and what of their co-texts? In enTenTen [2013], *same-sex marriage* alone has over 44k hits (1.93 HPM). In View Options, Second Level Domain is the most informative here.

> Recently seen on Facebook:
> I support gay marriage, or, as I call it, marriage.

---

[131] http://ske.li/eebe_doo_vb_1000
[132] http://www.helsinki.fi/varieng/CoRD/corpora/corpusfinder

Subcorpora

A subcorpus is a set of texts within a corpus. Selecting certain Text Types each time a search is performed can be simplified by creating a subcorpus. This helps with consistency. You can limit future searches, including word sketches and word lists to your subcorpora.

Criteria for a set include general things like a period of time, a domain, a genre, and more specific things like the works of a single author or a group of authors, or of fiction by female British authors. A subcorpus of a single text is also possible – this would qualify for idiolect studies whereas the types just exemplified fall into the dialect (domain and genre, etc.) category. A subcorpus can also be made of the results of a specific search, as mentioned on p.47.

To create a subcorpus, click the **Create New** button under the Text Types heading on the main query page as in this screenshot.

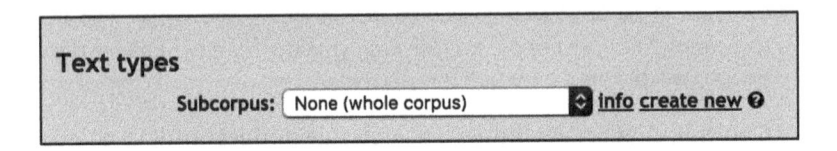

Give your subcorpus a name, e.g. Science texts. Select the relevant check boxes and click Create Subcorpus at the bottom of the page. Sets of texts can also be made from David Lee's Classification: type a letter in the field and select from the list that appears. To include more than one item from this list, enter a vertical bar after those you select, and type another letter.

Create a fiction subcorpus as well. People who read a lot of fiction as a part of their language learning may be surprised to discover how much language of this genre is not frequent in other genres.

We will use both the fiction and science subcorpora in later tasks.

Question 201	**How do authors report the way things are *said* in fiction?**
	To launch this investigation, enter *said* into the Word Form field and adverb into the POS filter, 1R. Select your Fiction subcorpus.
	Using Frequency with node and 1R, we can see which words authors have most frequently employed.
Question 202	**Which adverbs express the purpose of saying, and which indicate the way something was said?**
	Here are two examples of many thousands.
Corp ex.111	*It's nothing, she said reassuringly.*
Corp ex.112	*"Oh, far be it from me to pry," Rob said loftily, "I was merely paying you an indirect compliment."*

Search for *relate, recount, explain* in your subcorpus as well. You might also expand the adverb's range to 2R or 3R, in which case listing them will be more effective in Collocation than in Frequency.

Compare the results of these searches in fiction with those in science texts, or in Hansard, etc.

Question 203	**Which verbs are followed by *that* in science writing?**
	That clauses are a marked feature of academic prose. To observe the verbs that are typically involved, search for *that* in a Top level query and in the POS filter, verb 1

Left. Then choose your science subcorpus. Once you make a frequency list of the lemmas, you can start to observe patterns in their semantic domains (see p.109).

It may also be of interest to see which generally high frequency verbs are not among the top scorers in these contexts.

In the Frequency list, adding a column to the left shows a high proportion of *be* and *have*, which can only mean one thing! See the auxiliary verb chart on p.96. There are many infinitive markers, as well. These patterns of normal usage must be of interest.

Add another column and set the frequency limit to 10, for example. Click on the column headings e.g. lemma, word, to group the bundles that are appearing step by step.

Text Types Frequency Distribution

So far we have been constraining searches by text type. However, with frequency distribution we can create a list of the text types that the node occurs in. Remember that the node can be words and phrases, as well as grammatical structures. The Text Types button is under Frequency in the left panel. The lists that appear with text types also contain Relative Text Type frequencies, which often exceed 100% as explained in these notes adapted from the Sketch Engine site[133].

Relative Text Type Frequency

The number is the relative frequency of the query result divided by the relative size of the particular text type. The number grows the higher the frequency, and shrinks the greater the amount of text for the given text type. It can be interpreted as: how much more/less often is the result of the query in this text type in comparison to the whole corpus?

For example, *test* has 2,000 hits in the corpus and 400 of them are in the text type Spoken. Since the Spoken text type represents only 10 % of the corpus, the Relative Text Type frequency will be (400 / 2000) / 0.1 = 200 %. This means that *test* is twice as common in Spoken than in the whole corpus.

Question 204 *Ubiquitous* **looks like a rather specialised word. Is it?**

Perform a search in the whole corpus. Does it occur in specific fields only? Or is it ubiquitous? There are many different text types that *ubiquitous* occurs in according to David Lee's Classification[134]. The Visualize tool addresses the question of range, and in this case it illustrates its ubiquity[135] in the corpus.

Question 205 **Is *data* used as a singular noun, plural or both?**

Despite the fact that English has the singular form *datum* and the plural form *data*, it seems that the word form, *data,* is used both in the singular and plural.

Search for *data* in the Word Form field and click on Node tags. Click on the P beside each of the tags and make Text Types lists. Do you observe any correlation between the use of *data* as a singular noun in certain text types? Ditto plural?

For a kibbitzer on the word *data* from Tim Johns, see Kibbitzers 6/6a on this page[136].

---

[133] https://www.sketchengine.co.uk/rel
[134] ske.li/bnc_ubiquitous_tt
[135] ske.li/bnc_ubiquity
[136] http://lexically.net/TimJohns

Question 206 **Is the phrase *having said that* mostly at the beginning of utterances?**

It would be reasonable to assume that it is used in spoken language only, would it not?

Question 207 **Did I really hear someone say *could of done* something?**

Search for this in the BNC using Simple Query. If you set David Lee's Classification in View Options, the domain is instantly clear. Try *would of done* as well. Extend this to other verbs with *could | would* in the Word form field, *of* in Context's Lemma filter, and in POS filter, verb 1R [137]. Once you have the concordance, you could use the Filter tool to filter out the word *course* which appears of course.

Is *could| would of done* the normal spoken form? Repeat the above search replacing *of* with *have*. In Text Types, choose spoken forms only.

The London English Corpus (LEC) yields only several but nevertheless interesting results [138], thanks in no small part to its metadata. This Structures and Attributes screenshot shows the speaker metadata in the LEC.

What is the source of this *of* error?

Question 208 **Did I really hear someone say *never heard nothing*?**

Double negatives are said to be a crime in English. Search for *never* in Simple Query and *nothing* in Context (3R). What does the number of concordances suggest about this being a pattern of normal usage? Click on Text Types in the left panel and observe where they occur.

Repeat this with any other double negative expressions you are aware of.

Double negatives in some languages are a form of emphasis, while in others they cancel each other out and create a positive sense. Remember our litotes example of *isn't uninteresting* in Question 130?

This joke highlights our use of double negatives quite nicely:

> But there isn't a single language, not one, in which a double positive can express a negative.
>
> Yeah, right. [139]

Question 209 **Both *at the weekend* and *on the weekend* are in the BNC but with quite different frequencies.**

Can Text Types tell us anything about the contexts in which these two synonymous phrases are used?

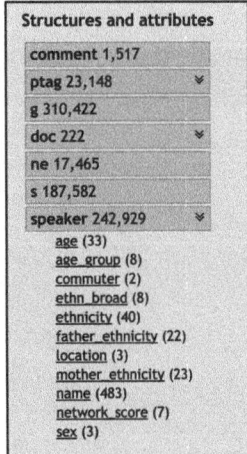

Structures and attributes
comment 1,517
ptag 23,148
g 310,422
doc 222
ne 17,465
s 187,582
speaker 242,929
  age (33)
  age_group (8)
  commuter (2)
  ethn_broad (8)
  ethnicity (40)
  father_ethnicity (22)
  location (3)
  mother_ethnicity (23)
  name (483)
  network_score (7)
  sex (3)

---

[137] Sketch Engine.li/bnc_w_could_of_verb
[138] ske.li/lec_would_of
[139] For the full joke, see *J is for Jokes* in the blog, An A-Z of ELT.

Is it true that *practice* is the noun and *practise* the verb?

Search the BNC for *practi?e* and then ask Frequency to create a list of Node forms using the Attribute, **lempos.** It should look like this [140], which means that the answer to the question is *yes.* But what about the mysterious 315? More tagging errors or is there another explanation?

lempos	Frequency
P | N practice-n	20,231
P | N practise-v	3,636
P | N Practice-n	841
P | N practice-v	315
P | N Practise-n	17
P | N PRACTISE-n	3

Across the pond, the answer to the *practice vs. practise* question is different. Use the 'am' English part of LEXMCI to discover what happens in the US.

Question 210 **Do men say *sorry* more than women?**

Saying sorry is one thing. What is meant by it is a different matter entirely.

To obtain a quantitative answer to the question, type *sorry* into Simple Query and select Spoken Demographic under Text Type.

Click Frequency and from the Text Type frequency distribution menu, choose menu, select Sex of Demographic Respondent, which is about 14th in the list, as in this screenshot.

You might like to repeat this search in the much smaller LEC which has spoken language only.

As we know, *sorry* is not only used to apologise, as can be seen in the following examples from the BNC.

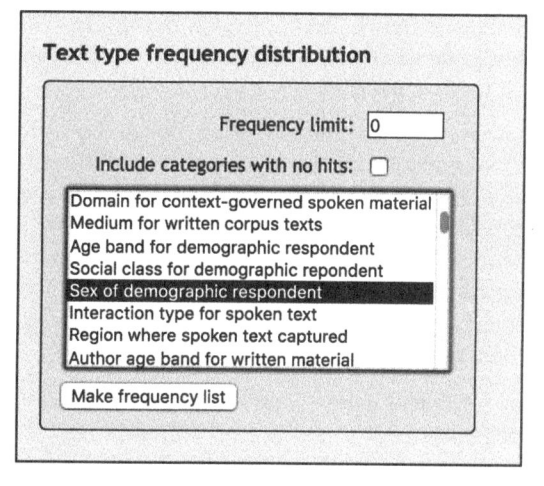

Can you guess which gender said them?

Corp ex.113 *hello, hello, I'm **sorry** to trouble you there's an ostrich on your phone line*

Corp ex.114 *Oh **sorry** I didn't mean to hit you that hard.*

In the London English Corpus, search for *sorry*. Click on Frequency Text types, where the gender breakdown is given.

The following examples from LEC are spoken by the same gender as the BNC examples above. They demonstrate various uses of *sorry* that are more to do with communication itself than with the denotative meaning of the word. Most of them also reveal quite a bit about the speaker. This is Pragmatics at work.

Corp ex.115 *he's just abusing her i'm **sorry** .. and i think i've got a right to call crimestoppers*

Corp ex.116 *no way. I'm **sorry** but that ain't happening .*

---

[140] ske.li/bnc_practi_e_freq

Corp ex.117   *it's only fucking raining now er I'm a good keeper* **sorry** *if I sweared you're allowed to swear ah yeah*

Question 211   **What are some common ways of starting sentences?**

This might not be a question that keeps you awake at night, but our previous observations have revealed some valuable findings.

It is not uninteresting to compare the use of stance adverbials, disjuncts, conjuncts, discourse markers, backchannels and sentence stems across different corpora, different text types and different contexts. This Organisation/Orientation language makes an indispensable contribution to communication, and until you have it under control, it should keep you awake at night!

The data can also be used for questions concerning given and new information, theme and rheme. See Tribble and Jones (1997:26).

As we have done before, create a CQL with just "SENT" and the Default attribute, "tag". This asks the software to generate concordances of sentence punctuation, making full stops, question marks and exclamation marks the node – new sentences follow. This screenshot was created from the two spoken text types in the BNC.

word	word	word	word	Frequency
P | N I	do	n't	know	2,369
P | N That	's	right	.	1,311
P | N Yeah	.	Yeah	.	1,165
P | N I	do	n't	think	1,065
P | N I	think	it	's	588
P | N Thank	you	very	much	551
P | N Mm	.	Mm	.	535
P | N That	's	right	,	469
P | N Yeah	.	That	's	463

It is then simply a matter of using the Frequency tool to make bundles up to four tokens long, starting with R1 in the first column. Some of the tokens in these four positions are not words – sometimes they are punctuation and we often see the negative particle separated from its stem, as in *do n't*, which makes one word two tokens. Click the **P** to see the sentences. The screenshot on the previous page shows a Frequency list of some spoken sentence beginnings, or utterances, to be more precise[141].

Quite different and informative data emerges when we process the data differently. For example, you can:

1. make a sample
2. include the Node in the Frequency list
3. select different attributes, e.g. a Frequency list of tags generates syntagms as we saw under Frequency on p.54
4. experiment with the Frequency limit at the top of the Multilevel frequency distribution
5. see the default sort according to frequency. Click the column headings and sort by the chosen attribute.

Question 212   **Does the enTenTen corpus hold Australian texts?**

As we saw in *Text types in web-crawled corpora* (p.127), .au is one of the top Top level domains (TLD), with over 400 million words. This is over four times the size of the BNC.

To make an Australian subcorpus within enTenTen, open Text Types under Simple Query and click **Create new** beside Subcorpus. Type *au* into the Top Level Domain field.

---

[141] http://ske.li/bnc_spok_sent_4

This will then be available for all searches, word sketches, thesaurus, etc. The second most frequent is .com.au. Open the full list [142] of SLDs and observe how many end in .au.

Question 213 **Is *battler* as Australian a word as many Australians think?**

Before we begin, would you expect the connotations of this word to be positive or negative?

Open enTenTen and search for *battler*, then create Text types frequency list. Among the TLDs, au is the top country code. In the SLDs, .com.au is the top code. How does it compare with other domains?

Click the P beside *battler* from where frequency lists, collocations etc. can be made, so as to see the constructions it is used in and its prosody.

In 1986, the Australian Corpus of English was created according to the Brown family sampling frame. This is not however, available in Sketch Engine. For more information, see this link [143].

---

[142] ske.li/ett_2nd_domains
[143] https://www.ausnc.org.au/corpora/ace

Your Notes

Chapter 8 Corpus Query Language – in detail

As we have seen many times, queries are generated by typing words into the three search levels that Sketch Engine offers. And as we saw on p.95, Sketch Engine automatically converts these into CQL in the background. A manual CQL query, however, enables searches that can be far more specific and complex, which brings a whole new range of flexibility and differentiation.

All examples in this chapter use Tree Tagger tags, which means that you can apply this to most corpora in the Sketch Engine stable, the main exception being the original BNC tagged with CLAWS.

The Essentials of CQL

A query consists of attributes and the elements pertaining to that attribute. For example, the attribute TAG uses part of speech tags as in the screenshot below. The attribute WORD can be any single word. The attribute, lempos, is a lemma and its single letter part of speech code joined with a hyphen, e.g. *incumbent-j*.

When a query uses one attribute only, it is enough to put the string of attributes between non-curly quotation marks and select the Default attribute, as in this screenshot. This particular example searches for a long string whose parts of speech can be seen in the table below.

| CQL: "RB" "DT" "NN" "VVZ" "JJ" "NN" "SENT" | Default attribute: tag |

Before you search for this string in a corpus, try to form some clauses yourself by writing words into this table. Then perform the search. While in enTenTen it occurs over 1,000 times, in the BNC, it yields a mere six! Compare the HPMs.

adverb	det.	noun	3rd p. s. verb	adjective	noun	sent.punc.

Such strings are referred to as syntagms (e.g. Halliday) and PoS-grams (e.g. Stubbs). Being syntactically fixed and lexically free, it is interesting to note the semantic consistency that emerges, as we shall observe shortly. See this linked abstract for an interesting foray into the phraseologies of syntagms [144] by Pinna and Brett (2014).

If, as is mostly the case, there are different attributes in the query, it must be formed with (a) each element in square brackets, (b) naming the type of attribute and then (c) specifying it between non-curly quotation marks. Here is an example of a query that includes many of the elements that we are about to learn to combine. This searches for the lemma *bias* as a noun, followed by either *towards* or *toward* followed by any type of noun within a span of three words:

[lemma = "bias" & tag = "N.*"] [word = "towards|toward"] []{1,3}[tag = "N.*"]

It returns 90 hits in the BNC, including this interesting example:

Corp ex.118   *Like Brooke-Rose, Jacques Derrida (1972b:277-8) and Paul Ricoeur (1975:19-24) trace the **bias toward noun-based views** of metaphor back to Aristotle's classification, but neither investigates the implications of an alternative view based on a different part of speech.*

We will now look at how to build such queries in linguistic contexts.

Question Tags

Question tags allow statements to be presented as obvious, dubious or open to challenge. Tags with the same polarity as the main clause (*it is, is it?*) refer to propositions whose source is the addressee. Tags with reversed polarity (*he is, isn't he?, he isn't, is he?*) refer to the speaker's own beliefs (Stubbs 1996:226). See examples of *isn't it* in the BNC here [145].

To quote the 'philosopher' Fats Waller, *One never knows, do one?* [146]

Question 214   **You can find examples of question tags, can't you? In which domains are they are used?**

While there are no particular corpus tags for question tags, there are several structures which a CQL query will identify. For example, the following query searches for the string: comma, modal verb, pronoun and sentence punctuation.

CQL: "," "MD" "PP" "SENT"   Default attribute: tag

To include the auxiliaries, *be* and *have*, we add the vertical bar to the second slot. Alas, Penn Treebank does not have a tag for *do*. CLAWS does.

"," "MD|VB.|VH." "PP" "SENT"

Useful observations can then be made by making a frequency list with the node in the last column: First level: 3L. Second level: 2L. Third level: 1L. Fourth level: Node.

---

[144] See Pinna and Brett here: http://palc.uni.lodz.pl/files/palc_abstracts.pdf p.96
[145] ske.li/bnc_isnt_it
[146] ske.li/LEXMCI_do_one

Question 215 **All question tags are contracted, are they not?**

Consider the elements of question tags without contractions, and create some searches to test this statement.

Word

Even though the following can be created with the word in quotation marks only, we will use the fully bracketed version here as building blocks.

Create a query searching for a particular word. This is case-sensitive. Note also that the spaces either side of the equals sign are optional, which is not the case in some formal languages.

[word = "secondly"]

[word = "Secondly"]

To search for more than one word, use the vertical bar, as we did on p.94.

[word = "amid|amidst"]

[word = "bright|clever|smart"]

These searches produce the same results as using the text fields. They are being introduced here as stepping stones to more complex queries.

To search for similar words, use tilde and lempos, as introduced on p.41.

[lempos~"smart-j"]

To produce the list of words like *smart*, click Node forms after performing the search. The results of the same queries in different corpora tells as much as the corpora as they do about English.

Part of speech

To create a POS search, put the tag between the inverted commas. Use capital letters. For example, [tag = "NNS"].

Question 216 **What would a list of the most frequent nouns tell me about a corpus?**

[tag = "N.*"] The full stop permits any one character – similar to a blank tile in Scrabble. The asterisk permits any number of 'blank tiles'. There are only four PTB tags starting with "N" as can be seen in the list of tags at the back of this book.

If a subcorpus or specific corpus is topic-related, the list can be expected to represent it and provides a good starting point for further enquiries. For example, a corpus of texts about the Czech composer, Leoš Janáček, with a mere 80,000 tokens, lists the following nouns as its most frequent, in this order:

music, opera, piano, composer, work, CD, violin, life, folk, viola, time, movement,

performance, love, string, quartet, year, style, death, world.

Question 217 **What would a list of the most frequent verbs in this subcorpus reveal?**

[tag = "V.*"] There are 18 tags starting with "V".

Finding many more state verbs than process verbs, for example, would imply quite different aspects of information structure.

The Janáček corpus has *writing* (102) more often than its troponym, *composing* (39).

In this corpus, he wrote a *concerto, sonata, ballet*, etc. but he composed *a masterpiece, trio, accompaniment*, etc. There are also references to writing texts, such as *novel, tragedy, essay, libretto*, though Janáček himself does not usually perform these verbs, i.e. he is not the subject.

Most of the verbs are general high frequency verbs, including auxiliaries, but expressing things that composers do.

be, have, write, do, make, take, see, give, perform, come, say, publish, play, go.

Question 218   **What do we like | love | etc. doing?**

[lempos~"like-v"][tag = "VVG"]

This CQL query produces over 2,000 hits in the BNC. Make a Node forms list, set the Frequency limit to 5, then click on the column heading, Word, to sort them alphabetically. Compare your result with this [147].

With such a list, it is worth seeing what goes either side of it. Using Frequency, make a list of items one to the left and one to the right, and observe the quite different types of subjects that *need* has.

CQL lemma queries

Create a query searching for a particular lemma …

[lemma = "impact"]

… or particular lemmas, e.g. synonyms or co-hyponyms

[lemma = "blink|wink|squint"]

or troponyms, such as:

[lemma = "cry|weep|sob"]

[lemma = "kill|stone|strangle|execute"]

[lemma = "go|drive|race|travel"]

Combining elements within brackets

Impact is a noun and a verb. To search for the lemma with a specific POS we use ampersand (&) as in the following examples:

[lemma = "impact" & tag = "V.*"]

[lemma = "going" & tag = "NNS"] searches for the noun *going* in the plural.

Note that the final S in the tag refers to the plural *s* – it does not mean singular.

This produces accurate results when the corpus has been correctly tagged: the word *sheep* is not tagged as singular or plural, despite a Simple Query of *sheep is* and another of *sheep are* returning separate concordances.

[147] ske.li/bnc_likevbs_vvg_freq

Question 219 **Are there any differences between adverbs that precede and follow verbs?**

In Question 12, we investigated *boldly go*. We didn't ask then if *go boldly* would be less marked. Let us now compare adverbs following *go* with those preceding it.

This query asks for words that end in *–ly* and are tagged as adverbs followed by the lemma *go*:

[word = ".*ly" & tag = "RB"][lemma = "go"]

This next query asks for the same items but in the reverse order:

[lemma = "go"][word = ".*ly" & tag = "RB"]

After performing these searches, make Node Forms lists and compare the types of adverbs that appear in the lists. Even though one of the searches yields many more than the other, a qualitative interpretation of the results is of greater value than a quantitative one.

When forming CQL queries, please note:

- put the search item between quotation marks, straight " not curly ones
- words in lower case
- tags in upper case

Question 220 **Can I have a list of nouns ending in "f"?**

Such a list is useful for working with such nouns that change to their voiced partners, "v" in the plural. This is both a spelling and pronunciation change, unlike the plural and 3rd person *s*, whose pronunciation systematically changes in certain environments but is only ever written as *s*.

[lemma = ".*f" & tag = "NN"]

Or you could cut straight to the search: [word = ".*ves" & tag = "NNS"] to get the plural forms.

In both cases, click on node forms to generate the lists. These appear in order of frequency by default, which is likely to be the most useful format. There are plenty of other /f/ ➔ /v/ alternations, e.g. *relief, relieve; belief, believe; themself, themselves; proof, prove.*

It is a moot point whether this is an irregular plural or a sub-pattern. The result of searching for nouns ending in 'f' is a list that can be scanned to find which ones do not undergo the voicing alternation. It may be equally correct to say that those which do follow the sub-pattern are the irregular nouns. As is well-known, every rule in English has an exception, except this one.

Question 221 **Did I just read the word *themself*?**

This is an interesting word: it looks like the first half is plural and the second half singular. When you see it in multiple contexts, it makes sense, does it not? What about the subject form, *theirself*?

By the way, does *selves* exist as a free morpheme?

These little digressions are moments of serendipity.

Strings of elements

Question 222 **What prepositions follow *impact*?**

[lemma = "impact"] [tag = "IN"]

A frequency listing – Level 1, lemma – produces convincing evidence for a bound preposition, as will be described on p.155.

What prepositions follows the noun *impact*?

[lemma = "impact" & tag = "N.."] [tag = "IN"]

Question 223 **What prepositions follow these near synonyms?**

[lemma = "struggle|battle|fight"] [tag = "IN"]

It is worth making a first level frequency list with lempos as the attribute.

A similar search can be created with [lempos~"struggle-v"][tag = "IN"].

Question 224 **Is it the case that verbs following prepositions always use the *–ing* form?**

This query provides all the verb forms that follow prepositions in the given corpus.

[tag = "IN"][tag = "V.*"]

To answer the question, it is necessary to look at the list of Node tags. Clearly the answer is *no*. To observe the counter-examples, make frequency lists with columns of words either side of it. It is also interesting to observe the chunks.

After the –ing forms, the second most frequent pair is preposition plus past participle. This harks back to Question 139, where we asked if past participles are only used with auxiliaries. In many cases, the auxiliary has been ellipted. In these three examples from the NMC, some of *be* and/or *have* is part of the intended meaning.

Corp ex.119 *... and the radical lesbian feminist model of heterosexual sex **as described** by Jensen is obviously flawed ...*

Corp ex.120 *The return message was coming in later **than expected**.*

Corp ex.121 *(I'll give them the benefit of the doubt **until proven** otherwise)*

The last of these examples is made up of two prefabricated chunks. it also has this whole clause in brackets – quite unusual, as we noted on p.89. The metadata reveals that it is from a blog entitled *Coding Horror*. Parenthetic statements typically contain secondary information, but often appear in text more like an afterthought or an aside. See the use of *aside* in the BNC [148].

Question 225 **We noted earlier that *way how* was not a pattern of normal usage. What nouns do precede *way*?**

What about the *possibility how, the manner how, the reason how ...*?

Try searching for Nouns followed by *way*: [tag = "N.*"][lemma = "way"]

[148] ske.li/bnc_parenthetic

Strings of elements 145

To find nouns similar to *way* that precede *how*, use the tilde.

[lempos~"way-n"][word = "how"]

Question 226 **Is this curious structure, noun + preposition +** *and* **+ noun + preposition, a pattern in English?**

This is the context in which it was met:

The Phonemic Chart is a widely-used resource for developing students' **sensitivity to and production of** *individual sounds.*

We need some more examples.

To search for this structure, use this query. Three examples follow.

[tag = "N."][tag = "IN"][word = "and"][tag = "N."][tag = "IN"]

Corp ex.122 *The process is helped by Eliot's* **reading of and reference to** *the works of Demant and Dawson.*

Corp ex.123 *Henry III's* **admiration for and emulation of** *Louis IX is well known.*

Corp ex.124 *The decisive role in the black youth's continued* **enthusiasm for, participation in and commitment to** *sport is played by others of similar inclination.*

The last of these three examples has the noun + preposition three times.

Question 227 **Is there any patterned use of *through* in passive structures?**

[lemma = "be"][tag = "V.N"][word = "through"]

Experiment with Sorting and Frequency.

The semantics of some of these verbs have a prepositional phrase that starts with *through*, e.g. *is passed through the brain, being dragged through the mud*, i.e. adverbial of place.

Other verbs use *through* to express the means by which something is done, as *by* traditionally does in passives, e.g. *sth. was acquired through long use, sth. is heightened through conflict*. Could *by* be replace *through* in these contexts?

Question 228 **Adverbs typically precede adjectives, but *enough* follows them. Is this typically followed by a *to* – inf structure?**

Using CQL, search for adj + enough + to + inf

Question 229 **What are the most frequent lemmas in a corpus?**

This and the following questions are of particular value in specialised corpora. These searches may also be conducted within specific text types and subcorpora.

To search for all the lemmas in a corpus, type this: ".*" (attribute Lemma).

For all the lemma bigrams, type ".*" ".*". A bigram is an adjacent pair of items.

For all the lemma trigrams, type ".*" ".*" ".*" etc.

Bigrams, trigram, 4-grams and beyond are referred to generally as n-grams. Sketch Engine has an n-gram tool that we explore in Chapter 13.

To generate lists of the findings, click Node Forms.

Lemma can be replaced with word and tag for quite different yet useful results, depending on your research question. This is followed up under the heading of Syntagms, p.151.

How to allow space between elements

Words often appear between your target elements. For example, we cannot expect meaningful results from a search for a specific collocation, e.g. *organise party*, because nouns are usually the last elements in noun phrases: determiners, adjectives and other nouns form compound nouns, e.g. *wedding party*, occur before head noun.

Empty square brackets force one token to appear in between. Remember that punctuation marks are tokens as are possessive and negative particles.

> [lemma= "organi.e"][][lemma = "party"]

The full stop here is the operator that allows any letter in that space: it is being used here to allow both *s* and *z*.

For a range of spaces between elements, use braces directly after the square brackets. The number between the braces {} indicates the number of tokens requested in between. This query asks for exactly three tokens between them:

> [lemma= "organi.e"][]{3}[lemma = "party"]

Using {1,3} gives the range from one to three. This allows one or two or three tokens between them.

> [lemma= "organi.e"][]{1,3}[lemma = "party"]

Corp ex.125   The officials **organized themselves into search parties**.

Corp ex.126   The strength of current protest is that there are no leaders, no **organised large party** and no hierarchies.

The question mark here makes the search zero or one.

> [lemma= "organi.e"][]?[lemma = "party"]

Question 230   **What can you expect from this collocation search, *develop ... approach*?**

Will *approach* be a verb as well a noun? If so, what could come between these two verbs? And when it is a noun, being singular or plural should influence what comes between them.

> [lemma = "develop"] [] [lemma = "approach"]

Question 231   **What can you expect from this delexical verb search, *make ... success*?**

> [lemma = "make"][]{3}[lemma ="success"]

What sort of adjectives would you expect to qualify *success*? Will the noun be in the plural?

How do the structures of the delexical form differ from those of the lexical verb, *succeed*, in terms of subject – verb – object and beyond?

Question 232 **What can you expect to learn from this phrasal verb search, *let ... down*?**

[lemma = "let"][]{0,3}[word ="down"]

Will the verb appear in the full gamut of tenses (past and present) and aspects (perfect and progressive)? Is the verb transitive? If so, do noun phrases 'interrupt' this phrasal verb? Are there any lexical adverbs describing the impact of letting someone down?

Question 233 **Is the structure *whether ... or not* typically accompanied by any type of phrase?**

Perhaps it tends to be at the end of information units.

This query asks for up to five tokens separating them.

[word = "whether"][]{1,5}[word ="or"][word ="not"]

Correlative conjunctions can be studied in the same way. For example, *either...or..., not only... but also..., both ... and ...*

Question 234 **Is the structure, *as ___ a ___ as,* frequent enough in the repertoire of native speakers to recognize it as a useful pattern?**

Here is one example:

Corp ex.127 *But the sea is not **as secure a barrier as** it might seem.*

Use this CQL and use Frequency to observe any patterns that occur. Right sort this page[149], and observe what follows it.

[word = "as"][][word = "a|an"][][word = "as"]

if you select *word* as the **Default attribute** beside CQL Field, it is enough to enter: "as" [] "a|an" [] "as"

This search reveals quite a few standard chunks, as Node forms shows.

How to exclude elements

The exclamation mark preceding the equals sign means *does not equal*.

Question 235 **What parts of speech does *fast* function in apart from adjective?**

The following query will find *fast* as any POS except as an adjective.

[lemma="fast" & tag != "JJ.*"]

The dot-asterisk operators are necessary here to exclude JJR and JJS which are used for comparative and superlative, respectively.

Click on Node tags to list its other pars of speech.

Similarly, we can search for a word not in the company of a specific word. The next example finds *dream* followed by any word but *about*.

[lemma="dream"][word !="about"]

[149] http://ske.li/bnc_as_a_as

The next example finds all forms of *break* followed by three words and then *like* not as a verb.

[lemma = "break"][]{3} [lemma="like" & tag !="V.."]

Question 236 **Is *which* always preceded by a comma?**

The first example here searches for *which* preceded by a comma. The second example without.

[word = ","][word = "which"]

[word != ","][word = "which"]

Given that punctuation is a feature of written language, it is worth limiting the search to Written text types.

Question 237 **The split infinitive is wrong. Says who?**

The split infinitive misdemeanour is as much loved by prescriptive linguists as it is by those who enjoy ridiculing them. As the search results show, it is a standard construction in English.

[tag = "TO"] [tag !="V.*"] [tag = "VV"]

This search starts with the infinitive marker followed by anything but a verb, followed by the base form of any lexical verb.

Click on Node forms and then the Word button at the top of the list to find out which words wedge themselves in between when an infinitive is split. Select some example sentences and try moving the "intruder" to another part of the sentence. When it is possible, does it affect the meaning?

Question 238 **Which adverbs do not end in *–ly*?**

This part of speech is a broad church. Adverbs that describe how verbs are performed mostly end in *–ly*. But there are many other very high frequency words which are classified as adverbs, and which have quite a different relationship with their verbs, as this search reveals.

[word != ".*ly" & tag = "RB"]

Set a frequency limit and sort by the Word column.

Generate some bundles that include items before and after these adverbs: consider their roles in relation to whole clauses.

Note that there are many adverbs ending in *–ly* that function at the clause level – these are disjuncts and stance adverbials.

How to make search items optional

Use the question mark to make various items optional.

Question 239 **What do these two spellings, *blond* and *blonde,* indicate?**

Are they random, alternative spellings? Different parts of speech? Something else?

Search either "blonde?" or "blond(e)?" with the Attribute set to Word – both return the same concordances. Then click on Frequency and choose First level Node, Second level 1R. The pairings in the list are pretty obvious. To be even more obvious, First level 1L, Second level Node, Third level 1R, and we can be in no doubt how these two spellings, *blond/e*, are used.

The question mark can also be used to make a whole CQL element optional: in this query, *not* is optional. See here [150].

[word="might"] [word="not"]? [word="think"]

word	Frequency
P | N might think	546
P | N might not think	15

Question 240 **Who or whom?**

Start with [word = "whom?"] in CQL, and then click Node Forms. Even though *who* is many times more frequent, *whom* is no slouch, with approximately the same frequency as words such as *travel, finally, announce, mile*.

When is *whom* preferred? Click on **P** beside *whom* in the frequency list. Then again in the concordance of *whom* only. To answer what precedes it, select 1L and Node. Try this with words, lemmas and tags. What is most salient?

Create four-word bundles with *whom* in different levels. There are interesting observations to be made.

Now that the question mark is in our skill set, we can simplify some earlier searches. For example,

[word = "towards|toward"] ➔ [word="toward?"]

[word = "amid|amidst"] ➔ [word="amid(st)?"]

Question 241 **How much sense can be made of a string of proforms?**

What linguistic peccadillos do you observe in the concordance results of this?

"and|but" "do" "it" "(s)?he" "did" (Attribute *lemma*)

enTenTen is recommended for such a search. Apart from the conjunction, all of the pronoun references need to be retrieved from the discourse.

In what domains is such language used?

How to search for punctuation

Question 242 **When *only* is used at the beginning of a sentence, what follows?**

[tag = "SENT"][word = "Only"]

The results can be summarised using Frequency lists of words or tags, both of which can also reveal patterns.

Question 243 **Do sentences in academic prose start with "I"?**

Use either an academic subcorpus, or academic text types.

---

[150] http://ske.li/bnc_might_think

Question 244 **How are things said in fiction?**

In Question 201, we asked this question to find the adverbs that describe *said*. Now we are going to look for other 'verbs of saying' that are used in fiction, as each of the troponyms expresses its own way of saying. The first element in the query searches for sentence punctuation. The next element is a single quotation mark. And the third is any type of verb. Choose *Imaginative* in BNC Text Types, make the concordance, then click on Node Forms, under Frequency [151].

[tag = "SENT"][word="'"][tag = "V.*"]

The Frequency list contains three columns, one for each of the elements in the query. It is of stylistic interest that despite not asking for any particular verb type, one is particularly salient.

Escape

Some punctuation is used as **operators** in the formal language of computer expressions. In order to search for them as items in text, it is necessary to 'escape' them by using the backslash: \. For our purposes, these include the full stop, question mark, exclamation mark, brackets and braces, double quotes, the vertical bar, asterisk and ampersand:

. ? ! [({ })] " | * &

For more on this, see for example, Wikipedia: Boolean expression. Its originator, George Boole (1815-1864), pictured here.

Question 245 **How is the ampersand used in English?**

Enter this query into the CQL Field:

[word = "\&"]

And make a Frequency list from the data returned: 1L Node 1R.

Question 246 **Which text types most typically have single words appearing between brackets?**

This query searches for an opening bracket (parenthesis) followed by any one item followed by a closing bracket. Then click on Text Types in the left panel.

[word ="\("][][word ="\)"]

Within a sentence

We can add **within <s/>** to the end of a query to ensure that the elements occur within the same sentence. For example,

[lemma = "arouse"][]{3,5}[tag = "N.."] within <s/>

This is particularly useful for ensuring that your collocation results occur in the same sentence.

Question 247 **How far apart can *whether ... or not* be within a sentence?**

This query asks for up to five tokens separating them.

---

[151] ske.li/bnc_fiction_verbsofsaying

[word = "whether"][]{0,5}[word ="or"][word ="not"] within <s/>

But to see them at a distance, try {10, 15}, for example, still within the sentence.

You might also wonder if they have to be in the same sentence.

Wildcards and/or operators

As mentioned on p.36, some operators return different results when used in CQL. In the following sections, we will explore the use of operators in combination with other CQL tools for exploring some traditional grammar structures.

Syntagms

A syntagm is a string of parts of speech, which can include function words (e.g. *if, would, way*). They are the skeletons of clauses and sentence types. As the table *Searching for constructions* (p.153) shows, they open the door to studying syntagms as structures.

If lexical words are included, however, we are no longer working with syntagms, but with grammar patterns or hybrid n-grams, both of which are used in building word templates (see chapters 5 and 9).

CQL is the only way to search for syntagms and hybrid n-grams in Sketch Engine.

Question 248 **What are the most frequent parts of speech in a corpus?**

And how often do they occur and in what relative proportions?

This is not strictly speaking a question that will reveal syntagms, rather it lays some foundations for doing so.

To search for all the tags in a corpus, type this [tag = ".*"] or ".*" Default attribute, tag.

To generate lists of the findings, click Node Tags.

Question 249 **What are the most frequent syntagms?**

For bigrams, type [tag = ".*"][tag = ".*"]

For trigrams, type [tag = ".*"][tag = ".*"][tag = ".*"]

Significant differences between text types can be observed using Text types fields.

Question 250 **How do I find grammar structures like the present perfect or the third conditional in corpora?**

In our introduction to CQL at the end of Chapter 4, we noted that some languages mark aspect (perfect and progressive) and voice (active and passive) with inflections, whereas English uses auxiliaries. Because these are separate words, it is quite straightforward to form queries that find examples of such structures. Refer to the chart on p.96 to remind yourself of the systematic nature of these forms. The table of constructions below shows how to construct queries for some of these grammatical structures. Remember that:

- these can be used with any corpora using the TreeTagger. And sub-corpora.
- searches can be constrained by items in the Context and Text types fields, e.g. search for third conditional in spoken language only.

The following questions put some of these queries to some use.

Question 251 **It is said that American English uses the present perfect less than British English.**

We can explore this using the LEXMCI corpus. The following CQL finds the present perfect without anything between the auxiliary and the past participle.

[word = "have|has"][tag = "VVN"]

Using Text Types, perform this search once with **am** and again with **br** as in this screenshot from LEXMCI.

```
DOC.LANGVARIETY
☐ am
☐ br
☐ ie
[Select All]
```

This may lead you to consider related questions about the verbs and adverbs used in these constructions.

Question 252 **Are there any particular adverbs used with the present perfect progressive?**

For this, we need to search for *have* or *has* + adv + been + -ing form, by creating the following query [152]:

[word = "have|has"][tag = "RB"][word = "been"][tag = "V.G"]

This has 5.6 hits per million in the BNC and is quite evenly distributed across the corpus. Click the Visualize button to observe its distribution.

Click on Node forms to summarize your findings. The answer is quite clear, but given that many words, both functional and lexical, are classed as adverbs, the function adverbs predominate. To limit it to adverbs ending in *–ly*, try [153]:

[word = "have|has"][word = ".*ly" & tag = "RB"][word = "been"][tag = "V.G"]

This has significantly fewer hits per million: 1.32. Once again, click Node Forms and click the Word column heading. What is missing when only adverbs ending in –ly are included?

Do you find that the semantics of the adverbs contribute to the semantics of the present perfect progressive?

This is a question that can be asked of many verb structures. The semantics of structures and of the words in them 'conspire' to create the desired effect, a.k.a. their illocutionary force.

[152] ske.li/bnc_pres_perf_cont_gen_adv
[153] ske.li/bnc_pres_perf_cont_adv_ly

Searching for constructions

Progressive	BE –ing	[tag = "VB."][tag = "V.G"]
Present progressive	am/are/is –ing	[tag="VBP|VBZ"][tag="V.G"]
Perfect progressive	HAVE been –ing	[lemma = "have"][word = "been"][tag = "V.G"]
Perfect progressive with "be"	HAVE been being	[lemma = "have"][word = "been"][tag = "VBG"]
Perfect passive	HAVE been past part.	[lemma = "have"][word = "been"][tag = "V.N"]
Have you ever ...?	HAVE pronoun *ever* past part.	[lemma = "have"][tag = "PP"][word = "ever"][tag = "V.N"]
Has someone done ...?	HAVE pronoun past tense	[lemma = "have"][tag = "PP"][tag = "V.N"]
Third conditional	IF ... HAD past part ... WOULD	[word = "if"][][word = "had"][tag = "V.N"][]{0,6}[word = "would"]
Passive with get	GET past part	[lemma = "get"][tag = "V.N"]
Mandative Subjunctive	Singular noun + base form	[word="that"] [word="he|she|it"][tag = "VV|VB"]
No name	NOUN of NOUN	[tag ="N.*"][word= "of"][tag ="N.*"]
No name	VERB on to NOUN	[tag = "V.N"][word = "on"][word = "to"][][tag = "N.."]
No name	if PROPER NOUN would	[word = "if"][tag = "NP0"][word = "would"]
No name	it VERB to INF	[word = "it"][tag ="V.."][tag = "TO"][tag = "VV"]
No name	as ADJ a NOUN as	[word = "as"][tag = "JJ"][word = "a"][tag = "N.*"][word = "as"]
Comparatives	the –re ... the -re [154]	[word = "the"][tag= "JJR"][]{1,3}[word = "the"][tag= "JJR"]

The distribution of these structures can be observed using the Visualize tool, e.g. third conditional here [155].

---

[154] ske.li/bnc_the_er_the_er
[155] e.g. ske.li/bnc_thirdconditional_vis

Question 253 **Do any lexical patterns appear in the third conditional?**

Using the appropriate CQL query from the table, you will obtain a set of third conditional clauses. Using the Node Forms button, you will obtain a screen that will simplify answering the question [156]. It will also provide you with a useful set of sentence stems.

Question 254 **Which words trigger the mandative subjunctive?**

English has three moods, indicative, imperative and subjunctive, the last of which is used for something that is not actual or factual. Some words and phrases 'mandate', or require, the use of the subjunctive.

Some studies have shown the subjunctive to be alive and well and living (primarily) in American English or that American English is leading in its revitalization and that British English is lagging behind. [157]

> The phrase *alive and well* is a binomial: it occurs in enTenTen 338 times, which qualifies it as a chunk. It is used significantly with one person (left sort) living somewhere.

Our task is to find words and phrases that are typically followed by the subjunctive. The periphrastic nature of English does not help us much in this regard, as there are no words (free morphemes) serving as markers, such as auxiliaries, but there is one grammatical marker (bound morpheme) that helps us: we will use this now.

We will use a CQL that requests (a) the word *that*, (b) 3rd person singular subject pronoun and (c) the base form of lexical verbs and of *be*. In the indicative mood, verbs following 3rd person pronouns have the 's' ending. The lack of this in the subjunctive permits this search.

[word="that"] [word="he|she|it"][tag = "VV|VB"]

Verbs in all persons and numbers can be followed by the subjunctive, but English conjugation can only help us with 3rd person singular.

Given its alleged distribution in UK and US English, it is worth performing this search in LEXMCI and observing the text types. Comparing its use in fiction, spoken, academic prose might also bring some useful findings.

To answer the original question, make a Frequency list with 1L lemma in the first level, followed by the node. Since BE is very frequent in the node, it is worth adding a Third level column with 1R to see what follows. Is BE ever used as a lexical verb in this context? Since BE is very frequent in the node, it can be deleted from the search: [word="that"] [word="he|she|it"][tag = "VV"]

To see what lexical verbs are active in the mandative subjunctive, make a frequency list and sort by the first level, i.e. the lemma that precedes the node [158].

We can find out if it was used more in earlier centuries by repeating these steps in EEBO. The Frequency list of references certainly indicates when it had its heyday.

Question 255 **Is it true that academic prose prefers the passive?**

After searching for the syntagm that forms the passive, check its distribution in Text Types. There is more to answering the question than this, but this is a good start.

---

[156] ske.li/bnc_3cond_stems
[157] From here: http://bit.ly/cambridge_mand_subj
[158] ske.li/LEXMCI_mandsubj_freq

Searching for constructions

Question 256 **Is the structure of the phrase, *drink someone beautiful,* a pattern of normal usage?**

I came across it once in my reading – is it a one off? This exemplifies the claim that an authentic occurrence of something does not make it typical (Gries 2008:425).

Is there a difference between drinking someone beautiful and drinking yourself beautiful, as in these only two examples in enTenTen?

Corp ex.128 *a lot of us are very shy, and if you are **drinking your date beautiful** or you're doing things that you would regret in the morning, ... (ETT12)*

Corp ex.129 *Feeding and Cultivating Beauty with chapters like **drink yourself beautiful**, and reclaiming the joy of eating. (ETT12)*

With only two hits, it is clearly not well-established in the language. But it is lovely. Are there any analogous instances of verb + person + adjective?

"VV." "NP.*|PP" "JJ" (attribute TAG)

Yes, in the BNC, 140.4 per million [159]: *drive me crazy, find it impossible, make me thirsty, prove me wrong, scare him shitless, see him drunk, set him free,* etc.

> Stop Press
> Recently spotted in London
> **Book yourself fabulous**, a poster for a website for making hair and beauty appointments. Google it.

Is the semantic harmony between *drink* and *beautiful* any more conspicuous than the common examples in the BNC?

Question 257 **Which verbs are used in ditransitive structures?**

Cognitive linguists argue that grammatical structures have their own meanings, and replace terms such as *pattern* and *rule* with *construction*, which in their definition recognises that form and function are linked. This is closely related to construction grammar, and is not incompatible with the grammar patterns of the Neo-Firthians.

The ditransitive construction has four elements: subject, verb, object, indirect object. Its essential meaning is *transfer*.

Using CQL we could create this simple query for each of those four slots:

"N.*" "V.*" "N.*" "N.*"

Click Node forms and we find this returns many items not germane to our research question, even though they may be patterns worthy of later investigation. Commonly occurring false positives can be filtered out using the Filter tool (p.53).

We need to allow for the noun slots to be noun phrases, not just single words. We can make the pre-noun slot either a determiner or an adjective using the vertical bar. We can optionally make the subject and indirect object pronouns, [tag = "N.*|PP"]. Making the verb lexical only, [tag = "VV.*"], removes high-frequency non-transfer verbs such as *be* and *have*.

In this structure, the two objects can go in either order, but if the indirect object is last in the construction, its role is indicated by *to*. To add a word, we need to return to using square brackets. Let us try the following [160]:

---

[159] ske.li/bnc_vb_n_jj_freq
[160] ske.li/bnc_ditrans

[tag = "N.*|PP"][tag = "VV."][tag = "DT|JJ"][tag = "N.*"][word = "to"]
[tag = "DT|JJ|PP"]

This, however, opens a can of worms: despite their being a tag for *to* functioning as an infinitive marker [tag = "TO"], no tags distinguish *to* as a particle marking the indirect object (dative case) from *to* as a preposition.

Considerably more manual processing of the data is required than we are used to.

Question 258 **Are there any patterns of normal usage associated with the order of verbs and their adverbs?**

Search for lexical verbs followed by words ending in *–ly*.

[tag = "VV."][word = ".*ly"]

Then reverse the search items.

Make nodes form lists of both concordances. Quite different and informative lists are generated when you add columns 1L and 1R of the node in Frequency lists. Using lemmas, set the frequency limit and sort by the column headings.

Question 259 **What can we learn about IFIDs?**

IFID is an acronym for illocutionary force indicating devices, an aspect of pragmatics that Searle worked on, following Austin's work on speech acts. For more on this, see e.g. O'Grady, 2010.

One type of IFID is the performative verb, i.e. those which express their intended force by saying so. For example, *I quit. I promise … I name this ship …* etc.

Here is one syntagm that gives examples of an IFID, by starting with a structure.

[word = "I"][tag = "VVD"][word = "you"][word = "that"]

Click on Node forms to see a summary of the results, some of which are clearly performative.

This brings to an end DESKE's introduction to CQL. As usual, we have studied not only the mechanics of this Sketch Engine tool, but have used it to find and structure data for many language questions. Despite the detail in this introduction, it is far from exhaustive – even more specialised CQL querying elements can be found in the Sketch Engine wiki[161].

Speech Acts

1. A locutionary act is the performance of a linguistic expression: syntax, phonology, etc. It is also the actual meaning of the utterance.

2. An illocutionary act is the function of an utterance, e.g. getting someone to do something, making a promise, expressing an opinion.

3. A perlocutionary act is the desired effect, e.g., to flatter, to insult, to impress, to express gratitude.

J.L. Austin, 1962

---

[161] ske.li/cql_guide

Chapter 9   Parallel Corpora

Sketch Engine define a parallel corpus as *a corpus of source texts plus translations into one or more languages*, as do McEnery et al. (2006:47). Others working with corpora containing more than one language use different terms such as multilingual, translation, comparable corpora, which may differ in their constitution and use.

The quality and reliability of a parallel corpus is always proportional to how accurately the texts in different languages are aligned. Alignment refers to the process of identifying certain *anchor points* in the parallel texts, linking together corresponding sentences, word clusters or even individual words (Obrusník 2012:1).

Parallel corpora are useful for observing how the same notions are expressed in two languages and are therefore of value to translation, lexicography and language teaching and learning. Although there is some risk of *translationese*, a large parallel corpus should be able to mitigate this with human intuition.

One such resource in Sketch Engine is the OPUS2 suite of parallel corpora, which is introduced on the OPUS website [162] thus:

> OPUS is a growing collection of translated texts from the web. In the OPUS project we try to convert and align free online data, to add linguistic annotation, and to provide the community with a publicly available parallel corpus. OPUS is based on open source products and the corpus is also delivered as an open content package. We used several tools to compile the current collection. All pre-processing is done automatically. No manual corrections have been carried out.

This is the corpus that we will be using in this chapter. At the time of writing it contains 1,139,515,048 words spread across a number of sub-corpora as can be seen here [163]. The figures express tokens. English is compared with Czech, German and Italian in this chapter as these are the foreign languages with which the author is familiar.

> TIP If the two columns on a parallel page are not balanced, click *Alignment* under View Options in the left panel. Experiment also with *KWIC* and *Sentence* to see how they affect a parallel concordance page. If your screen is narrow, click on *Menu position* at the bottom of the panel.

Very many of the linguistic concepts and language questions that we have explored so far in this book could be investigated again through the lens of other languages that you are familiar with. For example, *experience*.

---

[162] http://opus.lingfil.uu.se
[163] http://ske.li/op2_subcorpora

Question 260 **What might a parallel corpus contribute to our exploration of countability?**

On p.87 we observed some features of *experience*. Open this permalink[164] and observe how the two equivalents suggested, *Erlebnis* and *Erfarhung,* appear in German. Using CTRL F, find these two words. Then have a look at German sentences which contain neither. You could use the Select Lines check boxes to collect them for closer investigation.

Using parallel corpora

To try this with another language, go to Sketch Engine homepage, click the Parallel button and choose the OPUS2 English corpus. In the Lemma field, type *experience*, and choose Noun. In the list of languages below, choose yours. Leave the subfields blank and click Make concordance. Add your findings to this table.

How might you interpret the vastly different numbers that appear for the countable and uncountable forms?

experience	countable event	hits	uncountable knowledge expertise gained	hits
German	*Erlebnis*	2	*Erfahrung*	784
Czech	*zažitek*	1	*zkušenost*	463

Question 261 **How do the various meanings and uses of polysemous lexemes manifest in another language?**

In Question 144, we observed how the collocation and colligation of *put down* realised its different meanings. If we now look at this phrasal verb in a parallel corpus, we can see how many different translations it has. And why.

We also noted that the COBUILD Dictionary offered 17 meanings for the word *frame*, although there were some lumping and splitting issues to deal with. Have a look now in the parallel corpus to see how translators dealt with the verb *frame.*

Let us now explore *manage*, a verb with numerous grammar patterns, e.g.

   sb manages to do sth

   sb manages sth

   sb manages quantity

   sb | organisation manages sb

   sb manages

Since each of these structures realises a different meaning, depending on the extent you lump and split, they are likely to be translated variously.

[164] http://ske.li/op2eng_de_experience

Search for *manage* in the English OPUS2 and observe the equivalents it offers. The important question concerns the correlation between the patterns and the translation, i.e. is a pattern mostly translated in the same way?

Question 262 **Is there any consistency in the translation of grammar patterns?**

Given that words with the same pattern have similar semantics, do their syntax and semantics co-operate systematically in another language? This is an important consideration in using vocabulary accurately and learning it efficiently.

Let us take, for example, the highly frequent pattern in English, V n to-inf (Francis et al. 1998a:290), which is used with such semantic groups as:

tell e.g. advise, recommend
nag e.g. pester, encourage
inspire e.g. move, persuade
choose and use e.g. nominate, enlist
expect e.g. intend, require
Select some of these words and search for them in OPUS2, in their patterns. This requires CQL, e.g.

[lemma = "encourage"][]?[tag = "N.*"][tag = "TO"]

Corp ex.130 *How, otherwise, can we ensure a future for current farmers **and encourage young people to work** in the sector?*

If there are several translations of *encourage*, it may be necessary to enter your preferred foreign word into the lemma field beside the language, as in this screenshot. As a straightforward example, here is *motivieren*. As can be seen via this link [165], this translation pair has several patterns.

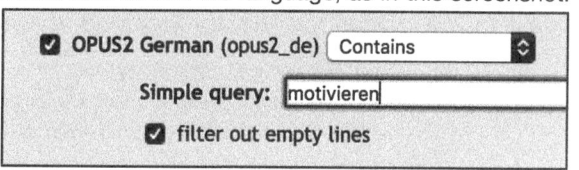

Question 263 **Do translated words have the same connotations and/or semantic prosody that they have in English?**

Search for some of these words in English OPUS2 with your language selected.

bachelor, spinster, harbour (verb), *gross* (adjective), *put down, etc.*

Question 264 **We have already explored some examples of litotes. Is this figure of speech peculiar to English?**

Search for un.* in the lemma field as an adjective, and *not* in the Context lemma 1L. As can be seen here, this structure is not unknown in German [166], nor in Czech [167] where *není* means *he/she/it is not*. Search for others such as those mentioned under Question 132.

English is fond of saying that something is *not very* 'something'. If someone says that they are not good at names, they mean that they are bad at names. But if they say

---

[165] http://ske.li/op2_eng_ger_encour_motivieren
[166] http://ske.li/op2_eng_ger_not_un
[167] http://ske.li/op2_eng_cz_not_un

that they are not very good at names, the implication is that they could be better and/or they regret it. On this page [168], there are three columns of translations of some English sentences containing *not very*. Use this or make your own and see if the pragmatics of *not very* are borne out in other languages. Are they in the translations even if the source language does not express this nuance?

Question 265 **How have translators dealt with common words and phrases that do not have one-to-one translation equivalents?**

Many requests and questions in English start with *I wonder* and the gentler, more hedged, *I was wondering*. Czech does not have a one-to-one translation for this. At this link [169], there are eight corpus examples of short English sentences and their Czech translations, each with a different realization of *I wonder*. Some of them back-translate as *I say to myself, I hope that, It would interest me, … just if …, I would like to know*.

Another example of something that does not have a one-to-one translation in some languages is *let alone* which occurs in the BNC 11.28 HPMs. Explore this in some languages you know.

The word *affectionate* appears not to have a one-to-one translation in either Czech or German. This concordance page [170] which has all three languages in parallel demonstrates the different translations that the translators arrived at in every sentence.

Some others you might like to explore: *chronological order, false alarm, be bound to* (p.52), *in cahoots with* (p.38), *clench teeth* (p.126), *positively dangerous* (p.110).

Question 266 **What are the applications of some common politeness expressions?**

See this text box for the technical use of *application*. Expressions for *please, sorry, thank you, excuse me* exhibit a range of applications in other languages, as can be explored in parallel corpora.

The phrase, *I'm so sorry*, expresses both sympathy and apology. Other languages have separate phrases for these speech acts. I once saw an English language film in which someone said *I'm so sorry* upon hearing of someone's death, but the Czech subtitles used the Czech expression for an apology *omlouvám se*, not for sympathy *je mi líto*.

> **Application**. A term used by some linguists to refer to the overall relationship which exists between language and non-linguistic entities, situations, etc. A lexical item may be applied to a range of situations which are not part of its normal denotation. This term is particularly useful in translation. (Crystal 2006:30)

Question 267 **How is the English future expressed when the source language has a future tense?**

On p.97 the conjugation table of *scrivere* (*to write* in Italian) shows a *Futuro semplice*, a form which English does not have. Searching for one of the conjugated forms will show how it is translated. For example, *scriveranno* becomes: *will be written, will be writing, come to write*, as can be seen here [171].

---

[168] http://ske.li/cys
[169] http://ske.li/op2eng_cz_i_wonder
[170] http://ske.li/op2eng_cz_ger_affectionate
[171] http://ske.li/op2eng_it_scriveranno

Although there is no metatag for future, all the future forms start *scriver*, which makes it possible to search for *scriver.** in the Word form field, and then use Filter (Word form) to exclude the infinitive, *scrivere*. It might be a long journey, but the tools exist that facilitate these complex searches. Now the research can begin.

Question 268   **How are the different meanings of *for the last time* expressed?**

The two meanings of this four word chunk are temporal and emotional. The following examples are from OPUS2 exemplify them.

Corp ex.131   *The reindeer has come **for the last time***.

Corp ex.132   *Daisy, **for the last time**, will you stop being so dramatic?*

The next two might be ambiguous, but with more context this is unlikely.

Corp ex.133   *You've poisoned me for the last time, you wretched girl.*

Corp ex.134   *For the last time I have a favor to ask.*

Despite their quite different meanings, this phrase is almost always translated with the same word in Czech. Is this the case in other languages?

Question 269   **How different are the meanings of *in the beginning* and *at the beginning*?**

Search for these in a monolingual English corpus and right sort the concordances. Their different colligations are immediately apparent. How is this reflected in other languages?

Question 270   **How are English grammatical structures expressed in other languages?**

Verb structures typically keep company with adverbs. In performing some of the following searches, you might choose to use the Context POS filter in addition to the top CQL field.

Because grammar structures often manifest differently in text types, you also might like to constrain the searches to some text types as well.

The table on p.153 has a number of structures that would be worth observing in translation. Use the CQL field in the OPUS2.

Try, for example, the '*get* passive'. It gets enough hits to justify making a sample. Does it have a negative prosody in English as well as in the translated language? Compare this with the unmarked *be* passive.

The perfect progressive, another compound verb structure, is very frequent in English. Search for this in your parallel corpus and observe any systematic patterns in the other language.

Question 271   **How do question tags manifest in translations in other languages?**

Use the CQL from Question 214 to observe this. If the other language does not typically use question tags or expresses their pragmatics differently, is there any evidence of *translationese*?

Question 272 **Do hypernyms extend across languages?**

Sometimes they do, sometimes they don't. On this short concordance page[172], we see English *dwelling* matched with German *Haus*. This was obtained using the Simple Query field beside the translation language. The German word covers greater sematic space than *house* in English, often being used as a hypernym for *building* or *dwelling*.

The idea of a *family house*, which is more continental than English, can be seen in these three columns of Czech, German and English[173]. On the concordance page, the lines marked *Not translated*, indicate that the Czech text containing the phrase has not been translated into English.

It is difficult to answer questions about the English translation of something that is not in English. Other lexical gaps include *professional deformation*, *habilitation*, as well as various ranks in the military and nobility. You can probably think of a number of things that exist in one language that do not have a convincing English translation. This lies at the heart of Malinowski's Context of Culture: see textbox.

> Malinowski's theories influenced linguists such as Firth (1957) and Halliday (1985) and language became to be considered meaningful only if considered within the language events in which it is used.

Question 273 **Would transliterating a phrase into another language sound idiomatic?**

For example, does *I have the feeling that...* work in other languages? If you know the foreign word for *feeling*, you can include it in your search beside the language in the Simple Query field. It turns out that in German, it translates word for word, but does not require *that*[174].

Conclusion

Using parallel corpora marks a considerable shift in the way we approach language questions. In our work up to this chapter, we have been dedicated to learning English from English and studying linguistics with English data only. Sketch Engine tools and corpora permit new dimensions to be added to our modus operandi.

In addition to the OPUS2 parallel suite, Sketch Engine also has Europarl in many languages as well as the Digital Translation Memory. See their information pages from the list of corpora.

For more on parallel corpora, see European and Comparable Corpora[175].

---

[172] http://ske.li/op2_eng_ger_dwelling_haus
[173] http://ske.li/op2_cz_ger_eng_rodinnydum
[174] http://ske.li/op2eng_ger_ihavethefeelingthat
[175] http://www.ecpc.uji.es/EN/links.php?language=en

Chapter 10   Collocation

In this section, we look at some of the ways that Sketch Engine generates collocation lists, and how we can work with them. The concept of Collocation was introduced on p.47.

The following examples are typical collocations we see in linguistics and teaching literature: *relatively independent, give opportunity, large numbers, handsome man, cushy job, go awry, abiding passion, run risk, bridge gap*. Foreign language learners need to study them because they are patterns of normal usage, and therefore should be part of our linguistic competence. As we saw in the previous chapter, things cannot be relied upon to translate well, and replacing one of the pair with a synonym or a translation equivalent could sound unidiomatic, stylistically inappropriate, or worse – the intended meaning could be distorted or lost.

Lexical items in a collocation are usually single words, but they may also be multi-word lexemes. If we take *open door policy* as a single semantic unit, a.k.a. lexeme, its collocating verbs (e.g. *implement*) and adjectives (e.g. *informal*) will form collocations that consist of more than two 'words'.

Thus the Two Lexeme definition of collocation emerges – TLC (Thomas 2015) – and is the core of the word templates that were introduced in Chapter 5. In this constrained definition, collocation does not permit function words as in *participate in, impact on* as these are an aspect of colligation – a separate term for a separate notion. Neither are compound forms such as *strike off* (V), *airport lounge* (N), *well-deserved* (Adj) considered collocations. In fact, these are multi-word lexemes in their own right. This issue arose on p.111 in connection with delexical verb structures.

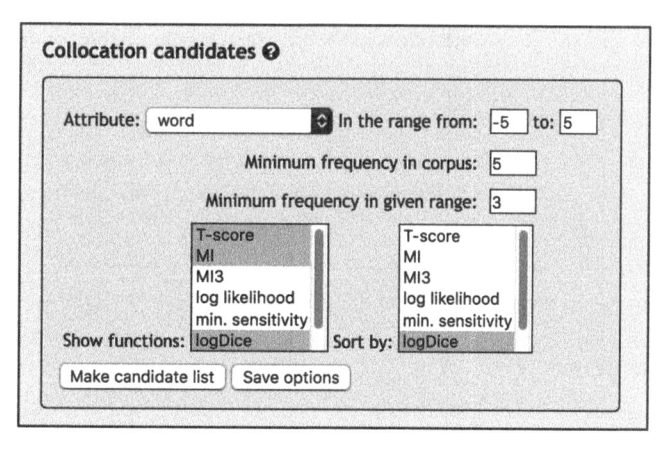

Since many of the linguistic patterns that revolve around collocation are more richly presented in word sketches, the subject of the next chapter, we will restrict ourselves here to some of the language questions that can be asked specifically of Sketch Engine's Collocation tool. Collocate lists can be generated for any mix of lemmas, word forms, phrases and parts of speech and within text types. The concordances that are returned from such searches provide the data from which collocation lists are built.

Question 274   **The Naked Gun! What else can be *naked* apart from people?**

> Before performing a search, make a list of words you would expect to occur significantly in the company of *naked*.

Using the BNC, perform a Simple Query for *naked* and when the concordance page appears, click the Collocation button in the left panel. This Collocation form allows you to customise the parameters for the collocation list. But for now, accept the default settings and click Make Candidate List. You will see words that *naked* clearly collocates with. Compare this with your own list.

In addition to body-related words, what other things can be *naked*?

As you look down the list of words, the data answers the question quite convincingly. Check in OPUS2 to see which of these *naked* collocations have literal or near translations in other languages.

Question 275   **What are the collocates of *open door policy*?**

Having only 16 hits in the BNC suggests how little open door policies were referred to in the BNC era, and predicts how little data we can expect. However, a search in the much larger LEXMCI corpus, for example, provides enough data to reveal its patterns of normal usage.

Click on the P beside an individual collocate to see the concordance. Quite revealing!

This is one example of how the collocation tool permits searches of multi-word units.

Collocation Candidates

The parameters you set affect not only the appearance and order of the list, but the actual content. Various linguists react to this fact in different ways. For example, Herbst (1996) called for collocates to be more sophisticated than lists sorted by frequency:

> The most frequent collocates of a word such as *house* include the determiners *the* and *of* and the verb *sell*, this is neither particularly surprisingly nor particularly interesting.

Fifteen years later, Groom, was arguing that:

> ... closed-class keywords can form a valid and even preferable basis for empirical linguistic research into specialized discourses (2010).

Thus, different linguistic fields and research goals make different uses of collocation lists. As we are about to see, the choices you make in setting the parameters are guided by the questions you ask. Exploring the effects of changing the parameters has on the resulting lists is time well spent.

Attribute

A dropdown list from which the type of item to be displayed is chosen. There are good reasons for choosing *word* or *lemma*, as a little experimentation will reveal.

Choosing Tag will generate a list of POS tags that occur in the set Range. Inevitably, there are many function words within a set span, so DT, CC and PP are among the most frequent in any frequency list.

Given that the TLC definition of *collocation* is lexically-oriented, these closed class function words instantiate colligation not collocation.

Range

Next to Attribute we see Range. The two figures express the distance from the node: a negative number is for items to the left and a positive one to the right. Consider the following example.

As we saw at the end of Ch.3 (p.67), *eagle* (lemma) occurs in the BNC 1,000 times[176]. If we set our range at -5 to +5, the program will collect the 10 tokens either side of all 1,000 lines. It then counts the recurring tokens from the 10,000 and presents them according to the **Attribute** you choose and in the order of frequency you specify in the **Sort by** box.

Much ink has been spilt debating the potential optimum ranges that will give the fairest general purpose list. "There is some consensus but no total agreement that significant collocates are usually found with a span of 4:4" (Stubbs 2001:29). Given the structures of English sentences, many words can occur between a node and its collocate, some of them being words in multi-word units. Given the nature of discourse, collocates also occur with pronouns. For example, this sentence contains three collocates of *exam*: *take place, give* and *sit*, only one of which is within the 4:4 range.:

> *The exams take place at your school and are given to you when you are ready to sit them.*

Furthermore, the issue of reference, as introduced on p.31 in connection with Shakespeare, makes it difficult to show that the verbs that *the playwright, Bill, the Bard* and *he* perform, are all actions of one person in one text.

Although there are some advances in anaphora recognition in corpus linguistics, our corpora have not yet been tagged to show pronoun references. It is therefore not possible to demonstrate that *sit* and *give* are collocates of *exams* when *them* is the referent. Range is a separate issue.

Question 276 **How far apart can a node and its collocates be?**

> The following query searches for between six and twelve intervening words. The **within <s/>** tag at the end ensures that the items occur in the same sentences.
>
> [lemma= "organi.e"][]{6,12}[lemma = "meeting"] within <s/>
>
> This yields 26 hits in the BNC, but without the *within sentence tag* there are 42[177]. Collocates do not typically appear across sentence boundaries, except in text linguistics which will have a different definition of collocation.

For specific purposes, ranges can be adjusted in the Candidates form. For example, in listing the objects of a verb, it is only necessary to list the items which follow it. We could allow for a determiner and an adjective to precede the noun: in the Range settings, we therefore set left 0 and right 3 or 4. On the other hand, to list the adverbs that collocate with an adjective, it is only necessary to list the items immediately to the left: in the Range settings we would set L1 and R0.

This screenshot has parameters set for the following question.

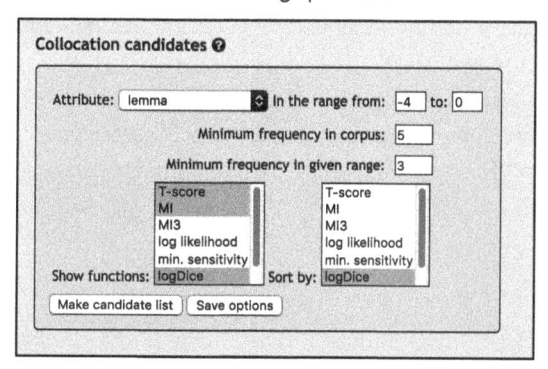

---

[176] http://ske.li/bnc_eagle_1000
[177] ske.li/bnc_organise_meeting_wide

Question 277 **Does *flying colours* refer to flags?**

Search for *fly colour* in Simple Query. Make a list of left collocates (Range -4 to 0) and see that the answer is a resounding no! What phrases does *flying colours* occur in? Can you therefore infer its meaning?

If you search in a corpus that has American spelling, make the search *fly colo*r*.

An internet image search finds a great many flying colours that are much more colourful than the idiom itself. Compare it also with *trooping the colour*, where the collocates clearly indicate what it refers to.

Functions

Functions in this context refers to the statistical processing of the collocates, which dramatically influences the content of the lists. We will consider here T-score, MI and logDice.

T-Score: "The t-score is a standard test to see if the results could be expected on the basis of chance" Charniak (1993: 122). The words that appear at the top of a T-score list are mostly function words, those that are common with any word, as noted by Herbst and Groom above. The now defunct COBUILD Corpus sampler website had this to say:

> T-score will get you significant collocates which have occurred frequently ("post office" "Washington Post" "post-war", "by post" "the post").

Mutual information as described in the original article by Church and Hanks (1990):

> MI compares the probability of observing x and y together (the joint probability) with the probabilities of observing x and y independently (chance). Joint probabilities, P(x,y), are estimated by counting the number of times that x is followed by y in a window of w words, fw (x,y), and normalizing by N. N is the size of the corpus.

> The window size parameter, *range*, allows us to look at different scales. Smaller window sizes will identify fixed expressions such as *bread and butter*, and other relations that hold over short ranges; larger window sizes will highlight semantic concepts and other relationships that hold over larger scales.

MI lists indicate that the most significant collocates are the words that are not necessarily common in the corpus, but are significant in the context (range) of this node. The items at the top of the MI lists are often rare, and being specific to the node makes them good candidates for *strong collocations*. The COBUILD Corpus sampler website again:

> MI (Mutual Information) will highlight the technical terms, oddities, weirdos, totally fixed phrases, etc. ("post mortem" "Laurens van der Post" "post-menopausal" "prepaid post" "post prepaid" "post-grad").

If a collocate appears in the top of both MI and T-score lists it is clearly a humdinger of a collocate, rock-solid, typical, frequent, strongly associated with its node word, recurrent, reliable, etc etc etc.[178].

LogDice: The LD list takes into account the grammatical relationships between pairs of words, which the other measures do not (Rychlý 2008). The software scours the corpus and generates so-called triples: [Word 1] [Gramrel] [Word 2], e.g. [versatile] [JJ-NN] [performer]. The node can be either Word 1 or 2. The list is then sorted according to the triples that contain the node.

> A Word Association Test consists of a list of words which are presented one at a time. For each word in the list you have to write down or say aloud the first word that comes to your mind. ... The word associations of normal adults are very unreveal-ing about their subconscious selves, and they show a surprisingly high degree of unoriginality.
> *(Meara 2009:6)*

This calculation does not take the size of the corpus into consideration, which permits comparison across corpora of different sizes, including subcorpora.

A list of collocates sorted by logDice column often contains words that tend to accord with word association data. While this is a casual observation awaiting further investigation, this coincidence is not true of T-score and only partially true of MI. Comparing psycholinguistic data, which word association is, with corpus-generated lexical statistics can inform our decisions about which ones to use in which situations. In the Edinburgh Association Thesaurus, the top associates of *eagle* most closely match logDice. For information about word association, see the text box on the previous page.

bird, golden, nest, hawk, comic, fly, star, wings, America, eye

Collocates of lemma *eagle*, Range -4 +4		
T-score	Mutual Information	logDice
the	Verreaux	owl
,	white-bellied	golden
.	white-tailed	Verreaux
and	Bubo	spotted
an	Callanish	Callanish
be	double-headed	birdie
of	eyrie	eagle
a	spotted	buzzard
golden	Aquila	bald
owl	chamois	tawny

Given that one swallow, or in this case *eagle*, does not a summer make, let's explore a possible general correlation between logDice and word associations.

Here are some of the single-word lexemes that we have explored so far in this book.

bold, wave, troubles, naked, exam, wonder, thatch, fish, positively, gross.

Draw up a four column table for each of the words that would like to study. Copy and paste say the first ten collocates from each of the columns (T score, MI, logDic).

Visit the Edinburgh Associations Thesaurus[179] and search for the words. In your fourth column paste word association data. Compare the list of associations with the lists of collocates. Does this influence your view of collocation statistics?

---

[178] Found on a website introducing the COBUILD Sampler (CCS): http://bit.ly/CCS_collocation. SKELL is the new CCS: skell.sketchengine.co.uk
[179] See here for WAT: http://www.eat.rl.ac.uk. In the Stimulus field, enter *eagle*.

In the table below, can you work out which noun these are the collocates of?

Write the column headings for the three statistical measures. Which of them is most useful in answering the question? You could add word associates to the last column.

.	SHOOTING	cause
be	teethe	trouble
the	Strife	serious
,	hamstring	lot
Have	waterworks	sport
in	bronchial	into
to	Ballater	worth
of	McManaman	get
that	Gender	stir
and	sinus	save

Question 278   **What do the top T-score items tell us about the adjective *eligible*?**

to be eligible, be eligible for something, be eligible to do something, etc.

Click **P** beside *be* in the collocate list and right sort the results. This word's patterns of normal usage almost jump off the page at you.

Compare this now with the top logDice items of *eligible*?

How many of the nouns in the list are described as *eligible*? If you are not sure which words are tagged as nouns, choose the Attribute *lempos* when making the list.

What do these two listings tell us about the attributive and predicative status of this adjective?

Question 279   **Is *inventing* something normally considered a positive act?**

Search for *invent** in Simple Query field. The wild card (*) extends the search from the lemma to the word family (see p.75).

Using the attribute *lempos* in the Collocation candidates form, make a list of collocates: logDice. Using your browser's Find, search for the adjectives, -j. Make three lists of them: (1) positive (2) negative (3) objective/factual. Does this answer the question?

In the Introduction, we discussed armchair linguists *inventing data* – very small quantities of it in comparison with corpus data. In the 40 concordances that enTenTen yields for this collocation[180], the semantic prosody emerges crystal clear from the company it keeps:

> *sloppy, be wary of, stupid, fraud, fabrication, manipulation, unjustified, liars, distort, to unnaturally hype, exploit, bypass validation check, to give the impression that, scientists become superstitious, discredit*

Note the several instances of *invent data storage*. Because this is a compound noun, *invent* is collocating with the multi-word lexeme, *data storage*. Be vigilant for this phenomenon – failure to recognise what is truly collocating can skew your interpretation.

---

[180] ske.li/ett_invent_data

Question 280 **What do we think of Edward Snowden?**

We here refers to the collective consciousness that is represented in the hundreds of documents in which he is mentioned in the enTenTen [2013] corpus. Compare this frequency with how frequently he is mentioned in enTenTen [2012].

Search for *Edward Snowden* and Save as Subcorpus. From this make a collocation list[181]. Scour the list for subjective, emotive terms like *hero, traitor*. Click on those you find to check how they are used. Beware litotes: there is no reason not to suspect that he is regarded as *no hero* or *no traitor*. Remember that *no* is unlikely at the top of a logDice or MI list of collocates. It may also be necessary to find out if *whistle blower* (hyphenated or not) is used emotively or objectively. Does any sense of a moral evaluation emerge from this community of idiolects? Does our corpus data indicate the extent to which Snowden's leaks have served or harmed public interest, in the words of those who write on the subject?

Hoey Procedure

Learners are known to react to their teacher's correction with, *but I've seen/heard it*, which deserves the response, *how often and in what contexts?*

From a book of papers entitled, *Teaching Collocation: Further Developments in the Lexical Approach*, (ed. Michael Lewis), comes:

> I was never sure whether the context was natural or typical. Unless one knows that the collocation one is learning is absolutely characteristic of the way the word is used, more than half the value one gets from learning the word in its context disappears.

So said Michael Hoey in 2000 (p.233). In order to consider something worth adding to our learning dossiers, we need to find out how typical it is, and a corpus can provide us with enough data to this end. It is also worth remembering that *Authenticity does not automatically entail typicality* (Gries 2008:425). In other words, we cannot say that a construction is representative just because it occurs in an authentic text.

How can we know if the language of a text we are reading contains enough patterns of normal usage to make it a worthy model for language learning? In the name of learning language from language, this is a very reasonable question to ask. To address this question empirically, we can find out if each chunk occurs significantly in a topic-related corpus or large general corpus. As you follow the next steps, you'll be doing the Hoey Procedure.

Here is one not overly long sentence from the BNC to work with:

Corp ex.135   *Large numbers of mentally handicapped people are willing and able to lead relatively independent lives if they are given the opportunities, support and encouragement they need.*

There are several ways to tackle this task.

---

[181] ske.li/ett_edward_snowden_colls

Search for each collocation using Simple Query with their lemmas, e.g. *lead life*. Write the number of times the chunks occur as lemmas and where appropriate, the exact word forms as they occur in the source sentence.

However, collocations are not necessarily contiguous, i.e. an adjacent pair. To search for these as collocations, instead of chunks, put one of the words in the appropriate field in the top section and the other word in Lemma Filter. To allow for words in between, set Window to ±3. Since collocates appear in either order so the lemma filter Window can be set to 'both'.

> **Original Concordance:** appears at the bottom of the left panel if you have refined your concordance. Click this to return to the original concordance.

A third approach is to choose the semantically richer word of each pair and create its collocation list.

Compare the above approaches, as you detail your findings beside these collocations:

> *large numbers*
>
> *relatively independent*
>
> *mentally handicapped*
>
> *give opportunity*
>
> *give support*
>
> *lead lives*
>
> *give encouragement*
>
> *willing and able*

Willing and able is actually a binomial, not a collocation, at least not in TLC terms.

Regardless of how you observe and explore language, it is difficult not to see that sentences in naturally occurring language contain a good many prefabricated chunks of language. The point is that as we produce language, we don't select individual items from our linguistic repertoire; rather, we co-select sets of items. *Co-select* is a key word in studies of idiomatic language use. This is the thrust of the Idiom Principle mentioned in the Introduction. As Bolinger said in 1974, "speakers do at least as much remembering as they do putting together."

We have arrived at this point on the basis of one sentence. Experiment also on sentences from your own writing and on samples written by learners. To make similar observations about spoken language, find transcribed speech in corpora using Text Types. You can also use the LEC of spoken language.

Observing polysemy

For distinctions between polysemy and homonymy, see p.50 and p.75.

Collocation lists do not distinguish between the meanings of polysemous words. On one hand, this might be seen as a shortcoming; on the other, this is data indicating that a word is in fact polysemous.

For example, the first logDice collocates of *bat* include:

> *baseball* and *cricket* pointing to *bat* as sporting equipment.
>
> *eyelid*. Click **P** here [182]. What POS is *bat* in this phrase? What is the phrase? It suggests a phlegmatic or indifferent attitude, perhaps even coquettish.
>
> *moth* invoking the nocturnal, flying creature meaning of *bat*.

[182] ske.li/bnc_bat_eyelid

In these cases, it only took one collocate to distinguish the various meanings of *bat*, part of which involves its part of speech. Not only is *bat* polysemous but it undergoes conversion. This is not unlike the minimal context needed to disambiguate the word *bar,* as we saw at the beginning of Ch.5.

Question 281 **Can you tell which meaning or use of your search word (node) is intended when it is paired with a collocate?**

Create collocation lists for some of the following polysemous words and consider the relationships between the nodes and their collocates.

chip, bank, lecture, retire, peer, advance, court, wave, frame, perfect.

Click on the **P** to see the concordances of the node and the collocate.

Text Types may be used to filter the original search. For example, the collocates of *wave* when filtered by natural science in David Lee's Classification has as the top logDice collocates *collide, gravitational, impulsive, polarization, electromagnetic, plane, align, collision* [183] whereas in a full BNC search, they are *tidal, wave, goodbye, collide, gravitational, shock, radio, flag, arm* [184]. As we saw on p.125, where general words are also field specific, it is the context of the field that disambiguates them.

Question 282 **How is the word *evidence* used differently in research and in law?**

Search for *evidence* and limit the text type to Law in David Lee's Classification. Then produce a list of collocates [185]. Repeat in another tab with some of the research fields in his classification. Can you account for the similarities and differences in the lists?

Question 283 **When a word is polysemous, what activates its meanings in context?**

Take the great insult, *He wouldn't give you a wave if he owned the ocean.* Read the following internal monologue as we talk this through.

Wave can refer to sound and light waves, waves crashing on a beach, gestures of hello and goodbye.

And we have the ditransitive structure: someone gives someone something.

And in this case it's a delexical verb, *to give a wave*. What else do people give: a sound, light or water? No, not really.

Can you give a gesture? Well, yes, we say we do. The verb could have been *show*, but it's not.

Who wouldn't give you a wave?

Someone who doesn't like giving. And the worst kind are those who are rich. Someone who has an ocean full of waves and still won't give you a wave.

Oh, so not the gesture now, rather those white frothy things crashing on the beach?

Yes, it's now another type of wave.

How do you know?

---

[183] ske.li/bnc_colls_wave_natsc
[184] ske.li/bnc_colls_wave
[185] ske.li/bnc_evidence_law_colls

I've seen him at his stingiest and I'm exploiting this hyperbole to exaggerate this unenviable trait.

So why is it a conditional structure?

He couldn't give you one of its waves because he doesn't own the ocean, or because such waves are quite intangible. He wouldn't give you one of its waves because he's downright stingy.

And do you kill all your jokes by analysing them out of existence?

You asked about polysemy – I am blameless.

Lexical Support

Collocation lists typically include words with similar connotations. We find that similar words are used near each other to reinforce the impression being created. Who could limit the expression of their enthusiasm for a footie goal, a performance, a gift, etc, to a single adjective? Or for oneself, as we see in the first corpus example here.

Corp ex.136   *It's only cos I'm handsome debonair suave sophisticated and fucking dead horny and hunky.*

Corp ex.137   *Come in and slobber over our fat ugly bimbos, bawled a fat ugly young man in jeans and a windbreaker ...*

Such strings of expressive words create a highly expressive image, the result of lexical support as was mentioned in relation to *pry* on p.62.

The difference between connotation and lexical support is that the former is a property of a word: the communal understanding of the connotations of a word in isolation can be shown through word association tasks. However, speakers and writers achieve their rhetorical effect by co-selecting words with similar connotations, and this adds up to lexical support.

Question 284   **Does lexical support manifest across texts, or hover around certain words?**

Choose some expressive words with the same POS – the Thesaurus tool may come in handy. Then make collocation lists of them. To make the lists consistent, once you have chosen your collocation list parameters, e.g. Attribute, Range, click on **Save Options.**

Decide if they keep company with words that support or reinforce their 'tone'. Some lists will offer a great many words with similar connotations, while others contain only a few.

Here are some candidate words that we have examined so far in this book.

troubles, naked, positively, gross, broken, harbour, concern, clench

To answer the question concerning text, it is necessary to explore the vocabulary of text types, e.g. espionage situations, cautionary tales, family celebrations, emotive pleas regarding climate change or preserving species. This can be done by making subcorpora or your own corpora, as described later in this book.

Question 285   **What do the collocates of *bachelor* in its *unmarried man* sense suggest about being one?**

After searching and noting the features of *bachelor*, compare them with those of *spinster*. Note especially *eligible* – does it collocate with both?

Even if you can imagine an *eligible spinster*, the English language only does so ironically and rarely. As they say, "an unmarried woman has a past, whereas an unmarried man has a future", as sexist as that sounds. Perhaps there is an analogy with Jack Kerouac's (pictured) observation in *On the Road* (1957):

Nothing behind me, everything ahead of me, as is ever so on the road.

1957 – what a year!

Kerouac *On the road*

Firth *Papers in Linguistics*

Chomsky *Syntactic Structures*

Skinner *Verbal Behaviour*

Your Notes

Chapter 11   Word Sketches

As the Sketch Engine website describes it, a word sketch is a one-page, automatic, corpus-derived summary of a word's grammatical and collocational behaviour[186]. A word sketch contains dozens of words – it is fascinating to observe that every word keeps so much regular company, although by this stage of our story, this can hardly come as a surprise. For anyone working in the Neo-Firthian tradition, the word sketch is an invaluable tool.

A word sketch is a table of collocates distributed into columns based on the grammatical relationship they have with the node, e.g. verbs used when *symptom* is the subject, and another column of verbs when it is the object. Significant prepositions have their own columns, e.g. *symptom* **of** *depression*, *patient* **with** *symptom*.

Whereas a list of collocates consists of lexical and function words that are presented in alphabetical or frequency order as the simple co-occurrences in a predefined window of words, a word sketch presents multiple lists of collocates that are the result of a special type of shallow parsing and statistical computing using the logDice score (Rychlý 2008).

A word sketch may be seen as a table of a word's paradigmatic and syntagmatic relations, which as noted on p.14, are represented by the vertical and horizontal readings of concordances respectively.

symptom (noun)
British National Corpus (TreeTagger) freq = **3,652** (32.32 per million)

object_of			subject_of			adj_subject_of			modifier			modifies		
	1,263	2.80		672	2.00		183	5.20		1,596	1.40		165	0.10
relieve	25	8.41	persist	12	8.11	suggestive	9	10.08	gastrointestinal	73	10.17	onset	10	10.10
alleviate	14	8.11	disappear	11	7.00	severe	9	9.25	withdrawal	58	10.08	score	25	8.24
suffer	29	7.28	occur	13	5.84	attributable	8	8.96	respiratory	25	8.64	picture	6	5.11
experience	24	7.23	include	27	5.66	free	13	7.29	obstructive	18	8.45	control	12	4.95
exhibit	11	7.22	appear	13	5.11	similar	15	7.19	bowel	26	8.35			
exacerbate	6	6.89	arise	6	5.02	present	6	6.24	dyspeptic	15	8.24			

and/or			pp_of			pp_obj_of			pp_obj_with			pp_in		
	554	1.20		682	3.60		580	3.00		138	4.40		80	0.80
sign	115	11.20	disease	50	9.22	onset	37	10.02	hospital	6	9.12	patient	17	7.76
diagnosis	8	8.14	poisoning	13	8.98	severity	29	9.89	present	14	9.07	case	6	4.55
treatment	10	7.16	depression	17	8.94	duration	22	9.00	patient	34	8.38			
disease	9	6.82	anxiety	17	8.93	relief	9	8.54	associate	7	5.29	pp_obj_to		
patient	7	6.39	stress	18	8.77	recurrence	8	8.49	deal	7	4.88		63	1.20
pain	6	6.37	reflux	9	8.60	prevalence	12	8.46				lead	8	4.32

[186] ske.li/wiki_wsketches

To obtain a word sketch, it is not necessary to perform any kind of query. Click on Word Sketch in the top left panel. It is then enough to type in your lemma and select the POS, or leave the default **auto** to choose it.

We will now explore the word sketch of *symptom*. Note that this word is used infrequently in the singular as you can see from a list of its word forms [187].

The first column in the word sketch of *symptom* shows the verbs of which it is the object. Thus we have the Verb + Noun collocations, e.g. *something alleviates symptom(s), something produces symptom(s)*. In the following BNC examples, the underlined phrases are the subjects about which the following verb + noun provides new information. This typically acts as predicate, as mentioned on p.27.

Corp ex.138   *The difficulty here is that simple lack of stress may also **alleviate the symptoms**.*

Corp ex.139   *Other alcohols such as wines did not **produce symptoms**. Gong et al reported that it was the congeners in alcohol and not alcohol itself that **produced symptoms** in asthmatic patients.*

Question 286   **What alleviates symptoms?**

People, actions or products? Click on the hyperlinked (underlined) frequency number beside *alleviate* and left sort the concordance page. Look at the subjects of *alleviate* to answer this question.

Try to complete this word template from the data, i.e. what sets of things occupy the subject role?

[_____] alleviates symptoms.

The second most significant verb here is *relieve*. The fact that both of these words have the Latin *levis* at their core might be of interest. For more on this, see these words at Etymology online [188]. *Alleviating symptoms* appears in EEBO, but curiously, only in the late 1700s [189].

Allay is also etymologically related. Is *allay symptoms* a collocation? What does *allay* collocate with?

The second gramrel column shows the verbs which follow *symptom*, i.e. when symptom is the subject. What do symptoms do? For example,

symptom(s) persist

symptom(s) disappear

It is worth observing the transitivity of the verbs in this column; when transitive, you can see their typical objects when they form S V O structures. In the case of *symptom*, however, the verbs which have *symptom* as the subject are rarely transitive.

Question 287   **How do sentences continue after intransitive verbs?**

Click on the frequencies of the verbs and right sort the concordances. Some patterns of normal usage emerge.

The transitive construction, *symptoms include something*, is an exception here, as we are about to see. Click on the hyperlinked frequency.

---

[187] ske.li/bnc_symptom_wordforms
[188] http://www.etymonline.com
[189] http://ske.li/eebo_alleviate_symptoms

Is the use of *include* similar to *for example*? Do *such as, etc, e.g.* appear in the context of *include*? This use of *include* has a textual function – *symptom* is not an Actor (in Halliday's terms e.g. 2004:58) performing an action in this context.

The third column shows predicative adjectives (Corp ex.140), i.e. those which give new information about *symptom*. The verbs in this structure are copular – mostly the verb *to be*, even if ellipted. This role of *predicate* is the same as the *Predicate* mentioned above.

Corp ex.140 *In general symptoms are **mild** and admission to hospital is necessary in only a few cases.*

The modifier column shows attributive adjectives. Their discourse function is quite different from predicative adjectives. An attributive adjective and its noun form a noun phrase, which can occupy a variety of syntactic slots. According to Chafe (1994), attributive adjectives have an important place in text flow because they provide sufficient or even unique definition and categorization to nouns and increase their contextual salience.

The following examples show three of these syntactic roles.

Subject

Corp ex.141 ***Severe withdrawal symptoms*** *(delirium tremens) are acute panic, delusions, exhaustion and trembling to the point of seizure.*

Corp ex.142 *There is evidence to suggest that **withdrawal symptoms** include heightened irritability, a tendency to drink too much and increased susceptibility to illness and depression.*

Object

Corp ex.143 *I'm experiencing **the expected withdrawal symptoms**.*

Corp ex.144 *On the other hand, few had witnessed another user undergoing **withdrawal symptoms**.*

Complement

Corp ex.145 *… it is part of dealing with problems in their lives, coping with stress, that part of that is also **withdrawal symptoms** from the nicotine, and …*

Corp ex.146 *It is not long before their imaginative faculties are reactivated and word-processing becomes **a universal withdrawal symptom**.*

The Modifies column contains nouns that often form compound nouns that start with *symptom*, e.g. *symptom control, symptom relief*. This takes us back to Compounding as we saw in the Taxonomy of Morphology (p.73).

The Modifies column also contains nouns that occur in binomials and trinomials, e.g. *symptoms, diagnosis and treatment*.

> Since each POS has its own syntactic relationships, it is inevitable that word sketches for nouns are structured differently from verbs, adjectives, etc

False friends

False friends is a term that refers to pairs of words that are the same, or almost the same in two languages but whose meanings and/or usage differ. They are a source of error in non-native speaker language and are an example of first language negative transfer, or interference. The French equivalent, *faux amis* (as mentioned in Question 17) is sometimes used in English with this meaning.

Let us make a word sketch of *sympathetic* so as to observe the following features:

Question 288 **How many things can you learn about *sympathetic* and about English in general from studying the word in this format?**

Admittedly a broad question, but its Sketch reveals:

Col 1: who and what is sympathetic

Col 2: how people are sympathetic

Col 3: what things are said to be sympathetic

Col 4: when joined by *and* or *or*, the other adjective maybe lending support to the notion of *sympathetic* or adding something new?

Col 5: someone or something is sympathetic to your ....

Col 6: we *feel* sympathetic, we *seem* sympathetic, we ...

Col 7: we can make someone sympathetic to ...

Do the words in each of the columns fall into any semantic groups? Look at the lists anew, and see which words you would group under the same headings. Even without thinking of a heading, some semantic notions are likely to form in your mind.

In the process of answering these questions for each column of the *sympathetic* word sketch, it is possible that your idea of this word has changed, especially if your first language has a cognate form with a different usage, e.g. *sympatisch, simpatico, sympathique, sympatický*. In any case, answering the questions forms connections between words you already know and new words – the process is said to strengthen connections in your brain.

Investigate some other false friends that you are familiar with.

Question 289 **Does *nuanced* have a place in your world view?**

Not all vocabulary is utilitarian. Hundreds of questions ago, the adjective *nuanced* flickered in and out of our kaleidoscopic investigation into English when we were considering the issue of rare words and phrases such as *germane*.

Boutique words do not generate large word sketches, nevertheless the handful of collocates in every column of *nuanced* gives a clear indication of its connotations and usage. Do you know any higher frequency words that do the same job as *nuanced*?

> There are no certainties, even grammatical ones ... only that which bears the imprint of our choice, our taste, our uncertainty, our desire and our weakness can be beautiful.
>
> From a letter by Proust quoted in de Botton (1997:104)

Question 290 **Which column gives the clearest positive associations of *wicked*?**

In Question 189 (p.127), we saw the word *wicked* being used positively in the BNC. Was this someone's idiolect, a group's slang usage, or something else?

The BNC word sketch of *wicked* reveals nothing positive about it. However, the more recent enTenTen word sketch certainly does. Compare them and consider this diachronic new direction. Do the collocates suggest that the earlier meaning has been lost altogether?

Do combinations like *deliciously wicked* and *wicked grin* change some aspect or nuance of the meaning of *wicked*? Does some element of the positive word weaken the negativity of *wicked*? Does it makes something bad less bad?

Do you think that this exemplifies language change as the student was enthusing about on p.127?

Question 291 **Do the most significant words that accompany *humdinger* reveal its meaning?**

We saw this word on p.166 in reference to collocation statistics in a sentence that also exhibits lexical support in an amusing way.

Make a word sketch of *humdinger* in, say, LEXMCI. Our intuition about this word's frequency is borne out by this word sketch. We can see that it is most frequently preceded by *real* and followed by *of a,* sometimes both. We can also observe other such features that give you confidence in using it, or even choosing not to.

How do we know who "He" is in this corpus extract?

Corp ex.147   *Or maybe He'd suddenly come up with a real* **humdinger** *of an 11th commandment,*

and/or

The second row of the *symptom* word sketch starts with **and/or**, which is a much undersung lexical relationship given the high frequencies it records with most words. *Symptom(s)* is accompanied 115 times by *sign(s),* left or right, joined in context by *and* or *or*. These conjunctions are not linking separate clauses, rather they are linking a pair of items that have a syntactic role. Semantically, the two items are often co-hyponyms, as we observed in the context of the Thesaurus.

Question 292   **Do the two words occur in the same order each time?**

Click on *sign*'s 115 to see the concordance page. In this case, the two words do not have a preferred order, but in many such phrases there is only one order.

Check this with some other words in the and/or column.

Question 293   **Why do people use *student* and *pupil* in the same syntactic slot?**

In a word sketch of *student*, click on *pupil* in the *and/or* column. Do they always occur in the same order? If they do, we have a candidate for a chunk.

If the words were true synonyms, it would not be necessary to use both, so what does this imply about people's conception of students and pupils? Some columns in the word sketches of *student* and *pupil* give some idea as to how differently they are used, which in turns implies why one word would be chosen over the other during actual language production.

Multi-word sketches

Multi-word sketches take us from collocation to collocations of collocations.

In the entire BNC word sketch of *symptom*, only one word has a frequency count higher than *sign* when sorted by significance (see *Sorting* below). These two words are the only ones in the whole word sketch in bold. Click on **sign** to see multi-word units that are formed with *symptom* and *sign*. There are four with *counteract*, one of which occurs in:

Corp ex.148   *This is the reverse of the conventional approach, which uses its remedies and drugs to* **counteract** *the symptoms and signs of disease.*

While there are very few words in this multi-word sketch which occur more than twice, this data can still inform writers of existing structures, even if there are not enough of them to be counted as patterns. With more frequent words and larger corpora, the multi-word sketches are richer, as we observe below.

Size matters

There is no data like more data – Sinclair (2001:ix)

Small corpora are preferred for genre studies and large corpora are preferred for observations across a broad spectrum of a language, and for obtaining enough instances of less common structures.

An important issue in language learning and teaching is prioritizing vocabulary. The first 3,000 words of core English are not negotiable and dealing with their multiple uses in their various structures deserves careful consideration. What is studied beyond this 3,000 essentially involves topic-based vocabulary, i.e. the words and phrases that articulate topics, and the functional language that articulates the genres of the field. We will develop this in Chapter 13 when we make our own corpora.

Symptom occurs almost exclusively in medical texts in the BNC. It occurs 3,653 times (32.3 HPM), which is why only a small number of multi-word sketches can be generated. However, in enTenTen it occurs almost 75 thousand times, which is 10 times less frequent when normalized: 3.2 HPM, yet dozens of multi-word sketches can be generated. This is a strong argument against the "curse of quantity" referred to on p.19.

The HPMs for *condom* in BNC and enTenTen are not very different: 4.5 and 5.8 respectively. Yet, more than 132 thousand occurrences of *condom* in enTenTen means that many multi-word sketches can be generated[190].

> [man | partner] uses a condom during [anal | extramarital] sex
>
> man (should | has to | always) use a condom or abstain from sex

Square brackets enclose syntactic elements and parenthesis indicate frequent though optional items.

One's ears might prick up upon finding that in the **PP on** column, *condoms* are more frequent *on banana* than *on penis*. To be fair, if we take into consideration other words doing duty for *penis*, its lexical set wins hands down[191]. This returns us to the issue of Reference, as exemplified by *Shakespeare* (p.31) and *exam* under Range (p.164).

We learn so much more from corpus study than mere language!

Advanced Options

By clicking on the Advanced options link, a submenu appears, offering many useful refinements. For example, the option to make a word sketch using data from one of the subcorpora you have created is quite valuable.

Select gramrels: ☐ All	☐ adj_comp	☐ adj_comp_of	☐ adj_subject	☐ adj_subject_of
	☐ and/or	☐ infin_comp	☐ ing_comp	☐ it+
	☐ modifier	☐ modifies	☐ np_adj_comp	☐ np_adj_comp_of
	☐ object	☐ object_of	☐ part_*	☐ part_intrans
	☐ part_trans	☐ passive	☐ possessed	☐ possessor
	☐ pp_*	☐ predicate	☐ predicate_of	☐ pro_object
	☐ pro_possessor	☐ pro_subject	☐ reflexive	☐ subject
	☐ subject_of	☐ wh_comp		

---

[190] ske.li/ett_use_condom_during
[191] Should you be looking for 1,300 English words doing this duty, see *The Lover's Tongue*, Mark Morton (2004).

Towards the bottom of the Advanced options, it is possible to choose which gramrels you want in your word sketch. As we have already seen, **All** is the default.

Prepositions in word sketches

Word sketches contain prepositional phrase columns headed **pp**...., as can be seen in the second row of the word sketch of *symptom*. This is an extremely valuable resource for studying and teaching an aspect of foreign language learning that continues to dog even the most advanced learners.

Let us take a look now at the word sketch of *decline* (noun). Generate its word sketch in enTenTen [2012].We will be using this one in several forthcoming questions.[192] And click on Less data in the left panel. Clicking on a word in pp-column shows the node, the preposition and the collocate:

> pp + preposition shows nouns that follow the node, e.g. *decline in revenue, decline into madness, decline of civilization/civilisation*
>
> pp + obj + preposition shows nouns that precede the node e.g. *cause of decline, result in decline, contribute to decline, responsible for decline*

Question 294   **Who or what is responsible for a *decline*?**

> What nouns are on the left of *responsible for decline*? Click on the number beside *responsible* in the *for* column. This opens the concordance page. To find the subject nouns, we can make a collocation list with a range of -7 to -4 and choose lempos as the Attribute. Using CTRL F in the browser for –n, the nouns to the left of responsible for decline can easily be identified.
>
> A word template emerges, e.g.
>
> [habitat] conditions are responsible for the decline in [productivity | population]

Question 295   **Is *is responsible for* the standard pattern of this adjective?**

> In the examples above, it is used predicatively, and with *for*. Is this its canonical form?
>
> In the word sketch of *responsible*, which column has the highest black number? This overall frequency count goes a long way to answering the question.
>
> Another question can be answered by considering why **adjective_subject** is the first column presented. Click on some of the frequency counts (blue) – an important word order observation can be made here.

Bilingual Word Sketches

In the left panel of word sketches in the enTenTen [2012] corpus, there are several languages which are available for making bilingual word sketches.

Click on German in the *decline* (noun) word sketch in this corpus. At the top of the page, the *best match* German equivalent is shown and the collocates on this page relate to it. However, *decline* translates into English variously, and Sketch Engine offers these underneath. Clicking on them generates new lists of collocates.

Since the English list does not change, it is clear that the English-German lists are not side-by-side translation lists. Rather, the lists are ordered by frequency or significance (see p.183). This is language data that users can work with to answer their questions.

---

[192] http://ske.li/ett_decline_ws

Prepositions bound and free

Cosme and Gilquin (2008: 259) observed that prepositions fall somewhere between grammar and the lexicon – they are often ignored by grammars and are regarded as lexically empty by lexicographers. The very natural process of chunking text reveals that prepositions are often components of lexical structures that take precedence over grammatical ones (Sinclair and Mauranen 2006:147).

For teaching and studying, a useful division of prepositions is those whose attachment is to the preceding word (left looking) and those which launch a prepositional phrase (right looking). These are referred to as **bound** and **free** respectively. Here are some examples of **bound** uses of preposition. It is often the case, that these prepositions have little independent meaning (see LGSWE p.74).

Nouns	an alternative **to**, a comment **on**, a decline **in**
Adjectives	be responsible **for**, be present **in**, be suitable **for**
Verbs	enter **into**, stumble **across**, be biased **towards**

Word sketches of these words testify to the significance of these prepositions. For example, the word sketch of *decline in* shows over 90,000 items in enTenTen [2012]. This is far more frequent than it being the object of verbs in a standard S V O construction as in *streamlining* ➔ *offset* ➔ *decline*:

Corp ex.149   *The streamlining has helped offset a 12 percent decline in Yahoo's revenue through the first nine months of this year.*

The second most frequent preposition after *decline* is *of*: Noun phrase of Noun phrase being the common pattern referred to several times already. There is a rapid decline after this, as the following screenshot shows.

The phrases that **free prepositions** launch are typically adverbials expressing circumstances such as manner, place and time.

Manner	caused **by** negligence, learn **through** experience, pay **through** the nose
Place	stroll **around** the garden, stroll **into** town, climb **through** the window
Time	stroll **before** breakfast, live **through** the winter

Question 296   **Do *decline*'s free prepositions launch adverbial phrases?**

This screenshot does not derive from a word sketch, but from a frequency list. Either make the list and click on the P beside each line to see what happens after the preposition, or use the PP gramrels in the word sketch.

With high frequency verbs in particular e.g. *get, make, take,* many of the prepositions are particles in phrasal verbs, which as we are about to see, is clearly accounted for in word sketches. Frequency lists and collocation lists do not make this explicit.

While bound and free is not a watertight distinction, it is

word	word	Frequency
P | N decline	in	14,797
P | N decline	of	6,010
P | N declined	by	1,324
P | N declines	in	1,188
P | N declined	in	1,167
P | N declined	to	813
P | N declined	from	626
P | N Decline	of	520
P | N decline	as	466
P | N decline	from	465
P | N declining	in	397
P | N decline	since	393
P | N declining	to	378
P | N decline	by	352
P | N decline	for	348

a very useful way of thinking about prepositions. As learners of foreign languages know, any help with prepositions is welcome.

This bipartite division often accounts for the salience of a preposition with a particular word or a set of words. The two-volume work, *COBUILD Grammar patterns* (1998 a-b) uses corpus data extensively to assemble sets of words that are in the same grammar pattern, about half of which are associated with prepositions. These patterns are form-meaning pairs, known elsewhere as constructions. With corpora at our fingertips and questions in our minds, we can make these observations ourselves and develop our word knowledge from word to collocation to chunks and templates.

Question 297 **How do we find a specific phrasal verb through word sketches?**

Let's try this example. Enter *carry* into the word sketch search form (BNC). Then search for the particle, *away*, using a browser search (CTRL F).

As mentioned above, **bold** words in word sketches are clickable. Thus, when you click on the particle(s) in bold, you get a word sketch for the phrasal verb. If there is enough data, something in its word sketch might also be bold. This is much more likely in large corpora.

(a) carry ➔ off ➔ prize

(b) carry ➔ out ➔ maintenance work.

part_trans	5,170	52.20
out	4,741	11.43
off	174	7.66
away	43	7.43
through	29	7.42
around	35	7.32
over	22	6.60
along	13	6.28
down	44	5.89
up	66	4.97

This screenshot from the word sketch of *carry* contains the particles with which it forms transitive phrasal verbs. There is another table in the full word sketch with the particles that form intransitive phrasal verbs with *carry*.

Question 298 **Are there other 'synonymous' verbs that can be used with the objects of *carry out*?**

For example, we *carry out work, task, survey, investigation*. The word sketches of these nouns shows many verbs of which they are the objects. The question asks if the meaning of *carried out* can be realized using different verbs. It is therefore necessary to explore word sketches of these nouns.

Word combinations are constrained by contextual and semantic factors and become matters of convention through exposure (input). And as we use them (output), the priming is strengthened in our own minds (intake) and across the language at large. In de Beaugrande's words, such combinations bear the stamp of collective approval (2.16 1991).

Question 299 **Is there any correlation between the transitivity and separability of phrasal verbs?**

As mentioned above, the word sketch of a verb includes tables of transitive and intransitive particles. In the case of *carry*, several particles appear in both tables. Click on them and see if the particles are always, sometimes or never separated.

Sorting Word Sketches

In the screenshot of *symptom* at the beginning of this chapter, the collocates are sorted according to logDice, the right column of numbers. For example, *alleviate* is the most significant verb which has *symptom* as its object, thus *alleviate symptom(s)* is at the top.

Word sketch collocates can be sorted using two statistics. The **Sort by** button in the left panel toggles the lists between frequency and significance scores. When the columns are sorted according to frequency, the blue numbers are in descending order; when sorted by significance, the black numbers are in descending order. Words occurring fewer than five times are indicated in grey and they remain grey, regardless of the sorting.

The differences in the lists seem to be more striking for nouns e.g. *examination*. Which of these sets of verbs are the strong and which are the light verb collocates of *examination*?

> resit, undergo, pass, retake, conduct
>
> take, pass, have, sit require, make

Yes, the semantically richer verbs are at the top of the significance sorts and semantically lighter verbs, often factotum, are at the top of frequency sorts, making different but complementary data. The lighter verbs collocate with a wider range of nouns than rich, strong verbs. Comparing the text types of strong and weak collocations reveals information that is important to word choice. The lists are also capable of stimulating ideas when writing.

By the way, does *exam* have the same word sketch as *examination*? Why is this so, or not so?

Make similar observations of other words from various parts of speech.

Question 300   Are nouns more often subjects than objects?

Firstly, create word sketches of some nouns of interest to you. The numbers at the top of the subject and object columns indicate how many items it found.

Then be more methodical in your selection of nouns: use hypernyms and co-hyponyms. For example, people (boy, pedestrian), jobs (baker), every day objects (car, shirt, library), abstractions (simulation, irony), factotum (fact, process). See Question 91 for other categories.

Do you notice any patterns? What do you learn from these observations?

Clustering

The Clustering button in the left panel of word sketches uses the Thesaurus tool algorithms to group words with similar properties into clusters. The degree of success varies, as described in the section on the Thesaurus (p.70).

Question 301   What things *indicate* in academic prose?

In other words, what are the subjects of this verb?

In the word sketch form, enter *indicate* and *verb*. Using Advanced Options, choose the subcorpus relevant to this query.

At the bottom of this form, select from GramRels *Subject* only. Click the Show Word Sketch button, then Clustering in the left panel.

Question 302   The phrasal verb, *blow up,* is quite polysemous – what things blow up?

Before asking the corpus, ask your intuition: make a list of things that blow up, and group them. Repeat the *indicate* steps, including the use of the Clustering button to group similar items. This is what lumpers and splitters do when creating definitions.

Then compare its subjects when it is transitive, i.e. someone/something blows up someone/something.

See Question 144 for finding phrasal verbs through standard searches, and Question 297 for observing phrasal verbs in word sketches.

Question 303 **Who or what *analyses*?**

Using enTenTen, use the word sketch tool to search for the verb, *analyse*. At the bottom, Advanced Options, choose **Subject** only in Gramrels. Then in the word sketch, select **More data** and cluster it.

Word Sketches and Lexicography

> James Murray, editor of the **Oxford English Dictionary** from 1879 to his death in 1915, realised that for dictionaries to get good coverage of a language, they needed very large amounts of data and tools to support finding all the words and phrases in them.
>
> Murray resorted to an army of volunteers to gather twenty million slips – examples of words in use, with a sentence written out, with details of where it had been found, on an index card. These were then filed under the word being exemplified, so when he started work on the word, he would go to the filing system, find all the slips for it, and use them as the basis for the entry. (Adapted from Kilgarriff et.al 2015)
>
> *The Surgeon of Crowthorne* by Simon Winchester (1998) is a historical biography that deals with Murray and one of its most prolific early contributors. It is subtitled, *A Tale of Murder, Madness and the Love of Words*.

Word sketches were developed with lexicography in mind, and if we reflect on the ramifications of the patterns that emerge around *sympathetic* (p.178), it is not difficult to see how useful such structured data is to dictionary making. They permit emphases on frequency, collocation and phraseology, variation, lexis in grammar and on authenticity (see Hunston 2002:96).

Contemporary lexicographers use corpus data to create definitions of words: the result is a word-by-word description of the language according to the findings in the corpus chosen or created for the purpose. The alternative, traditional practice relied on the personal linguistic intuition of the lexicographers and their relationships with existing dictionaries. Instead of reflecting current usage, pre-corpus dictionaries prescribe how words should be used and are generally conservative in nature. Thus we have had both prescriptive and descriptive dictionaries, but the latter are inexorably in the ascendant. The most authoritative English dictionary, the Oxford English Dictionary, predates electronic corpora. For a summary of its construction, see the text box.

Hanks, one of England's most important lexicographers, has developed some useful procedures that use collocation and colligation in the process of formulating definitions. He also happens to be half of the team, Church and Hanks, that devised the highly influential collocation statistic, Mutual Information (MI) as we saw on p.166.

The first of these procedures involves verb patterns, which can be seen at Hanks's website, *Pattern Dictionary of English Verbs* (PDEV). Go to the site[193] and sort by patterns. The first thing to notice is the number of patterns that verbs have. How many patterns do the top verbs have? Which verbs have many patterns, and which have few? For example, *follow* has 20 and *achieve* has one. The next thing to notice is the structure of each entry.

This screenshot depicts one pattern of *follow*. The subjects and objects are hypernyms, derived from the CPA Ontology, which is linked from the PDEV site.

1	*Pattern:* **Human 1** *or* **Animal 1** *or* **Vehicle 1 follows** **Human 2** *or* **Animal 2** *or* **Vehicle 2**	6.4%
	Implicature: Human 1 *or* Animal 1 *or* Vehicle 1 moves in the same direction as that selected by Human 2 *or* Animal 2 or the driver of Vehicle 2	...More data
	Example: They cluster around him in a dense shoal and **follow** him as he moves about.	FrameNet

[193] http://www.pdev.org.uk

Hanks's approach involves analysing word sketches of BNC data to reveal the syntactic (syntagmatic) patterns of a word. Most instantiate literal uses, while others figurative and metaphorical. He refers to these as Norms and Exploitations, respectively.

It is crucial to our understanding of language that we recognise that the meanings of words come not only from the central meaning(s) of words themselves, but from the patterns in which they operate. This is why vocabulary cannot be studied separately from its grammar patterns, its patterns of normal usage. This relates directly to Halliday's grammar-vocabulary continuum first mentioned in the Introduction.

From these patterns, data-based definitions are written. As we have seen, verbs are the pivots around which clauses operate. The PDEV site has set a target of 5,602 *All Verbs.* Hanks (2013:33) argues that there will be comparatively few new verbs added to the language. Nouns make up the bulk of the word types in a language and new nouns are of three types: proper names, technical terminology and multi-word expressions. Most of the recent coinages we saw on p.131 are nouns.

A pattern dictionary of English verbs obviously does not deal with noun patterns. However, Book 2 of COBUILD Grammar Patterns, deals with patterns of nouns and adjectives, but not as full lexicogrammatical patterns. We noted the different definitions of pattern on p.116. Word templates are attempting to provide analogous structures for nouns, for pedagogical purposes.

Hanks developed a separate procedure for preparing data-based definitions of nouns. It involves taking semantically rich collocates of the word under discussion and inventing factual sentences that use the two words. For example, his example of *spider* includes:

Spiders have eight **legs**.

Spiders **lurk** in the centre of their **webs**.

Some spiders **bite**.

Some species of spiders hunt **prey**.

Some species of spiders are **poisonous**.

Hanks has named this format and procedure Cognitive Profiles

Collocates are used as a basis for building up a 'cognitive profile' that consists of phraseologically well-formed, idiomatic statements for the noun (Hanks 2012:66).

Question 304 **What do you notice about the constructions in *spider*'s cognitive profile?**

Is simple present the most likely tense and aspect for word profiles?

Do the verbs collocate with *spider* or with the other noun collocates?

What parts of speech are the collocates?

Question 305 **Make word profiles that represent a topic of interest.**

Choose a word and make a word sketch. Choose key words from it and write your own "phraseologically well-formed, idiomatic statements".

Both the PDEV and cognitive profile procedures use data which is readily derived from corpora, but they both require 'manual labour' and linguistic intuition, something which need not be viewed negatively.

Word templates (2)

The introduction to Word templates in Ch.6 ended with a promise to follow this up once some additional Sketch Engine skills had been acquired. Since then, we have worked with Text Types, CQL, Collocation and Word Sketches. And importantly, we have studied Hanks' patterns. Let us continue.

In a lot of the work done so far, we have explored various aspects of *Who said What to Whom under What circumstances*, a mantra of Systemic Functional Grammar. This mantra encapsulates unmarked word order, as can be seen in the second row of the table below. The elements in the third row realize the mantra in terms of its grammatical constituents. This particular one represents ditransitive verbs, whose semantics often express *transfer* in Construction Grammar terms.

Who	said	what	to whom	under what circumstances?
subject	Verb	direct object	indirect object	adverbials
NP	VP	NP	NP	adverbs/PP
det + adj + noun	aux + lex vb	det + adj + noun	det + adj + noun	adv | prep + det + adj + noun

A noun phrase (NP) consists of a single lexeme e.g. *enemy, collateral damage,* optionally accompanied by determiners and adjectives. Similarly, the verb phrase (VP) can be single or multi-word lexical verbs (e.g. *open, sit up*) and verb phrases may contain auxiliaries and lexical verbs (e.g. *be about to, declare*), as shown in the fourth row of the table.

Clause structure is governed by the verb's pattern. For example, the patterns of these four semantically related verbs show how central the verb is to clause structure and how their predicates differ accordingly.

> someone **asks** someone about something
>
> someone **questions** someone about something
>
> someone **wonders** wh…
>
> someone **queries** something

It is not only what follows the verbs that differ, so do their 'someones': the people who *question* someone about something are usually in authority, typically the police. Therefore, the object 'someone' is typically a suspect, as we see in this word template.

> **[authority] questions [suspect] about [something suspicious | criminal activity]**

Word templates articulate the collocations and colligations that constitute a word's construction. For native speakers this knowledge is subconscious. It could be an interesting study to compare the word templates of the four verbs above with their translations using bilingual word sketches.

Despite the importance of the verb, nouns are inevitably more frequent in the language and in text, given that most of the other elements in the clauses are, or contain, noun phrases.

When we speak and write, we grammatize word templates. This is therefore a process of extending a bare collocation with the elements of noun and verb phrases that situate it in the context of the discourse. This is what determiners, tense, aspect, modality, etc, do.

The impetus for a word template is our observation of its presence in text, and generalising this using word sketch data allows a word template to be empirically drawn.

Question 306 **Which columns in a word sketch are relevant to *who does what to whom under what circumstances*?**

Choose your verb. We need to observe the subject and object columns for *who* does *what*; those that express the circumstances, are the adverbials. Given that adverbials are typically either adverbs or prepositional phrases, we need to look adverbs and the preposition columns and identify the relevant ones. Remember that bound prepositions look left to their noun, verb or adjective, while free prepositions launch preposition phrases, "rightly".

Let us now explore the collocates of *lecture* in the object position, as can be seen in the text box below. We will use enTenTen, since all of the verbs have enough data to generate multi-word sketches when the word sketch is sorted by frequency. This allows us to explore these collocations in depth.

Question 307 **Who *gave, attended, got* etc. a lecture?**

Click on these verbs in the word sketch of *lecture*, the noun. If there is not enough data to form a subject column in the multi-word sketch, which is sometimes the case, click on the frequency number to see the concordances. Or use a bigger corpus.

For example, some of the subjects of *give a lecture* are *professor, researcher, philosopher*. These can be automatically clustered, as we saw above. And a label for the group can be used, typically a hypernym, e.g. *experts*.

Now we have *experts give a lecture*. Next, **to whom**?

Question 308 **To whom are *lectures* given?**

In the word sketch of the noun *lecture*, *give* has enough hits to permit a multi-word sketch. Click on *give* and see what the **PP to** column contains.

Question 309 **In what circumstances are lectures given, entitled, published, etc?**

Search now for adverbials in the guise of adverbs and prepositional phrases. For example, the topic of the lecture and when the lecture was given, e.g. *during the semester, at a conference*.

```
_____ give a lecture
_____ attend a lecture
_____ deliver a lecture
_____ get a lecture
_____ entitle a lecture
_____ include a lecture
_____ organise a lecture
_____ publish a lecture
```

Some of the word templates of *lecture* will look like this:

[Expert] gives a lecture [to students | fellow professionals] [on | about topic] [when | event]

[Institution] includes a lecture [in event | publication]

[Miscreant] gets a lecture [from rule | law enforcer]

Word templates show how the different meanings and uses of lecture emerge. They make sense as units of meaning and they sound like a pattern of normal usage. They also reveal the extent to which they need to be grammatized in discourse.

Question 310 **What do sentences that contain these templates look like?**

We now reverse the process of distilling language to form word templates. To find out how they exist in discourse, search for them using a CQL query. For example,

[tag = "N.*"][lemma = "give"][][lemma = "lecture"]

This query searches for nouns followed by *give* then a space and the word *lecture*. It permits anything to precede the first noun, such as items that constitute a noun phrase, i.e. articles, adjectives and other nouns. You can use the similarity search in this slot, e.g. [lempos~"expert-n"]

You might also like to limit your search to certain text types. Remember to choose your corpus wisely: size matters as much as its domain.

Here are two examples:

Corp ex.150   *In March, about 8 weeks from surgery,* **David gave a public lecture** *to his old academic colleagues. (ukWaC)*

Corp ex.151   *the course proved so popular that* **Müller gave each lecture** *twice. (BNC)*

The following examples show some multi-word noun phrases occupying the slots.

Corp ex.152   *Masaryk (subsequently president of Czechoslovakia) was appointed a professor in the School and, in October 1915, delivered <u>a highly influential lecture</u> entitled 'The Problem of Small Nations in the European Crisis'.*

Corp ex.153   <u>*A rather unusual lecture*</u>, *because in devising these lectures we've actually worked with local school teachers in working out what ...*

Corp ex.154   *The meeting was brought to a fitting climax by Professor Brian Johnson (Edinburgh), who gave <u>a highly entertaining lecture</u> on how studies of metal ...*

Question 311   **How do the text types in which *get a lecture* occurs support its non-academic tendencies?**

Create a similar query using *get* and observe the subjects and objects, and especially the text types.

Question 312   **Is distinguishing the objects of verbs enough to disambiguate them?**

Do a CQL query similar to struggle|battle|fight (Question 223) with "alleviate|relieve|allay" and the attribute set to *lemma*. Then make a frequency list, setting the frequency limit to 5. The first level - Node/lemma. Second level 1R/word. The resulting list can be sorted by clicking on the column heading *word*. This will show you if any of the three verbs share objects and to what extent.

Click on the P beside the nouns which both verbs share to see the left context and the metadata.

This brings to an end the second half of this introduction to my word templates. The primary inspiration has been Patrick Hanks' *Pattern Dictionary of English Verbs* [194].

When is enough too much?

Who wants to know all this about a word? First, as noted at the outset, data is not knowledge. The data has to be assembled, structured and interpreted, which is precisely what we do throughout this book. The answer to 'who wants to know' is anyone interested in the patterns of normal usage of a word and their exploitations. This includes lexicographers, authors of books about language and course books, teachers and students of foreign languages, translators and programmers developing human-machine interaction and machine translation. These applied linguists seek answers from corpora for practical everyday purposes, which are not at all "restricted to the ways in which (corpus) linguistics like to use them." (Braun 2010:92).

[194] Hanks 2000-2014. http://deb.fi.muni.cz/cpa/#

Isn't this overkill? Not if you can answer language questions that you couldn't otherwise. Perhaps even more important is learning what questions to ask.

Can a language learner process all of this data? Nobody can. Programs process the data and serve it to us in more digestible formats – the word sketch is one such format. The collocates in a word sketch are not just words, but instances of the **types** of things that fill a word's syntactic slot: this is where the human capacity for grouping things and finding connections plays a role.

Furthermore, it is the job of lexicographers and authors to serve learners with manageable portions, and the job of teachers to instruct their learners how to learn: this includes prioritizing what needs to be learnt and when. Training students to be research workers (see p.98) and in metacognitive skills and strategies develops their ability to learn independently.

Thanks for that. Can we continue now?

Chapter 12 Word Sketch Differences

What motivates a speaker to select *flawless* instead of *faultless*, *consist* instead of *comprise*, *accident* instead of *incident, foursome* instead of *quartet, collaborate* instead of *cooperate*, *feedback* instead of *criticism*, *student* instead of *pupil*, and *countless* or *innumerable* other such pairs of similar words.

Several things come to mind when considering the differences between synonyms and co-hyponyms. One question concerns what is similar enough about them that the question can be asked. Compare asking about the differences between *billiards* and *meatballs* with the differences between *billiards* and *pool*. Another thing is the facet of word meaning/use that can best differentiate the words, e.g. the words' connotations, register, regional variety, etc. There is little real-world difference between *an aisle, a corridor* and *a hallway*, or between *a footpath, a sidewalk* and *a pavement*, or between an *umpire, a judge* and *a referee*, or between *an intermission, interval* and *half-time,* or between *overweight, fat* and *corpulent*, or between *furthermore, in addition* and *what's more*. The effect of referring to someone as one's *ladyfriend* instead of *girlfriend*, however, says more about the speaker than about the friend.

As we have seen, a word's meaning potential is realised in the company it keeps. We saw this in the uses of *bar* (p.100) in reference to its meaning potential, in the double meaning of *arresting officer* (p.56), as well as in the various meanings of *blow up* (p.184). It is therefore reasonable to compare the collocates and grammatical relationships pairs of words.

Sketch Differences is a tool that generates combined word sketches for pairs of words. It uses colours to show which collocates are associated with which of the two words. The colours are shaded to depict the strength of association between a word and its collocates.

Question 313   **What is the difference between *be interested* and *be interesting*?**

Click on Sketch-Diff in the left panel. Type *interested* into Lemma, choose adjective and type *interesting* into Second Lemma. Under Advanced Options, choose All in one block, the default option. The maximum number of items of the common block was set to 10 for this screenshot.

This shows the modifier column only. The top row is blue and identifies the gramrel, modifier and then some summary data. The next four rows are green and are collocates of *interested*, while the bottom two are red and are collocates of *interesting*. The middle four are

modifier	2,483	1,579	0.90	0.70
keenly	23	0	8.1	--
genuinely	30	0	7.9	--
primarily	30	0	7.5	--
principally	14	0	7.2	--
deeply	41	5	7.7	4.9
remotely	20	5	7.9	6.4
particularly	187	152	8.7	8.5
especially	23	36	6.9	7.7
very	327	615	6.8	7.7
quite	34	171	5.2	7.6
extraordinarily	0	10	--	7.3
intrinsically	0	9	--	7.3

white and collocate with both. This is the standard format of Sketch Differences.

The first two columns of numbers are the occurrences of the collocates. It is clear how differently the two words collocate. Clicking the numbers takes you to the concordance page of the collocation.

The other two columns are the logDice scores. You can see that the table is sorted according to the logDice of the word you entered first.

Once you have the full Sketch-Diff for these two words, you will notice that not only do they collocate differently, but they also colligate differently. This is apparent from no collocates of one of the search words in some of the gramrels tables, e.g. pp_in.

The *interested* vs. *interesting* question we are asking is the same question as Question 66. Compare your earlier findings with what can be gleaned from Sketch Differences.

There are many such pairs of adjectives ending with –ed and –ing that you can compare in this way.

Question 314 **Should I describe something as *random* or *arbitrary*?**

Click Sketch Differences in the left panel, fill in the form with these two words and choose their POS. Click Show Diffs.

Study the form [195] and observe the colour coding described above. Notice the white middle sections of some tables indicating that there is no preference of association. Study the numbers and see how they determine the colour shadings.

In the *random* vs. *arbitrary* Sketch Differences, are there any noteworthy tendencies in the uses of the two words?

Question 315 **How differently are *sexy* and *sexual* used?**

Tipping is sexy according to my cash register receipt at lunch today. It was written in English in a Czech restaurant and I wondered if non-native speakers might think of *sexy* as *sexual* or *erotic*. Do Sketch Diffs reveal significant differences between these two adjectives? Open this link and see what is regarded as *sexy* [196]. Chronologically sorted concordances of the two words in the Brown Family clearly indicates changes.

Question 316 **What are the similarities and differences between the uses of *convincing* and *persuasive*?**

Do we say a *convincing person* and *persuasive person*? Do their similar and different collocates reveal anything about their meaning or usage? Do we have to look further afield, e.g. into their extended collocations or text types?

Question 317 **What does English do with *co-operate* and *collaborate*?**

opera (in *co-operate*) and *labour* (in *collaborate*) both derive from Latin words for *work*. How did English end up with both words and are they put to different uses?

> Facilis descensus Averni:
> Noctes atque dies patet atri ianua Ditis;
> Sed revocare gradium superasque evadere ad auras,
> Hoc **opus**, hic **labor** est.

---

[195] ske.li/ukwac_sd_random_arbitrary
[196] ske.li/lexmci_noun_is_sexy

> The gates of hell are open night and day;
> Smooth the descent, and easy is the way:
> But to return, and view the cheerful skies,
> In this the **task** and mighty **labour** lies.

The Aeneid Book VI Lines 126–129, translated by John Dryden, 1631-1700.

The most common meaning of *opus* was fortifications, and it was also used to mean need or work. The primary meaning of *labor* was preoccupation or concern, and it also denoted struggle, suffering, distress, hardship or stress. By the time of Dryden's translation, *opus* had become a single piece of work, while *labor* was the larger, more general term. Both words occur in the top 1,000 words in all elementary Latin textbooks (Pulverness 2015).

In Question 96, we investigated *elaborate,* also containing the Latin *labor*. What do Sketch Diffs offer?

Question 318　**How do singular and plural forms differ in their usage?**

In *Reading Concordances*, Sinclair devotes considerable space to the difference between *eye* and *eyes* (2003:167ff). He observes that the collocates of the plural form express *eyes* as a body part, e.g. *blue, green, lips, mouth, open, staring,* whereas the collocates of the singular form are involved in idiomatic expressions, e.g. *bird's eye view, private eye, sharp eye, keep an eye on someone.*

Does this extend to other parts of the body such as *fingers, hands, ears?*

To search for pairs of word forms, it is necessary to enter the lemma into the top field. Select the Word Form radio button and put the two forms into their respective fields.

Question 319　**How is *discover* used in fiction and science?**

Before performing this search, give some thought to:

　　Who discovers what under what circumstances in FICTION?

　　Who discovers what under what circumstances in SCIENCE?

It would be reasonable to expect different collocates of *discover* in these two fields.

Using the subcorpora we created on p.132, type *discover* into the Lemma field, and choose *verb*. Select Subcorpus and choose *Science* from the first drop list and *Fiction* from the second.

Does the data accord with your intuition?

As we noted in the Thesaurus chapter, clicking on words in the lists or word clouds leads to this Sketch Diffs tool.

Your Notes

Chapter 13   Word List

The Word List tool is a powerful tool capable of generating many types of lists. These can provide an overview of a whole corpus, unlike most of the tools we have explored up to this point. The searches in this section can be conducted in any corpus or subcorpus.

Many of the following questions ask about the most frequent instances of a feature. Despite the fact that all of the listed items meet the search parameters, the frequency question is answered at the top of the list. It is often the case, however, that less frequent items answer more interesting questions.

Click on Word List near the top of the left panel.

Question 320   **Can I have a list of all the words in a corpus?**

Yes. This is a frequently asked question of subcorpora and of specialised corpora in particular.

Whichever corpus you have open, click Word List in the left panel. Then without changing any of the defaults on the Word List form, simply click the Make Word List button at the bottom.

Explore some of the smaller corpora, such as CHILDES, Brown Family, Science blogs, TED. Generate these lists in separate browser tabs so that you can compare the lists. What the tops of the lists have in common is useful in accounting for core English, while the points at which they diverge reveal features of their tenors, fields and modes.

Question 321   **Can I have a list of all the collocations in a corpus?**

The drop list of Attributes includes collocations. Choose a small, specialist corpus and make the list of collocations. Click through some pages until less frequent words start appearing. They probably reveal more about the nature of a corpus than lists of single word forms or lemmas.

Question 322   **What strings of words most frequently occur in the corpus?**

Using any of the smaller corpora mentioned above, choose Word as the Search attribute, tick the check box and use n-grams with a value of 3 in both the **from** and **to** drop lists. The resulting lists are bundles. They show considerable divergence in their levels of formality, word length, negative particles, verb tenses, use of proper nouns, etc.

Despite the fact that longer n-grams in large corpora take quite some time to process, the data is invaluable and unlikely to be generated anywhere but Sketch Engine.

Question 323 **Are the most frequent words in written English more or less the same as in spoken English?**

With a subcorpus of written language and another of spoken language, use the same procedure as in Question 320.

The transcriptions of spoken English that make up the LEC prove an interesting contrast to corpora of written English. What features of spoken English can you observe in a list such as these trigrams from LEC? [197]

Question 324 **What are the most frequent tags in the corpus?**

Select **Tag** from the drop list Search Attribute and click Make Word List. If you haven't memorised all the tags yet, click on Corpus Info in the left panel – best opened in a new tab.

A more instructive question asks if different types of corpora or subcorpora have the same most frequent tags, and at what points the lists diverge.

Does finding similarities in the most frequent POS in a variety of domains reveal anything of stylistic interest? Compare, for example, journalism, academic, political, fiction, spoken and blogs.

Question 325 **Do n-grams represent or instantiate the tenors, fields and modes of corpora?**

Generate these lists in a variety of corpora or subcorpora. Use the n-grams drop lists to obtain the length of n-grams that you would like to compare. The attribute *word* generates lexical bundles while *tag* generates syntagms.

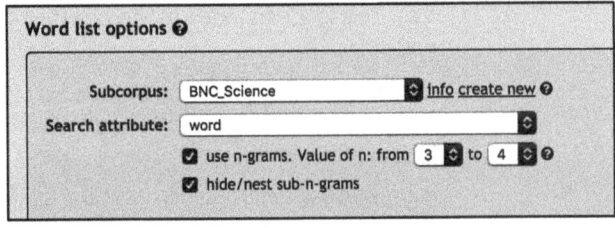

Question 326 **What are the most frequent syntagms in the corpus?**

An article entitled *Towards an n-gram grammar of English* by Cappelle and Grabar (2015:7) found that,

> the most frequent POS 4-grams in COCA is the one instantiated by *at the end of, in the middle of* and 6,984 other sequences of a preposition (other than *of*), the definite article, a singular common noun and the preposition *of*.

Their work was undertaken using the pre-constructed, downloadable lists from COCA, the Corpus of Contemporary American English [198]. Their very interesting methodology can be easily replicated in Sketch Engine using the Word List tool with any corpus.

Using Sketch Engine, the most frequent 4-gram syntagm is NN IN DT NN in both the

---

[197] ske.li/lec_3grams
[198] http://corpus.byu.edu/coca

BNC[199] and in the academic corpus, ARC[200]. The preposition tag, IN, is mostly *of*. However, in the LEC, this syntagm is the second most frequent[201], while in CHILDES it is the 12th most frequent[202] where the high number of SENT tag points to the very short utterances that young children produce.

To make these lists in Sketch Engine, go to Word list and in **Search attribute**, select tag, and tick **use n-grams** making the value 4.

The first syntagm in CHILDES with a verb is the 11th, and few of these are spoken by children, as this list shows[203]. This list was created by clicking on the first syntagm with a verb, then clicking on Frequency. In the Text Type Frequency Distribution, choose WhoLong. We can find such sub-field information by clicking on Corpus Info, and under Structures and Attributes, click on **u**, which shows the list.

As Capelle and Grabar (2015) point out (p.10), the specificity of the tags influenced the levels of generality of the syntagms. Nouns have four tags: NN is not a tag that covers all nouns – it excludes plural nouns and proper nouns, singular and plural. This phenomenon is even more significant in the case of verbs, which have 18 tags.

Question 327 **How balanced are the attributes in the corpus?**

The drop list of search attributes is derived from the metadata in the corpus. For example in the BNC, you can see the gender balance by selecting *Sex of demographic respondent*. Choose various attributes and see what they offer, e.g. Written: perceived level of difficulty; Interaction type for spoken texts.

Filter Options

Just as Filter options in concordance searches enable more refined searches, the same is true of Filter Options in the Word List tool.

The items entered in the Regular Expression field depend on the Search attribute above. For example, N.* will list noun tags if the Attribute is *tag*, and words starting with N if the Attribute is *word*. Regular expressions include: ^ $. * ? \ [...]

Question 328 **What noun tags are in the corpus and in what numbers?**

Select Attribute *Tag* and in the filter, N.* to find not only the tags that start with N, but the frequency of each one.

Repeat with V.* to answer the same question about verbs. These lists can also be used to isolate a particular sub-part of speech.

Filter word list by: Regular expression: N.*

Question 329 **Which lemmas occur at least 2,000 times?**

Select Attribute Lemma and set Minimum frequency to 2,000.

---

[199] http://ske.li/bnc_4_pos
[200] http://ske.li/arc_4_pos
[201] http://ske.li/lec_4_pos
[202] http://ske.li/childes_4_syntagm
[203] http://ske.li/childes_4_pos_who

Which words starting with *z* occur not more than 2,000 times?

Attribute: word. Regular Expression: z.*. Maximum frequency: 2,000.

Question 330 **Which words starting with *mega* are in the corpus once only?**

See p. 91 for a note about *nonce words* and *hapax legomena*.

```
Filter options:
  Filter word list by:  Regular expression: mega.*
                        Minimum frequency: 1
                        Maximum frequency: 1
```

Question 331 **How many hapax legomena are there in a corpus?**

With *Word* as the Attribute and the Minimum and Maximum frequencies set to one, a list of hapax legomena is generated.

Sketch Engine does not number listed items nor state how many items there are. One approach to answering this question is saving the list and importing it into a spreadsheet. Use **Save** in the left panel. There are over 52,000 in the BNC fiction subcorpus.

Question 332 **How many of the documents in the BNC are emails?**

Set the Word List form as in the following screenshot and under Output options, choose **Document counts**. There are very few. Compare this with later corpora that include this text type.

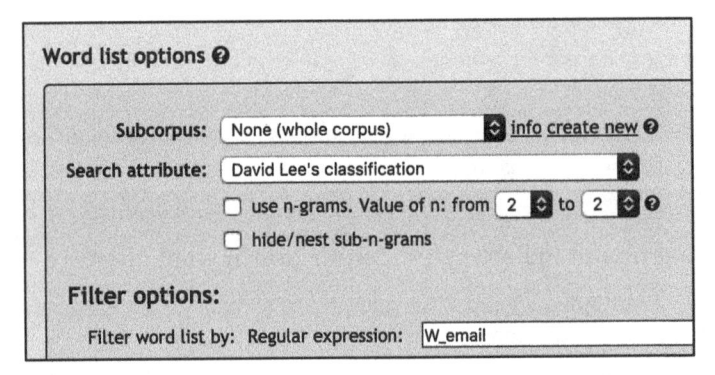

```
Word list options
  Subcorpus:         None (whole corpus)    info create new
  Search attribute:  David Lee's classification
                     □ use n-grams. Value of n: from 2 to 2
                     □ hide/nest sub-n-grams
  Filter options:
    Filter word list by:  Regular expression: W_email
```

White list, black list

Question 333 **What are the features of a particular set of words?**

In order to derive data about a set of specific words, use the **White List function**. For example, you might be working with discourse markers, *however, therefore, moreover,* or some troponyms of *kill* such as *stab, drown, choke, strangle,* or a set of irregular verbs.

Create a list in an ordinary text file with each word on a separate line. In Word List, choose the Attribute (e.g. lemma, lempos, collocations) you would like to see for your words and upload your file using White List. Click Make word list.

To find the n-grams of the words in the White list, select the n-gram number from the drop list to see your words in chunks, choosing Word Form or Lemma as appropriate. Open this permalink [204] to see the list of four-word bundles of the above troponyms.

The check box, **Include non-words,** permits words that start with characters other than letters.

Question 334 **Are words with the feminine suffix, -ess, fading from use?**

The word *actress* seems to be fading from use, as most male and female thespians refer to themselves as actors. It is, for example, much less frequent in 2006 than in 1991 in the Brown Family[205]. In this corpus example (Brown 2006), the pronoun indicates the gender of *actor:*

Corp ex.155 *Featuring mime, magic, stand-up and trapeze, it is a trip through her experiences as an actor, woman, wife and mother.*

What other nouns end with the, -ess? A search for nouns ending in –ess returns a list containing thousands of words, only some of which represent the feminine suffix. There is a list of them to copy into a text file to make your white list here[206].

Can we conclude that using this feminine marker is a marked choice these days?

Question 335 **Which words in a corpus occur with a frequency similar to a given word?**

It can be useful to find other words which occur with a similar frequency to the word you are working on. Select the attribute *word* or *lemma*, depending on your needs, then type your word into the Regular Expression field.

If your word has a frequency of 1,500, you can set both Minimum and Maximum frequency at 1,500. To allow a range instead, set them at say 1,450 and 1,550.

Output Options

Question 336 **What nouns are in a corpus?**

As the most frequent open-class part of speech in text, and those that carry most of the surface meaning, a list of nouns is a valuable resource, especially in specialised corpora.

Set the Attribute to tag and the Regular expression to N.*, then in Output options, click Change output and select *lemma* from the first drop list. Selecting tag from the second drop list will show the noun tags as well.

Create WLT lists by selecting Word in the first, Lemma in the second and Tag in the third.

> When we look at the type-token relationship in very large collections of text, ... all the other parts of speech (verbs and function words) pale into insignificance in comparison with nouns. ... Nouns make up the bulk of the word types in a language; the other parts of speech make up the bulk of the word tokens.
>
> (Hanks 2013:33).

The most frequent words are factotum. It is worth looking down the list to see when the first topic-specific words start appearing.

---

[204] http://ske.li/bnc_4gram_trop_kill
[205] http://ske.li/bf_actress_freq
[206] From versatile.pub, click on DESKE under books, and click on **List of –ess nouns**.

Most new words are nouns. Our observation of words starting with *faux* (p.91) demonstrated an aspect of language creativity, one of the motivations for new coinages. As Hanks points out, most new words in a language are nouns, and words starting with *faux* are by and large nouns. Observe this by setting the Search attribute to *lemma*, the Regular expression to *faux.** and change the Output options to *lemma* and *tag*. A relatively insignificant number of verbs appear on this list.

This procedure can be adapted for other related research questions.

Question 337   Which words in a corpus are most 'key'?

Scott's work on keyness in text defines a key word as one which occurs with unusual frequency in a given text. This does not mean high frequency but *unusual* frequency, by comparison with a reference corpus of some kind (Scott 1997:236). Thus as Stubbs points out, the study of recurrent wordings is of central importance in the study of language and ideology, and can provide empirical evidence of how the culture is expressed in lexical patterns (Stubbs, 1996: p. 169).

As we saw in the previous question, the high frequency words are factotum. Open a topic-specific corpus or subcorpus and in Word list, choose Lemma as the Search attribute. In the Output Options, choose Keywords.

```
● Keywords
    Reference (sub)corpus  [ ukWaC ]
```

Comparing your corpus with a large general corpus will identify 'unusual' words. Choose one of Sketch Engine's reference corpora. Click the Make word list button.

This screenshot shows the top findings comparing the BNC Science subcorpus with the full ukWaC. The scientific flavour of the data is undeniable.

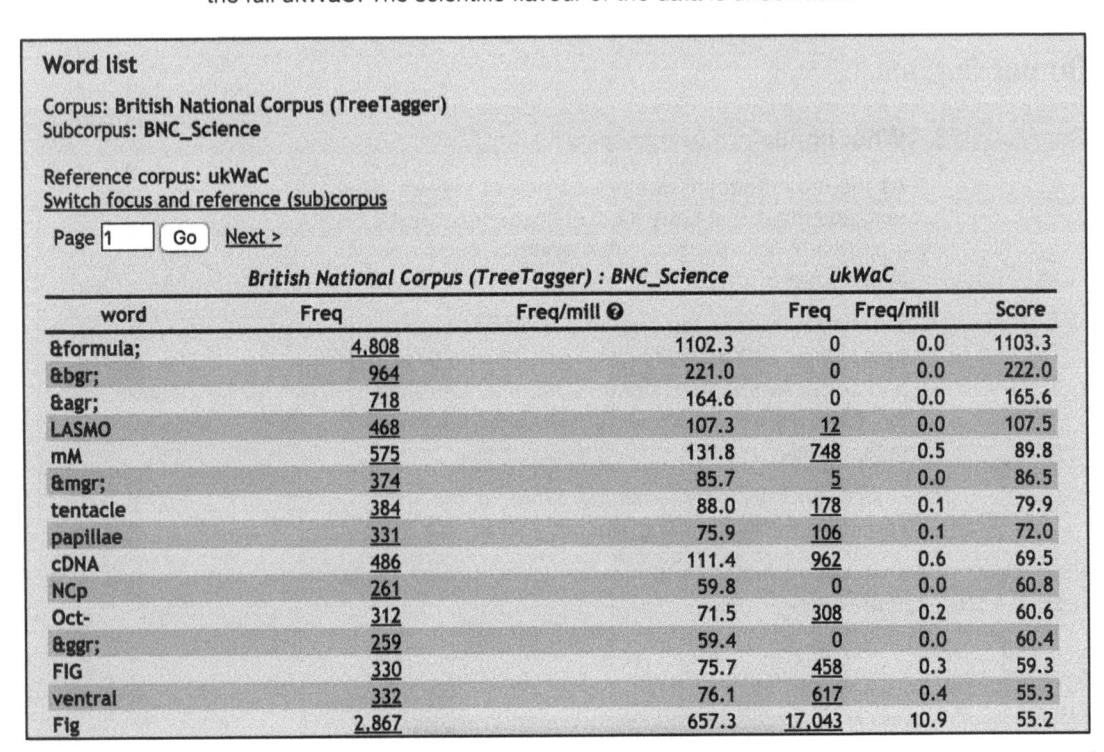

Word list

Corpus: **British National Corpus (TreeTagger)**
Subcorpus: **BNC_Science**

Reference corpus: ukWaC
Switch focus and reference (sub)corpus

Page 1 Go Next >

word	British National Corpus (TreeTagger) : BNC_Science		ukWaC		Score
	Freq	Freq/mill	Freq	Freq/mill	
&formula;	4,808	1102.3	0	0.0	1103.3
&bgr;	964	221.0	0	0.0	222.0
&agr;	718	164.6	0	0.0	165.6
LASMO	468	107.3	12	0.0	107.5
mM	575	131.8	748	0.5	89.8
&mgr;	374	85.7	5	0.0	86.5
tentacle	384	88.0	178	0.1	79.9
papillae	331	75.9	106	0.1	72.0
cDNA	486	111.4	962	0.6	69.5
NCp	261	59.8	0	0.0	60.8
Oct-	312	71.5	308	0.2	60.6
&ggr;	259	59.4	0	0.0	60.4
FIG	330	75.7	458	0.3	59.3
ventral	332	76.1	617	0.4	55.3
Fig	2,867	657.3	17,043	10.9	55.2

Question 338 **What are the key words in the Australian subcorpus?**

Word list will also compare the contents of a subcorpus with another corpus.

To answer the question, choose the subcorpus at the top and the Attribute that you want to compare and select a reference corpus, such as the whole enTenTen.

When you click Make word list, it starts a long, arduous process. Be patient – the results are invaluable and are not easily obtained elsewhere.

These steps can also be employed to compare n-grams across corpora. Choose the n-gram parameters at the top of the Word list form and set the reference corpus. And then what? Scott suggests:

The most appropriate interpretation of these key words or key word clusters is as pointers; they suggest some statistical anomaly which itself merits further research (2010:150).

Question 339 **Which verbs occur not more than 2,000 times?**

When we ask this question of a general corpus, we obtain data that provides information about the language in general.

Select Attribute *Tag*, type V.* (no inverted commas) into the Regular Expression field, set Maximum frequency to 2,000, and in the Change output attributes at the bottom, Lemma in the left drop list.

Alternatively, lists of WLTs can be generated using the other drop lists here.

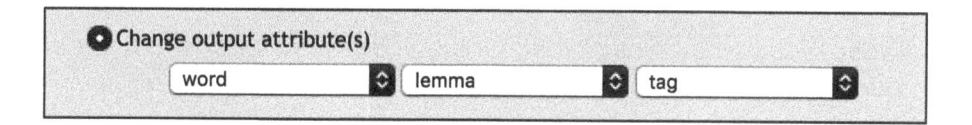

Question 340 **Which adjectives occur between 1,450 and 1,550 times?**

Finding out what other words or structures are in a similar frequency range can be useful in preparing teaching and research resources.

Set Attribute: Tag, RE expression: JJ and the Frequencies 1450 and 1550. At the bottom, set Change Output to word.

Question 341 **How new and how frequent is the question tag, *innit*?**

As we explore this question, also consider if it is used as a substitute for *isn't it* only?

Search for *innit* it in the LEC. It is around the 110th most frequent lemma in this corpus. To observe the quite revealing speaker profiles, click on Text Types under Frequency in the left panel.

Right sorting puts the question mark at the top of the concordance page. Almost one fifth of *innit* in LEC are followed by question marks.

Scan these uses of *innit* and use the Select Lines checkboxes to mark those in which it is not substituting for *isn't it*?

This screenshot compares its frequency of use in LEC and NMC, using the Word list tool. Attribute – words. Regular expression – *innit*. Output options – Keywords – NMC as the reference corpus.

Word list

Corpus: **London English Corpus**

Reference corpus: **New Model Corpus**
Switch focus and reference (sub)corpus

word	*London English Corpus* Freq	Freq/mill	*New Model Corpus* Freq	Freq/mill	Score
innit	3,180	1074.6	37	0.3	813.1

There are still more options available in Word List. See the Sketch Engine wiki for more information.

Chapter 14   DIY corpora

The BNC, NMC and enTenTen are corpora of general English and we have used them for discovering features of general, core English. At times, we have also observed patterns in parliamentary debates, academic prose, spoken language, Australian English and many others that can be isolated in these large reference corpora thanks to their metadata. But they were not designed to represent specific topics, domains or genres of English.

However, someone writing or translating a text within a sub-field of sports psychology, economics or musicology, for example, will find a corpus of closely related texts containing key words and terms in their patterns of normal usage invaluable. If someone, whether native or non-native speaker, is writing a chemistry essay, for example, and is aware that the appropriate verb for the chemical process is *coalesce,* but is not sure how the verb should be used, none of the main online dictionaries gives us a chemistry example (Kilgarriff et.al. 2015). And if a course book author is preparing teaching resources for topics such as Australian aborigines, the environment or capital punishment, the data in specialised corpora is invaluable. In a classroom context, teachers and students can use such corpora as well, thereby cutting out the middle man, as mentioned in reference to DDL on p.20.

Following Kennedy and Miceli (2000), the writing process can be given a nudge if authors consult a corpus on the topic about which they are to compose a text: lists provide words and phrases used with their context-appropriate collocations and colligations. Writing cognitive profiles (see Hanks' *spiders* p.186) is a practical realisation of this. Novice writers are as likely to find out how to express something as they are to find ideas on what to write about. For example, the collocation lists for *Charles and Diana* in the BNC [207] and for *Robin Hood* in enTenTen [208] read like brainstorming sessions.

There are two tools in Sketch Engine for creating your own corpora. WebBootCat (Baroni et al. 2006) crawls the web and gathers texts for the corpus, while Corpus Builder allows you to upload your own texts. Once you have a corpus, you can add more texts by crawling the web and/or by uploading your own documents, regardless of which of these tools your corpus was originally created with.

The corpora you create can rightfully be called your corpora, but bear in mind that they are not your texts. Unless the corpus creator has permission to use texts in a corpus, there are copyright issues to be taken seriously. McEnery and Hardie devote a whole chapter to this matter: *The web, laws and ethics* in their 2012 book, *Corpus Linguistics.* And Baker (2006:38) cautions that discourse analysis of a text or the work of a particular author might present it or them in an unfavourable light, which may tempt the litigious into action.

Before creating a corpus, read about corpus design: an online article by John Sinclair is available here [209], and the first chapter of Corpus Linguistics (McEnery and Hardie) provides a wealth of information.

---

[207] ske.li/bnc_charles_diana_colls
[208] ske.li/ett_robinhood_colls
[209] http://bit.ly/sinclair_corp_design

Use this information to plan your modes of text collection and metadata.

Creating a corpus from the web

Start from the Sketch Engine Homepage and choose **WebBootCaT** from the left panel. Give your corpus a name and choose the language.

This tool crawls the web looking for documents that contain combinations of your so-called *seed words*. It is enough to enter up to about twenty of these. This screenshot shows seed words for a corpus about *environmental issues*. Note the advice provided under its field.

Alternatively, use URLs if you want to create a corpus of a particular set of webpages. A list of articles about using corpora published in the online journal, *Language Learning and Technology,* may be of interest to readers of this book.[210].

Clicking *Next* initiates the process of web crawling. You can watch it build as the green progress bar extends from left to right. The corpus is then compiled, which involves POS tagging with Penn Treebank, lemmatizing and preparing the word sketches and Thesaurus. Click OK. You will then see a folder with the name of your corpus.

Working with your corpus

New menus of corpus management tools appear once the corpus exists.

Add new file: choose a document from your computer, download something from the web, or paste some text that has been copied to your computer's clipboard.

Add data from web using WebBootCaT: create a name for the next round (iteration) of web crawling. And provide some seed words. See *Forward Planning* below.

Compile corpus: this is necessary whenever new texts are added. The Structures and Attributes that are selected in the list of checkbox items are those that appear when you perform a search that includes Text Types.

Search corpus: this permits searching using the Sketch Engine search fields and tools that this book has been extolling.

Advanced Features in the left panel includes **User Groups**. These can be created so that a group of users can be granted access at the same time. This is particularly handy when corpora are shared with the same group or class of users repeatedly.

---

[210] Accessible from http://llt.msu.edu/archives under Topic.

Manage Corpus includes the following tools and more:

Configure corpus contains fields for regular and advanced users. The top field allows you to edit the name of your corpus. The **Info field** allows you to describe it. This information may be of use to the corpus creator upon returning to it after some time, and to anyone you share it with. Corpora you share with other people will display these icons beside the name of shared corpora. Clicking on the first of them shows the text from the Information field. The magnifying glass icon takes you to the standard queries page and the tools icon takes you to the corpus management page.

Download corpus if you want to use the data with other concordancers or for any other processing.

Share corpus allows you to share your corpus with other registered users. Choose between three categories on this page depending on what we want to allow them to do. For example, if a group of people are going to contribute to the same corpus, use **Upload File Privilege**. This can be modified at any time. **Type pattern** simply means: start typing the person's name or their username in Sketch Engine. Once you select the people you are sharing your corpus with, it appears on their list of corpora **Shared with me** on the Home Page.

Search Corpus includes **Keywords and Terms**. These are two lists generated by comparing the content of your corpus with a large general reference corpus, as we saw on p.199 in the Word list chapter. The Keywords and Terms screenshot below shows the top section of those extracted from a corpus of this book.

Any of the key words and Terms can be selected and used to perform another iteration of 'corpus growing'. As you read through your list, select those that you would like to form a new set of seed words.

DESKE 2nd ed Feb 16: Extracted keywords and terms

Change extraction options Download keywords: TBX CSV. Download terms: TBX CSV.

Keywords	Score	F	RefF	Terms	Score	F	RefF
corpora	1,382.14	279	6,428	word sketch	437.94	59	5
bnc	1,337.15	231	3,633	normal usage	349.10	52	1,381
lemma	1,265.71	190	1,459	concordance page	312.04	42	2
xe	813.07	175	7,719	frequency list	309.88	42	98
corpus	793.50	514	49,260	left panel	227.54	34	1,444
collocation	740.93	167	8,696	form field	225.11	34	1,596
collocates	729.28	99	87	phrasal verb	191.26	26	166
lexical	685.22	146	7,514	academic prose	155.28	21	105

Change extraction options appears at the bottom of this page. One of the options is to **Exclude stop words**. Click on the link on that page or here[211] to see what items are included on the list of stop words.

---
[211] https://the.sketchengine.co.uk/stopwords/english

It is clear that these are highly frequent words which appear in every corpus. The other items on this screen are self-explanatory and unless there is good reason to change them, use the default settings. Click OK to generate a table of keywords and terms.

Then click the button at the bottom, Use WebBootCaT with selected words, to expand the corpus.

Note that it is not possible to share subcorpora. If, for example, you distributed a permalink that linked to the results of a search within a subcorpus, the recipient would not be able to access it. In fact, advanced users can share subcorpora: see how here [212].

Forward Planning

Each iteration of 'corpus growing' is stored as a separate folder. When you click on *Add data from web using WebBootCaT,* you are prompted to provide a *Name of collection*. If, for example, you are creating a corpus of articles about the environment, your seed words for one iteration might concern energy, another might be about causes, etc. This screenshot comes from a DIY *environment corpus*.

Original file	Plain text	Vertical	Tokens
Causes (75 files)			225,987
Energy (73 files)			146,260
environment (63 files)			87,696

When you compile the corpus, all of the folders are combined into one corpus, but the folder names (collections) are used as metadata. This can then be used in these situations:

- Use Text Types to filter a search within selected folders
- Show the folder names as References in concordances – set in View Options
- Create subcorpora based on the folder names.

Creating a corpus from selected documents

Your own documents can be a set of texts that students have written, the song lyrics of an artist, emails you have received from an institution or company, the novel you are writing, a set of articles you work with, or the complete works of Shakespeare (see p.51).

Preparation of texts: Although the software extracts the text from these files, it does not always remove hyphens that text processors add for the purposes of paragraph alignment. As this Keywords screenshot shows, there are some problems with automatic character recognition that can be so consistent that they become statistically significant! All of these incomplete words are due to -fi- being wrongly converted. This problem does not always occur – it depends on the source document.

Keywords
- corpora
- corpus
- dif
- bene
- speci
- dence
- concordancing
- culty
- cial
- rst

There may also be text in articles that can be excluded, such as contact details of authors and bibliographies.

To begin creating a corpus, click Create Corpus at the top of the left panel. Give your corpus a name and select the language.

On the next screen, upload your first text using one of the four options: from disk, from location, directory on the server, paste text. Then click Next. The message, *File added successfully,* means that it is ready to be incorporated into the corpus.

Click Finish. This is the point at which it would be best to add the metadata – see below.

---

[212] https://www.sketchengine.co.uk/creating-subcorpora-for-sharing-with-all-users

Metadata

Every search and sort in this book that has involved Text Types has been possible because of the metadata that is provided when texts are added to the corpus. For example, the Informatics Reading Corpus that my students contribute texts to has data for the following Attributes: author, lab, year, title, section. The *Values* for the **Sections** attribute can be seen in this screenshot. This allows us to search for linguistic features of these Sections across the corpus and to make subcorpora of them as well.

```
background
results
procedure
methodology
introduction
conclusion
abstract
futurework
experiments
acknowledgements
```

Adding metadata After clicking Add new file, a list of texts appears. In the right-hand column, these three buttons appear beside each text. The middle button, as hovering over it shows, is for metadata. Click it. The first time you add metadata to a corpus, you need to enter the **attributes** as well as the **values**. The metadata for subsequent texts can be selected from the drop lists that are created as you enter it. Typically, there are only several Attributes, but many values.

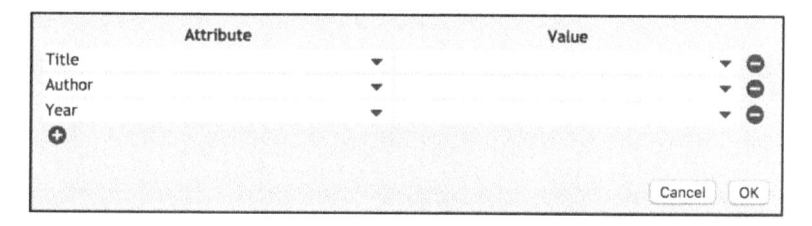

Attribute	Value
Title	
Author	
Year	

To add more texts, click Add new file, and choose one of the four options for adding text.

When you have finished adding your current set of texts, click Compile corpus and accept the defaults unless you have reason not to. Click the Compile button and wait for the OK button, which you should then click. The corpus is ready to be used with the full range of Sketch Engine tools.

> For a linguist, to describe language without accounting for text is sterile; to describe text without relating it to language is vacuous.
>
> Halliday, 1985, p.10.

Your Notes

Chapter 15   Pride and Prejudice

This is the final section of this book and we are going to garner many of our Sketch Engine skills, and much of our linguistic and language knowledge to answer some questions about literature. The study of literature using corpus analysis is called corpus stylistics.

Stylistics in Crystal's words, is "a branch of linguistics which studies the features of situationally distinctive uses (varieties) of language, and tries to establish principles capable of accounting for particular choices made by individual and social groups in their use of language" (1992:332). Halliday's field, tenor and mode have been used as reliable indicators of stylistic differences. They are factors influencing the choice of language means and posing limitations on the repertoire of phonological, grammatical and lexical devices.

Analysing the linguistic patterns of a text gives answers to questions such as how literary effects are encoded in language (Fischer-Starcke, B. 2010:2).

We will now create a corpus of Jane Austen's 1813 novel, *Pride and Prejudice* to address some general language questions and some matters of stylistics using a variety of tools and techniques we have encountered in this book.

The Gutenberg Project has many novels in plain text UTF-8 covering a wide timespan, including things published this year.

In Sketch Engine, create a new corpus. Then go to the Gutenberg Project homepage[213] and locate *Pride and Prejudice*, open its UTF-8 version and copy the URL. By pasting it into the URLs field and following the next steps, you will have a corpus of this novel in a matter minutes. However, this will contain a lot of so-called *noise*: Gutenberg Project information at the top and almost 3,000 words of copyright information at the end.

To omit this, download the whole webpage into a text document and delete everything before and after the novel starts. Then upload the file. Alternatively, copy only the text of the novel from the webpage, and paste it into the text field under Create corpus. This only takes a little longer and in the case of a novel, is quite manageable. For a very large work, copy and paste would not be appropriate.

Open the *Pride and Prejudice* corpus.

Question 342   **Does studying the language of classic literature cause learners to use words, phrase and structures in non-standard ways?**

Foreign language learners have been known to complain about picking up mistakes from their peers when they are asked to communicate with each other. We could

[213] http://www.gutenberg.org

similarly ask whether learners acquire archaisms by reading and studying Austen et al. However, with this "threat" in mind, it would be a valuable exercise to compare suspect archaisms with contemporary corpora.

For example, *good humour* occurs 14 times in Pride and Prejudice. In what templates is it used in this novel and how is it used nowadays? This is a valuable research approach to addressing the issue of acquiring language that is used differently today.

Similar research could be undertaken into these adjective-noun collocations from the novel: *great pleasure* (9x), *humble abode* (5x), *perfect indifference* (4), *good breeding* (4), *disagreeable man* (3).

Make list of 4-grams and try to identify any that you suspect of not being typical of contemporary English. Then compare with their 4-grams in a contemporary corpus.

Question 343 **What key words emerge when the novel is compared with enTenTen?**

Use the Word list tools to observe this.

Question 344 **What grammar, vocabulary and discourse features emerge from the novel's n-grams?**

Use the Word list tools to explore this with different lengths of n-grams. Some of them will belong to the novel's dialogue. Some frequent n-grams instantiate adverbial phrases, others tense and aspect verb groups.

How frequent are proper nouns in these n-grams?

Does the n-grams list contain anything you would not expect in contemporary language?

Question 345 **Does Austen use *handsome* to describe both men and women, and non-living things?**

The 'handsome question' was first raised on p.25. We can explore it a little further now. There are quite a few words denoting *man* and *woman* in this novel. You can discover this using the Thesaurus tool. This may lead to a richer answer to the question.

In the EEBO corpus, we can observe the use of *handsome* in the decades around 1813 to see if her use is idiosyncratic or conventional. In Text Types, select the decades then make frequency or collocation lists.

Might these uses of *handsome* be another candidate for problematic language acquisition, as raised in Question 342?

Question 346 **What does *amends* mean?**

Search for this word in the Pride and Prejudice corpus. It occurs often enough for a reader to become at least aware of it, if not acquire it. Is *amends* associated with any particular character or situation? If it is used in direct speech, who says it and who is being referred to?

Note however, that its template differs from its 20th century template. Compare it in a contemporary corpus. In the process of syntactic observations, can the meaning be inferred from its collocations and colligations?

Question 347 **Do question tags feature in the dialogue?**

If this is an interesting question, how interesting is the answer?

Question 348 **To what use are modal verbs put in this novel?**

To search for the central modals, make a CQL query of "MD" then generate a node forms list. Clicking the Ps and making frequency lists leads to more specific questions. For example, why is *she could* more than three times more frequent in this novel than *he could*? Are the modals used in hedging, for politeness, etc?

Question 349 **Is *shall* used exclusively with first person pronouns?**

Read the information in this text box and then see the entry linked below [214] for the rest of this explanation.

> *Will and shall* according to the Oxford Dictionary Online:
>
> The traditional rule in standard British English is that *shall* is used with first person pronouns (i.e. I and we) to form the future tense, while *will* is used with second and third person forms (i.e. you, he, she, it, they).

Question 350 **What features of reported speech can be observed in this novel?**

After a search has been performed, the filter tool can be used to locate direct speech. Put an inverted comma in the Filter's Simple Query field and set the range to say ±7. Back on the concordance page, View options – sentence.

It might be noted that after reported speech, Austen uses *returned she, replied he, cried he*, etc. Compare this with a current corpus and observe the systematic differences.

Question 351 **What positive adjectives does Austen use to describe people?**

Use Thesaurus with the word *happy,* for example. How is the opposite expressed?

Do we learn anything about Austen's view of the world by looking at the adjective + noun collocates?

For example, do the adjectives used with people (e.g. man, lady, person) show them in a positive light?

Do the adjective + noun collocates that occur once use uncommon words and do they express a positive or negative attitude?

Question 352 **Are the D'Arcys ever referred to with their first names?**

Is this standard practice in this novel? Compare with the literary text types in contemporary corpora.

Question 353 **Does Austen typify her characters by what she has them do?**

To generate a list of proper nouns in the novel, use the NP tag in Word List and change the output options to Word.

Investigate what verbs each of the characters perform. Enter one of the characters into the Simple Query field, and in POS filter select Verb on the right. Elizabeth, for example, does almost 500 things, but not 500 different things as right sorting reveals.

---

[214] http://www.oxforddictionaries.com/words/shall-or-will

Do their verbs indicate emotion, physical activity, modes of communication, reflection, work, etc? You might like to categorise them in the semantic categories that LGSWE offers: activity, mental, communication, existence, occurrence, causative, aspectual (1999: 365).

For a more detailed approach to this type of question, see Halliday's study into transitivity in his analysis of Golding's *The Inheritors,* a classic in stylistics (Fischer-Starcke 2010:47).

Question 354 **Are some characters more prone to not making answers than others?**

Having spent the last 200 or so pages of this book answering questions, let us see how Jane Austen permitted her characters to leave questions unanswered.

```
from all his life." Darcy made no answer , and seemed desirous of
like a ball." Miss Bingley made no answer , and soon afterwards she
y such expectation, she made no answer . "Well, Lizzy," continued
ly displeased." Elizabeth made no answer ; and without attempting
 be repaid?" Mr. Bennet made no answer , and each of them, deep
all about it." Mr. Bennet made no answer . "Do you not want to kno
ceive such a letter!" He made no answer . "You write uncommonly
rchase offers." Elizabeth made no answer . She was afraid of talkin
retched mistake!" Darcy made no answer . He seemed scarcely to
y own performance." He made no answer , and they were again sil
consequence. Elizabeth made no answer , and took her place in th
e was disconcerted, and made no answer ; but Lydia, with perfect
. "You forget that I have made no answer . Let me do it without fu
now told you." Elizabeth made no answer , and walked on, her hea
```

The end.

Afterword

This brings us to the end of our long journey of discovery. As they say, *travel broadens the mind* (66 times in enTenTen12) and it is hoped that you have found *Discovering English with Sketch Engine* an enriching experience. If this book were meant only as a guide to using Sketch Engine, we could say that it has been like using a *sledge hammer to crack a nut* (7 times in enTenTen12 but 114 when not hyphenated). But we have explored many aspects of language and linguistics, demonstrated the framing of questions and deriving information from data.

I sincerely hope that this kaleidoscopic treatment of language and linguistics has not been a source of irritation to you, the reader. Indeed there have been occasions when flitting from one branch to another has intended to exploit the inevitable links and associations between them. For me, the opportunities for cross fertilization that corpus linguistics offers applied linguists is a blessing, not a curse. For language teachers dealing with the full gamut of linguistic phenomena, this teacher trainer firmly believes in the value of such a broad overview. Hopefully knowledge has been created in the minds of the readers.

Parts of Sketch Engine have not been covered, in some cases because they are still under development, and in other cases because they are more oriented towards translation and lexicography than language learning and linguistics.

It is time now to close this book and reap the benefits of the hard work that has led you to this final page.

References

Adams, D. (1980). *The hitchhiker's guide to the galaxy*. New York: Harmony Books.

Anderson, L. W., Krathwohl, D. R., & Bloom, B. S. (2001). *A taxonomy for learning, teaching, and assessing: A revision of Bloom's taxonomy of educational objectives*. London: Longman.

Aston, G. (1998). Learning English with the British National Corpus. *6th Jornada de Corpus, UPF, Barcelona*.

Austin, J. L. (1962). *How to do things with words* (2nd ed.). Cambridge M.A.: Harvard University Press.

Baker, P. (2006). *Using Corpora in Discourse Analysis*. London: A & C Black.

Baker, M. (1992). *In Other Words*. London: Routledge.

Baroni, M., Kilgarriff, A., Pomikálek, J., & Rychlý, P. (2006). WebBootCaT: a web tool for instant corpora. In *Proceedings of the EuraLex Conference* (pp. 123–132). Torino.

Bemadini, S. (2000). Systematising serendipity: proposals for large-corpora concordancing with language learners. In *Rethinking Pedagogy from a Corpus Perspective*. New York: Peter Lang.

Benson, M., Benson, E., & Ilson, R. (1986). *The BBI Combinatory Dictionary of English: a guide to word combinations*. Amsterdam: John Benjamins.

Biber, D., Johannson, S., Leech, G., Conrad, S., & Finegan, E. (1999). *Longman grammar of spoken and written English*. London: Longman.

Bolinger, D. (1976). Meaning and memory. *Forum Linguisticum, 1*, 1–14.

Boulton, A. (2009). Data-driven learning: Reasonable fears and rational reassurance. *Indian Journal of Applied Linguistics, 35*(1), 81–106.

Boulton, A. (2010). Data-driven learning: Taking the computer out of the equation. *Language Learning, 60*(3), 534–572.

Boulton, A. (2015). Applying data-driven learning to the web. *Multiple Affordances of Language Corpora for Data-Driven Learning*.

Braun, S. (2010). Getting past 'Groundhog Day': Spoken multimedia corpora for student-centred corpus exploration. *Corpus Linguistics in Language Teaching. Linguistics Insights, 128*, 75–98.

Burnard, L. (2005). Developing Linguistic Corpora: Metadata for Corpus Work. In *Developing linguistic corpora: a guide to good practice* (pp. 30–46). Oxford: Oxbow Books.

Cameron, D., & Kulick, D. (2003). *Language and sexuality*. Cambridge: Cambridge University Press.

Cappelle, B., & Grabar, N. (forthcoming). Towards an n-grammar of English. In *Applied Construction Grammar*. Mouton De Gruyter.

Carstairs-McCarthy, A. (2002). *An introduction to English morphology: words and their structure*. Edinburgh: Edinburgh University Press.

Carter, R., & McCarthy, M. (1995). Grammar and the Spoken Language. *Applied Linguistics, 16*(2), 141–158. http://doi.org/10.1093/applin/16.2.141

Carter, R., & McCarthy, M. (2006). *Cambridge grammar of English: a comprehensive guide: spoken and written English grammar and usage*. Cambridge: Cambridge University Press.

Chafe, W. (1994). *Discourse, consciousness, and time*. Chicago: University of Chicago Press.

Charniak, E. (1993). *Statistical language learning*. Cambridge, MA: MIT Press.

Chomsky, N. (1957). *Syntactic structures*. The Hague: Mouton.

Chujo, K., Anthony, L., Oghigian, K., & Uchibori, A. (2012). Paper-based, computer-based, and combined data-driven learning using a web-based concordancer. *Language Education in Asia, 3*(2), 132–145.

Church, K. W., & Hanks, P. (1990). Word association norms, mutual information, and lexicography. *Computational Linguistics*, *16*(1), 22–29.

Clark, R., & Ivanič, R. (1997). *The Politics of Writing*. London: Routledge.

Cobb, T. (2005). Foundations of linguistics–Approaches and concepts: Constructivism, applied linguistics, and language education. In *Encyclopedia of Language and Linguistics* (2nd ed.). Amsterdam: Elvisier.

Cobb, T. (2006). Review of Nadja Nesselhauf (2005), Collocations in a Learner Corpus. *Canadian Modern Language Review*, *62*(2), 293–5.

Conrad, S., & Biber, D. (2004). The frequency and use of lexical bundles in conversation and academic prose. *Lexicographica*, *20*, 56–71.

Cosme, C., & Gilquin, G. (2008). Free and bound prepositions in a contrastive perspective. *Phraseology: An Interdisciplinary Perspective*, 259–274.

Coxhead, A. (2000). A new academic word list. *TESOL Quarterly*, *34*(2), 213–238.

Crystal, D. (2008). *A Dictionary of Linguistics and Phonetics* (6th ed.). Oxford: Wiley-Blackwell.

Csomay, E. (2013). Lexical bundles in discourse structure: A corpus-based study of classroom discourse. *Applied Linguistics*, *34*(3), 369–388.

De Beaugrande, R. (1991). *Linguistic theory: the discourse of fundamental works*. London: Longman.

Ellis, N. C. (2008). Usage-based and form-focused language acquisition: The associative learning of constructions, learned attention, and the L2 endstate. In *Handbook of Cognitive Linguistics and Second Language Acquisition*. London: Routledge.

Fillmore, C. J. (1992). Corpus linguistics or computer-aided armchair linguistics. In *Directions in corpus linguistics. Proceedings of Nobel Symposium* (Vol. 82, pp. 35–60).

Firth, J. R. (1948). Sounds and Prosodies. *Transactions of the Philological Society*, *47*(1), 127–152. http://doi.org/10.1111/j.1467-968X.1948.tb00556.x

Firth, J. R. (1957). *Papers in Linguistics 1934-1951: Repr*. Oxford: Oxford University Press.

Flowerdew, L. (2009). Applying corpus linguistics to pedagogy: A critical evaluation. *International Journal of Corpus Linguistics*, *14*(3), 393–417. http://doi.org/10.1075/ijcl.14.3.05flo

Flowerdew, L. (2015). Data-driven learning and language learning theories. In *Multiple Affordances of Language Corpora for Data-driven Learning*. Amsterdam: John Benjamins.

Francis, G., Hunston, S., & Manning, E. (1998a). *Collins COBUILD Grammar patterns: 1. Verbs*. London: HarperCollins.

Francis, G., Hunston, S., & Manning, E. (1998b). *Collins COBUILD Grammar patterns: 2. Nouns and adjectives*. London: HarperCollins.

Gabrielatos, C. (2015). The lexicogrammar of 'BE interested': Complementation patterns and pedagogical implications. In *ICAME 36*. Trier: University of Trier. Retrieved from http://repository.edgehill.ac.uk/6436/1/ICAME36.Gabrielatos.pdf

Geeraerts, D. (2010). *Theories of lexical semantics*. Oxford: Oxford University Press.

Gleiser, M. (2005). *The Dancing Universe: From Creation Myths to the Big Bang*. Hanover, NH: Dartmouth College Press.

Goldberg, A. E. (2006). *Constructions at work: The nature of generalization in language*. Oxford: Oxford University Press.

Gries, S. T. (2008). Corpus-based methods in analysis of second language acquisition data. In *Handbook of Cognitive Linguistics and Second Language Acquisition* (pp. 406–431). London: Routledge.

Groom, N. (2010). Closed-class keywords and corpus-driven discourse analysis. In *Keyness In Texts* (pp. 59–78). Amsterdam: John Benjamins.

Haig, G., Schnell, S., & Wegener, C. (2011). Comparing corpora from endangered language projects: Explorations in language typology based on original texts. *Documenting Endangered Languages: Achievements and Perspectives*, *240*, 55.

Halliday, M. A. K. (1971). Linguistic function and literary style: an inquiry into the language of William Golding's The Inheritors. In *Literary style: A symposium* (pp. 330–368). London: Oxford University Press.

Halliday, M. A. K. (1985). *An introduction to functional grammar*. London: Edward Arnold.

Halliday, M. A. K., & Hasan, R. (1976). *Cohesion in English*. London: Longman.

Halliday, M. A. K., Matthiessen, C. M., & Matthiessen, C. (2004). *An introduction to functional grammar* (3rd ed.). London: Edward Arnold.

Hanks, P. (2012). How people use words to make meanings: Semantic types and valencies. In *Input, process and product: developments in teaching and language corpora* (pp. 54–69). Brno: Masaryk University Press.

Hanks, P. (2013). *Lexical analysis norms and exploitations*. Cambridge, MA: MIT Press.

Hanks, P. (2015). Pattern Dictionary of English Verbs. Retrieved from http://pdev.org.uk

Herbst, T. (1996). What are collocations: sandy beaches or false teeth? *English Studies*, *77*(4), 379–393.

Hoey, M. (2000). A world beyond collocation: New perspectives on vocabulary teaching. In *Teaching collocation: further developments in the Lexical Approach* (pp. 224–243). Hove: Language Teaching Publications.

Hoey, M. (2005). *Lexical priming: a new theory of words and language*. London; New York: Routledge.

Hoey, M., Mahlberg, M., Stubbs, M., & Teubert, W. (2007). *Text, Discourse and Corpora* (1st ed.). London: Bloomsbury Publishing.

Hopper, P. (1998). Emergent Grammar. In *The new psychology of language: Cognitive and functional approaches to language structure* (pp. 155–76). London: Psychology Press.

Hunston, S. (2002). *Corpora in applied linguistics*. Cambridge: Cambridge University Press.

Jakobson, R. (1971). *Studies on child language and aphasia*. The Hague: Mouton.

Johns, T. (1991). Should you be persuaded: Two samples of data-driven learning materials. *English Language Research Journal*, *4*, 1–16.

Johns, T. (1994). From printout to handout: Grammar and vocabulary teaching in the context of Data-driven Learning. In *Perspectives on Pedagogical Grammar*. Cambridge: Cambridge University Press.

Kerouac, J. (1957). *On the Road*. Signet.

Kilgarriff, A. (2005). Language is never, ever, ever, random. *Corpus Linguistics and Linguistic Theory*, *1*(2), 263–276.

Kilgarriff, A., Busta, J., & Rychlý, P. (2015). *DIACRAN: a framework for diachronic analysis*. Retrieved from https://www.sketchengine.co.uk/wp-content/uploads/Diacran_CL2015.pdf

Kilgarriff, A., Marcowitz, F., Smith, S., & Thomas, J. (2015). Corpora and Language Learning with the Sketch Engine and SKELL. *Revue Française de Linguistique Appliquée*, *20*(1), 61–80.

Kilgarriff, A., Rychlý, P., Smrz, P., & Tugwell, D. (2004). The Sketch Engine. Presented at the 11th Euralex International Congres, Lorient, FR.

King, A. (1993). From sage on the stage to guide on the side. *College Teaching*, *41*(1), 30–35.

Lee, D. Y. (2001). Genres, registers, text types, domains and styles: Clarifying the concepts and nevigating a path through the BNC jungle. *Language Learning & Technology*, *41*(1), 37–72.

Levin, B. (1993). *English verb classes and alternations: a preliminary investigation*. Chicago: University of Chicago Press.

Lewis, M. (1993). *The lexical approach: the state of ELT and a way forward*. Hove: Language Teaching Publications.

Lewis, M. (2000). *Teaching collocation: further developments in the Lexical Approach*. Hove: Language Teaching Publications.

Löbner, S. (2013). *Understanding Semantics, Second Edition*. Routledge.

Macaulay, A., Seaton, M., & Gautier, P. (2011). *Collins COBUILD Phrasal Verbs Dictionary* (2nd ed.). Glasgow: HarperCollins.

MacEnery, T., & Hardie, A. (2012). *Corpus linguistics: method, theory and practice*. Cambridge: Cambridge University Press.

Mahlberg, M. (2005). *English general nouns: A corpus theoretical approach*. Amsterdam: John Benjamins.

Mair, C. (2008). *English linguistics: an introduction*. Tübingen: Gunter Narr Verlag.

Makaryk, I. R. (1993). *Encyclopedia of Contemporary Literary Theory: Approaches, Scholars, Terms*. Toronto: University of Toronto Press.

Malinowski, B. (1923). The problem of meaning in primitive languages. In *The meaning of meaning*. London: Routledge.

Manca, E. (2012). *Cantext and Language*. Leece: Salento University.

McEnery, T., & Hardie, A. (2012). *Corpus linguistics: method, theory and practice*. Cambridge: Cambridge University Press.

McEnery, T., & Wilson, A. G. (1996). *Corpus linguistics: An Introduction* (2nd ed.). Edinburgh: Edinburgh University Press.

McEnery, T., Xiao, R., & Tono, Y. (2006). *Corpus-based language studies: An advanced resource book*. London: Routledge.

Meara, P. M. (2009). *Connected words word associations and second language vocabulary acquisition*. Amsterdam: John Benjamins.

Morton, M. S. (2003). *The lover's tongue a merry romp through the language of love and sex*. Toronto: Insomniac Press.

Obrusník, A. (2012). *A hybrid approach to parallel text alignment* (Bachelor's Thesis). Masaryk University, Faculty of Arts, Brno.

O'Grady, G. (2010). *A grammar of spoken English discourse the intonation of increments*. London: Continuum.

O'Malley, J. M., & Chamot, A. U. (1990). *Learning strategies in second language acquisition*. Cambridge: Cambridge University Press.

Piaget, J. (1972). Some Aspects of Operations. In *Play and Development*. New York: Norton.

Pinna, A., & Brett, D. (2014). PoS-grams: an extra tool for the corpus linguist's kit? Presented at the Practical Applications of Language Corpora, Łódz, Poland: University of Lodz. Retrieved from http://palc.uni.lodz.pl/files/palc_abstracts.pdf

Potts, J. (2013). Think differently? Think different! *English Teaching Professional, 88*.

Prodromou, L. (2008). *English as a lingua franca a corpus-based analysis*. London: Continuum.

Rychlý, P. (2008). A lexicographer-friendly association score (pp. 6–9). Presented at the Recent Advances in Slavonic Natural Language Processing, Brno: Masaryk University Press.

Schmitt, N. (2010). Key issues in teaching and learning vocabulary. *Insights into Non-Native Vocabulary Teaching and Learning. Multilingual Matters.*, 28–40.

Scott, M. (1997). PC analysis of key words—and key key words. *System, 25*(2), 233–245.

Scott, M. (2010). What can corpus software do? In *The Routledge handbook of corpus linguistics*. London: Routledge.

Scott, M., & Tribble, C. (2006). *Textual patterns key words and corpus analysis in language education*. Amsterdam: John Benjamins.

Simpson-Vlach, R., & Ellis, N. C. (2010). An academic formulas list: New methods in phraseology research. *Applied Linguistics, 31*(4), 487–512.

Sinclair, J. M. (Ed.). (1987). *Collins COBUILD English language dictionary* (1st ed.). London: Harper Collins.

Sinclair, J. M. (1991). *Corpus, concordance, collocation*. Oxford: Oxford University Press.

Sinclair, J. M. (Ed.). (1995). *Collins COBUILD English language dictionary* (2nd ed.). London: Harper Collins.

Sinclair, J. M. (2001). Preface. In *Small corpus studies and ELT theory and practice*. Amsterdam: John Benjamins.

Sinclair, J. M. (2003). *Reading concordances: an introduction*. London: Longman.

Sinclair, J. M. (2005). Corpus and Text - Basic Principles. In *Developing Linguistic Corpora: a Guide to Good Practice* (pp. 1–16). Oxford: Oxbow Books.

Sinclair, J. M., & Mauranen, A. (2006). *Linear unit grammar integrating speech and writing*. Amsterdam: John Benjamins.

Stefanowitsch, A., & Gries, S. T. (2003). Collostructions: Investigating the interaction of words and constructions. *International Journal of Corpus Linguistics, 8*(2), 209–243.

Stubbs, M. (1996). *Text and corpus analysis: computer-assisted studies of language and culture*. Oxford: Blackwell Publishers.

Stubbs, M. (2001). *Words and phrases: corpus studies of lexical semantics*. Oxford: Blackwell Publishers.

Stubbs, M. (2002). Two quantitative methods of studying phraseology in English. *International Journal of Corpus Linguistics, 7*(2), 215–244. http://doi.org/10.1075/ijcl.7.2.04stu

Thomas, J. (2003). Teaching with concordancers: just imagine! Liberec: *The Proceedings of the ATECR 3rd International and 7th National Conference*.

Thomas, J. (2015). Stealing a march on collocation: Deriving extended collocations from full text for student analysis and synthesis. In *Multiple affordances of language corpora for data-driven learning*. Amsterdam: John Benjamins.

Thornbury, S. (n.d.). An A-Z of ELT. Retrieved from http://scottthornbury.wordpress.com

Tribble, C., & Jones, G. (1997). *Concordances in the classroom: A resource guide for teachers*. Houston TX: Athelstan.

Tversky, A., & Kahneman, D. (1973). Availability: A heuristic for judging frequency and probability. *Cognitive Psychology, 5*(2), 207–232. http://doi.org/10.1016/0010-0285(73)90033-9

Vygotsky, L. S., & Cole, M. (1978). *Mind in Society*. Cambridge, MA: Harvard University Press.

Widdowson, H. (2004). *Text, context, pretext: critical issues in discourse analysis*. Malden M.A.: Blackwell Publishing.

Widdowson, H. (2007). JR Firth, 1957, Papers in Linguistics 1934-51. *International Journal of Applied Linguistics, 17*(3), 402–413.

Wray, A., & Bloomer, A. (2013). *Projects in linguistics and language studies: a practical guide to researching language*. London: Routledge.

Index of Names and Notions

1st Hit in Doc, 101
academic prose, 102, 124, 132, 149, 154, 184
acquire
    language acquisition, 84
Adjective
    attributive, 56, 168, 177
    comparative, 34, 97, 107, 147, 153
    compound, 32
    frequency, 201
    in delexical verb structures, 112
    irregular, 15
    multi-word, 83
    predicative, 48, 56, 168, 177, 181
    present participle, 57
    superlative, 61, 97, 107, 147
    well + adj, 127
Adverb
    attitude, 49, 110
    circumstance, 188
    collocation, 108
    collocation, 81, 165
    degree, 110
    functional, 148
    in phrasal verbs, 102
    inflection, 97
    manner, 80, 149
    manner, 32, 106, 132, 147
    tense aspect, 19, 152
    without -*ly*, 148
    word order, 145
adverbial
    circumstance, 182, 188
    conjunct, 136
    disjunct, 136
    multi-word, 85
    spatial, 145
    stance, 136
affix, 17, 56, 73, 74, 91, 92
    prefix, 62, 63, 64, 91, 92, 93
    suffix, 63, 91, 108, 130, 199
affordance, 18, 19
agreement, 88
anaphora, 55, 165
    cataphora, 55
and/or relationship, 69, 70, 80
antonym, 70, 211
archaism, 28, 128, 210

armchair linguists, 10, 11, 168
article, 126
    country names, 34
    definite, 34
    in delexical verb structures, 111
aside, an, 89
attested, 10, 11, 109, 119
Austen, Jane, 209
Austin, J.L., 31, 156
Australia. *See* English and subcorpora
authentic, 8, 10, 12, 19, 27, 155, 169, 185
Bible, 29
binomial, 101, 154, 170, 177
Boulton, A., 5, 18, 20, 35, 39
breadcrumb trail, 27, 44, 48
Bruner, J., 1, 98
bundle, 66, 109, 116
    definition, 54, 84, 115, 120
    spoken vs. written, 126
choice, 7, 8, 11, 27, 28, 30, 31, 33, 107, 110, 121, 126, 191
Chomsky, N., 7, 32
chunk, 8, 37, 85
    definition, 84
    function, 85
    Hoey Procedure, 169
    holistic, 105
    using, 84
cluster, 70, 75, 184, 188
Cobb, T, 98
Cobb, T., 83
COBUILD
    corpus sampler, 166
    dictionary, 8, 10, 75, 102, 158
    grammar patterns, 116, 183, 186
    project, 8, 20
cognate, 30, 178
cognitive profile, 186, 203
colligation, 7, 8, 14, 48, 56, 65, 99, 163
    in word templates, 117
collocation, 7, 8, 13, 14, 18, 56, 65, 66, 69, 99, 100, 111, 126, 146, 163
    across a corpus, 195
    and polysemy, 170, 191
    and semantic prosody, 168
    and word templates, 117, 187
    definition, 65, 84

examples, 25, 56, 66, 87, 91, 106, 110,
    126, 146, 163, 164, 210
  Hoey Procedure, 170
  range, 164, 165
  register, 164, 171, 192
  strong and weak, 184
  two lexeme collocation, 115, 163, 164, 170
collocation statistics, 166, 170
  logDice, 167, 168, 171, 175, 183, 192
  mutual information (MI), 166
  T-score, 166, 167, 168
company names, 39
company words keep, 39, 40, 54, 60, 106,
    172, 191
componential analysis, 80, 83
compounding, 74, 177
conjugation, 15, 73, 154
conjunction, 147, 179
connotation, 28, 49, 63, 94, 159
construction, 97, 119, 155, 176, 183, 185, 187
Construction Grammar, 118, 155, 187
contractions, 35, 141
conversion, 32, 60, 62, 74, 75, 111, 113, 171
copyright, 203
core English, 12, 23, 39, 54, 126, 195, 203
Corpora
  British National Corpus (about), 13
  British National Corpus (first of many), 10
  Brown Family, 104, 129, 192, 195, 199
  CHILDES, 28, 195, 197
  EEBO, 130, 210
  enTenTen (first of many), 6
  FeedCorpus, 39, 130, 131
  Janáček, 141
  London English Corpus, 38, 134, 135
  New Model Corpus, 38, 39, 81, 94, 144,
      202
  OPUS2 (parallel), 157–62
  Pride and Prejudice, 209–12
  Science blogs, 195
  TED, 195
  ukWaC, 126, 200
Corpus Builder, 203
Corpus type
  learner corpora, 12, 28
  parallel, 157–62
  parallel (alignment), 157
  reference, 10, 200, 201, 202, 203, 205
countability, 87, 158
Crystal, D., 97, 209
curse of quality, 19

curse of quantity, 19, 180
data-driven learning, 16, 20, 39, 86
David Lee's Classification, 43, 51, 64, 125,
    133
  sorting, 50
declension, 15, 74, 76
deixis, 126
derivation, 74
descriptive linguistics, 86, 185
dictionary, 69
discourse, 85, 126, 164, 187, 188
discourse markers, 85, 86, 136, 198
domain, 13, 51, 64, 67, 75, 84, 115, 125, 126,
    127, 140, 196, 203
  semantic, 109, 133
domain (web), 128, 131, 136
double negative, 93, 134
email, 13, 89, 122, 198
English
  Australian, 136, 137, 201
  spoken, 29
  spoken and written, 125
  UK US, 41, 50, 103, 152
  US, 19, 109
English as a lingua franca, 98
escaping, 90, 150
etymology, 108, 176
exploitations, 7, 9, 34, 54, 94, 189
factotum vocabulary, 115, 184, 199, 200
false friend, 177
false positive, 104
FASI, 8, 19, 84
Firth, J.R., 7, 8, 40, 48
Flaubert, G., 33
Fronting, 107
functional language, 19, 61, 180
GDEX, 19, 44
gender, 135, 197, 199
gender neutral language, 27, 60, 104, 130
genre, 43, 49, 67, 85, 115, 123, 125, 126, 129,
    130, 131, 132, 180, 203
Goldberg, A., 119
grammar pattern, 8, 118, 151, 155, 158, 159,
    183, 186
grammatization, 97, 119, 124, 126, 187, 188
guided discovery, 1, 4, 18, 19, 20, 30, 40, 98
Gutenberg Project, 209
Halliday, M.A.K., 7, 8, 10, 30, 65, 120, 139,
    177, 186, 207, 212
Hanks, P., 8, 9, 15, 30, 91, 99, 116, 166, 185,
    186, 189, 200, 203

Hansard, 118, 132
hapax legomenon, 64, 91, 93, 198
Hierarchy of Language, 6, 31, 65, 73
Hoey Procedure, 169
Hoey, M., 8, 49, 65, 169
Hunston, S., 8, 116
hypernym, 28, 69, 70, 113, 114, 115, 118, 162, 184, 185, 188
hyponym, 70, 114, 115
    co-hyponym, 70, 113, 114, 142, 179, 184, 191
idiolect, 11, 101, 122, 178
idiom, 16, 24, 28, 29, 30, 81, 166
Idiom Principle, 8, 170
illustrative sentences, 10, 87
    selection criteria, 44
indirect question, 82
infer meaning, 33, 39, 50, 69, 78, 166, 210
Inflection, 31, 61, 73, 74, 75, 97, 108, 151
interlanguage, 12
internet search, 23, 25, 33
intuition, 1, 7, 10, 23, 25, 38, 80, 86, 87, 105, 185, 186, 193
inversion, 82
Johns, T., 20, 21, 58, 98, 133
jump to, 44
key word in context (KWIC), 14, 17, 42, 44, 47, 84
key words, 42, 116, 119, 120, 201, 203, 210
kibbitzer, 133
Killgarriff, A., 5, 6, 8, 30
knowledge creation, 1, 98
knowledge of the world, 87
language acquisition, 12, 18
    first, 119
    first, 28
    input, 183, 210
    intake, 183
    negative transfer, 177, 210
    output, 183
language change, 92, 126, 179
    diachronic, 115, 128, 131, 178
language pedagogy, 14, 18, 33, 39, 54, 125
    collocation, 163
    FASI. See FASI
    inductive learning, 20, 21
    learner as researcher, 21, 98
    learner autonomy, 20
    metacognitive strategies, 20, 21, 190
    prioritizing, 84
    vocabulary size, 180

Languages
    Czech, 77, 87, 157
    French, 33, 34, 58, 148
    German, 33, 34, 87, 157, 158, 159, 160, 162
    Greek, 34
    Italian, 97, 160
    Latin, 176, 192
Leech, G., 1, 129
lemma - defined
    (first of hundreds), 15
lempos – definition, 42
Levin, B., 81
Lewis, M., 20, 30, 65, 169
lexeme, 65, 74, 75, 111, 163, 187
Lexical Approach, 20, 30, 65, 169
lexical gap, 33, 162
lexical priming, 28, 183
    hypotheses, 49, 65, 70
lexical set, 41, 79, 117, 180
lexical support, 63, 172, 179
lexicogrammar, 7, 61, 79, 119, 120, 125, 146
lexicography, 6, 7, 9, 44, 75, 98, 157, 182, 185
LGSWE, 8, 91, 101, 109, 115, 182, 212
Linear Unit Grammar, 85, 86, 115
linguistic competence, 121, 163
litotes, 93, 134, 159, 169
lumpers and splitters, 7, 75, 158, 184
Malinowski, B., 7, 162
marked. See unmarked
meaning potential, 99, 100, 103, 116, 117, 119, 191
metadata, 15, 38, 41, 42, 43, 50, 51, 60, 64, 84, 121, 122, 123, 125, 197, 206, 207
metaphor, 9, 41, 58, 102, 140
morpheme, 73
    bound, 73, 154
    derivational, 108
    free, 64, 92, 108, 143, 154
    productive, 108
morphology
    taxonomy, 74, 108, 177
multi-word unit, 18, 54, 60, 65, 84, 91, 111, 163, 164, 165, 179
multiword unit, 83
neologism, 13, 19, 91, 186
n-gram, 11, 84, 115, 120, 145, 195, 196, 197, 198, 201, 210
    hybrid, 54, 151
nonce word, 91, 198
normalization, 24, 166, 180

noun
    compound, 112, 168
    contability, 87
    general noun, 115
    irregular plural, 76, 143
    mass, 87
    of quantity, 87
    phrase. See phrase, noun
    singular, 88, 91, 133
operator, 36, 37, 64, 74, 75, 90, 91, 93, 146, 147, 150, 151
    apostrophe, 35, 50
paradigmatic, 14, 65, 70, 175
particle, 65, 97, 119, 125, 183
    dative vs. prep, 156
    instrumental, 62, 119
    negative, 93, 136, 146, 195
    phrasal verb, 62, 102, 182, 183
pattern
    definition, 120
Pattern Dictionary of English Verbs, 15, 117, 185, 189
Pattern Dictionary of English Verbs (PDEV), 30
periphrasis, 29, 97, 101, 108, 131, 154
permalinks, about, 17, 45, 104, 206
phonology
    I-mutation, 76
phrase, 81–84
    adverbial, 182, 210
    definition, 84
    fixed, 32, 56, 82, 100, 105, 166
    noun, 29, 52, 111, 114, 146, 147, 155, 165, 177, 182, 187, 189
    prepositional, 50, 79, 116, 118, 145, 181, 182, 188
    semi-fixed, 8, 66
    verb, 79, 126, 187
Piaget, J., 20, 98
polysemy, 57, 70, 79, 80, 158, 170, 171, 172
polysemy vs. homonymy, 75
POS tagging
    CLAWS, 140
    Penn Treebank, 62
possible and probable, 27, 31, 33, 38, 39, 107
pragmatics, 10, 31, 85, 126, 135, 156
    hedging, 114, 160, 211
    reference, 31, 165, 180
predicate, 27, 176, 177, 187
preposition, 94
    bound, 144, 182
    bound and free, 182, 188

priming. See lexical priming
pronoun, 89, 107, 117, 140, 149, 154, 165, 199
pronunciation, 34, 55
    conversion, 79
    minimal pairs, 90
    voicing, 36, 76, 143
punctuation
    apostrophe, 35, 77, 82
    capitalisation, 34, 35, 77
    colon, 89
    comma, 59, 101, 148
    parentheses, 88, 89, 144, 150
    semicolon, 89
    sentence punctuation, 59, 95, 136, 140
question tag, 140, 141, 161, 201, 211
regular expression, 94, 131, 197, 199, 200, 201, 202
rhyme, 90
sampling frame, 129
seed word, 204, 206
Selinker, 12
semantic prosody, 48, 49, 66, 94, 159, 161
semantic type, 15, 110, 113, 115, 116, 118, 120
sentence stem, 35, 82, 85, 136, 154
serendipity, 9, 25, 63, 143
Sex of Demographic Respondent, 135
Shakespeare, 29, 31, 61
similarity search, 141, 142, 145, 189
Sinclair, 1, 7, 8, 20, 65, 85, 193
Snowden, E., 60, 169
speech act, 160
    illocutionary, 106, 118, 152, 156
    locutionary, 31
    perlocutionary, 31, 101, 106
    verb, 109
spelling, 38, 91, 126, 143, 148
    historical, 130
    UK US, 36, 94, 135, 166
split infinitive, 148
Stubbs, M., 8, 139, 140, 165
subcorpora, 18, 19, 47, 132, 145, 157, 167, 195, 206, 207
    Australian, 201
    fiction, 132
    science, 132
subjunctive
    mandative, 30, 153, 154
surnames, 86
SVOMPT, 27, 30, 124, 176

synonym, 63, 69, 70, 94, 113, 114, 142, 144, 163, 179, 183, 191
syntagm, 136, 139, 151, 154, 156
    definition, 54
syntagmatic, 14, 54, 175
syntax, 111, 120, 159, 184
Systemic Functional Grammar, 7, 187
tagging, 15
    CLAWS, 13, 61, 95, 139
    error, 42, 75, 142
    Penn Treebank, 15, 61, 140, 204
    semantic, 15
Text Types, 16, 23, 121, 123, 133, 171
thesaurus, 26, 69, 94, 184, 210, 211
    Roget, 69
    word association, 167
translation, 157, 158, 159, 160, 161, 164, 181, 187
    translationese, 157, 161
trinomial, 100, 177
troponym, 28, 79, 81, 119, 141, 142, 198
unmarked, 27, 28, 29, 30, 97, 107, 116, 117, 130, 187, 199
Verb
    argument, 116, 119
    auxiliary, 95, 97, 144
    copular, 27, 48, 110, 177
    delexical, 29, 81, 97, 111, 112, 146, 171
    ditransitive, 155, 171
    frequency, 201
    future, 97, 160
    infinitive marker, 56
    irregular, 198
    lexical, 62, 187
    light, 111, 184
    modal, 52, 62, 140, 211
    mood, 154
    of motion, 80
    passive, 49, 79, 95, 125, 145, 154
    passive (get), 161
    past participle, 15, 42, 74, 95, 105, 144, 152
    performative, 156
    phrasal, 38, 50, 65, 79, 81, 102–4, 103, 146, 158, 183
    phrasal (particles). See particle
    phrasal (polysemy), 103, 184
    phrasal (separable), 103, 183
    phrasal (transitivity), 183
    phrase. See phrase
    present participle, 15, 74
    process, 141
    reflexive, 104
    state, 141
    transitive, 81, 105, 124, 176, 184
vertical bar, 94, 125
visualize, 67, 77, 78, 133, 152, 153
Vygotsky, L., 1, 20, 98
WebBootCat, 203, 204, 206
Widdowson, H., 7
WLT, 57, 76, 201
    definition, 54
word association, 99, 167, 172
word cloud, 71, 193
    versatile, 71
word family, 75, 168
word order, 27, 28, 30, 82, 100, 107, 116, 117, 181, 187
word template, 115, 117, 119, 120, 124, 126, 151, 163, 187, 189
    definition, 120
Zipf, 58, 91, 93, 108
Zone of Proximal Development, 98

Word Focus Index

above-mentioned, 127
according to, 59
actress, 199
advantage, 75
affectionate, 160
allay, 176
alleviate, 176
although/though, 86
amid, 94
analyse, 185
and other, 114
approach, 146
arresting, 57
at all, 53
bachelor, 173
bar, 100
battler, 137
be bound to, 52
be sat down, 109
befriend, 92
beginning (in/at the), 161
bias, 140
blench, 64
blond(e), 148
blow up, 184
blue, 70
boldly go, 32, 143
break, 147
broken, 42, 60
cahoots, 38
carry, 183
carry out, 183
clench teeth, 126
company names, 39
compare, 69
concern, 105
convincing vs. persuasive, 192
curiosity, 87
curiouser, 34
data, 133
decline, 181
department, 94
device, 115
discover, 193
do, 101
do (auxiliary), 29
doth, 29
dream, 147

dwelling, 113, 162
eagle, 67, 167
ecstasy, 38
elaborate, 79, 106
eligible, 168
encourage, 159
enough, 145
examination, 184
experience, 87
eye vs. eyes, 193
fast, 147
faux (prefix), 91
first vs. firstly, 86
flying colours, 166
for the last time, 161
frame, 75
friend, 92, 191
friend (verb), 13, 61
germane, 33
Given that, 54
go fish, 81
going (noun), 142
hamper, 49
handsome, 25, 27, 108, 163, 172, 210
harbour, 49
harmony, 64
have a * day, 38
high street, 128
holiday, 26, 77
hook, line and sinker, 100
house, 162
humdinger, 167, 179
I had to laugh, 82
I was sat, 109
impact, 142, 144
include, 177
innit, 201
interested vs. interesting, 61, 191
invent, 168
kill, 198
kith and kin, 14
knife, fork and spoon, 100
lecture, 188
let * down, 38
let alone, 160
let down, 146
like, 60
likest, 61

liking, 113
make, 28
manage, 158
mankind, 130
moot point, 25, 86
more than likely, 83
moreover, 126
multitude, 87
naked, 163
not uninteresting, 51, 93
not very, 159
not, n't, 35
nuanced, 178
once in a lifetime, 83, 84, 113
only ... did, 101
open door policy, 164
open to, 52
ornament, 105
ownership, 41
pack, 63
painfully, 110
parts of the body, 80, 193
party, 146
positively, 109
practice, 135
problem lie, 25, 56
prove, 123
pry, 62, 63
put, 53
put down, 103, 158
question-v, 187
random vs. arbitrary, 192
rather, 105
responsible, 181
said, 109
scholarship, 87
secondly, 141
see, 127
seize control, 100
shall, 211
shared, 67
sleep furiously, 32
slouch, 78

smart, 141
sorry, 135
spider, 186
spinster, 173
struggle, battle, fight, 94
success, 146
such as, 115
sympathetic, 177
symptom, 176, 177, 179, 183
take * breath away, 38
their (3rd p.s. reference), 104
themself, 143
thingamabob, 37
think big, 108
through, 145
to (inf vs. prep), 33, 62
troubles, 51, 53
turkey, 53
tweet, 39
ubiquitous, 133
unthinkable, 48
versatile, 167
wave, 171
way how, 83, 144
weekend, 134
well pleased, 127
whatsoever, 49
whereas, 126
whether, 147, 150
which, 148
while, 101
whom, 149
whose, 23, 82
Why can't ..., 36
wicked, 178
wonder, 82, 160
wont, 50

Penn Treebank Tags as used in Sketch Engine

POS Tag	Description	Example
CC	coordinating conjunction	and
CD	cardinal number	1, third
DT	determiner	the
EX	existential there	there is
FW	foreign word	d'hoevre
IN	preposition, subordinating conjunction	in, of, like
IN/that	that as subordinator	that
JJ	adjective	green
JJR	adjective, comparative	greener
JJS	adjective, superlative	greenest
LS	list marker	1)
MD	modal	could, will
NN	noun, singular or mass	table
NNS	noun plural	tables
NP	proper noun, singular	John
NPS	proper noun, plural	Vikings
PDT	predeterminer	both the boys
POS	possessive ending	friend's
PP	personal pronoun	I, he, it
PP$	possessive pronoun	my, his
RB	adverb	however, usually, naturally, here, good
RBR	adverb, comparative	better
RBS	adverb, superlative	best
RP	particle	give up
SENT	Sentence-break punctuation	. ! ?
SYM	Symbol	/ [= *
TO	infinitive 'to'	togo
UH	interjection	uhhuhhuhh
VB	verb be, base form	be

Tag	Description	Example
VBD	verb be, past tense	was, were
VBG	verb be, gerund/present participle	being
VBN	verb be, past participle	been
VBP	verb be, sing. present, non-3d	am, are
VBZ	verb be, 3rd person sing. present	is
VH	verb have, base form	have
VHD	verb have, past tense	had
VHG	verb have, gerund/present participle	having
VHN	verb have, past participle	had
VHP	verb have, sing. present, non-3d	have
VHZ	verb have, 3rd person sing. present	has
VV	lexical verb, base form	take
VVD	lexical verb, past tense	took
VVG	lexical verb, gerund/present participle	taking
VVN	lexical verb, past participle	taken
VVP	lexical verb, sing. present, non-3d	take
VVZ	lexical verb, 3rd person sing. present	takes
WDT	wh-determiner	which
WP	wh-pronoun	who, what
WP$	possessive wh-pronoun	whose
WRB	wh-abverb	where, when
#	#	#
$	$	$
"	Quotation marks	' "
``	Opening quotation marks	' "
(	Opening brackets	({
)	Closing brackets	) }
,	Comma	,
:	Punctuation	- ; : -- ...

Abbreviations used in this book

BNC	British National Corpus
CHILDES	Child Language Data Exchange System
DESKE	Discovering English with Sketch Engine
DLC	David Lee's Classification
ETT	English TenTen
FASI	Fluency, Accuracy, Sophistication, Idiomaticity
FLA	First language acquisition
FLD	First Level Domain
IFID	Illocutionary Force Indicating Device (Pragmatics)
HPM	Hits per million
LEXMCI	See the Dante website
LGSWE	Longman Grammar of Spoken and Written English
LUG	Linear Unit Grammar
MAELT	Methodologies and Approaches in English Language Teaching
MLD	Monolingual Learner's Dictionary
NMC	New Model Corpus
POS	Part of Speech
SFG	Systemic Functional Grammar
SLA	Second language acquisition
SVOMPT	Subject Verb Object Manner Place Time
TLC	Two lexeme collocation
TLD	Top level domain
ukWaC	UK Web as Corpus
WLT	Word Lemma Tag